Political MIND GAMES

Political
MIND
GAMES

*How the 1% manipulate
our understanding of what's happening,
what's right, and what's possible*

ROY EIDELSON

GREEN HALL BOOKS

For Judy, Josh, Ben, and Sarah

CONTENTS

1

AMERICA'S PLUTOCRATS
WHO THEY ARE AND HOW THEY SUCCEED

"A lie can travel halfway around the world while the truth is putting on its shoes."

—ANONYMOUS

Smooth-talking con artists are familiar figures in American folklore. The well-dressed hustler arrives in an unsuspecting town. He pitches some miracle cure or get-rich-quick scheme, door to door or from atop a soapbox. Then, before his customers realize they've been duped, he steals away in search of his next mark. It's a risky vocation, one that demands quick feet, a keen understanding of human nature, and a talent for telling tales that both arouse and reassure.

But when it comes to profiting off people's hopes and fears, golden-tongued peddlers like these are mere gnats in a land of giants. By far the most successful purveyors of lucrative lies and false promises can be found among the denizens of America's palatial estates, corporate boardrooms, and corridors of political power. And unlike their small-time counterparts, they're rarely on the run—despite the misery and despair they leave in their wake.

How is it that these super-sized hucksters are able to accumulate ever-greater wealth and influence—at everyone else's expense—without provoking a broad backlash? As the pages ahead will show, they accomplish this by using manipulative psychological appeals that target five fundamental questions in our individual and collective lives: Are we safe? Are we treated fairly? Who should we trust? Are we good enough? Can we control what happens to us? These "mind games" are carefully designed to defuse and misdirect our outrage. When they're effective, we lose our bearings about what's gone wrong, who's to blame, and how we can turn things around.

The disingenuous claims of fat-cat profiteers took on even greater significance with the election of Donald J. Trump as the 45th president of the United States. On the campaign trail, the country's premier hustler offered voters a wagonload of beguiling accounts and assurances while breaking almost every rule of evidence, logic, and propriety. He sought to persuade not through rational argument, analysis, and truth-telling, but rather by manipulating our imperfect reasoning and our unreasoning emotions. The same strategic ploys that brought him to the White House certainly flourished during his first year in office.

But perspective is important here, because Trump's propaganda playbook isn't really anything new. In various guises, it's been around for a long time—even if most Americans haven't seen his level of mastery in their lifetimes, especially with the stakes so high. Ultimately, then, this political moment brings to the fore a clear and compelling message: We can't wait any longer to confront and debunk the destructive mind games of the country's millionaire and billionaire snake-oil vendors. And that's what this book is about.

FACTS ON THE GROUND: AMERICA'S EXTREME INEQUALITY

Let's begin with an inescapable truth. We live in a country where extraordinary wealth is concentrated in remarkably few hands. The financial assets of the richest 1% of Americans equal those of the bottom 90% of all U.S. households combined.[1] The Walton family alone, heirs to the Walmart fortune, has more wealth than the bottom 40% of all Americans, a group comprised of nearly 50 million families.[2] And top executives of S&P 500 companies each receive, on average, over $10 million in annual compensation, making roughly as much in a single day as their typical employees earn in a full year.[3]

Research shows that such extreme inequality between rich and poor—now at historic levels in the United States—is a driving force behind many of society's most profound and corrosive ills. These disparities are associated with *diminished* levels of physical health, mental health, educational achievement, social mobility, trust, community life, and economic growth. They're also linked to *heightened* levels of infant mortality, obesity, crime, violence, drug abuse, and incarceration.[4]

The ugly realities of extreme inequality are visible almost everywhere we look. Giant corporations are raking in record profits, while millions of Americans remain scarred by the Great Recession and a recovery that has left them behind. Mammoth defense contractors push for more of everything military, while programs for the needy are on life support. Global polluters are blocking effective responses to climate change, while the poor suffer disproportionately from environmental disasters and devastation. Influential voices ridicule those who are disadvantaged by prejudice, by discrimination, and by dwindling resources. All the while, our middle class is shrinking, imperiled, and insecure.

At the same time, the American public favors greater economic equality. Polls reveal that most of us recognize that the income gap between "haves" and "have nots" has been steadily rising, that our economic system unjustly rewards the wealthy, that large corporations have too much influence, and that hard work doesn't guarantee an escape from poverty.[5] Even so, researchers have found that most Americans still significantly *underestimate* the magnitude of the disparities between rich and poor in this country.[6]

The adverse consequences of our enormous economic divide are magnified even further by another crucial fact: There are striking differences in policy preferences between the super-rich and the rest of us. Compared to the extraordinarily wealthy, most Americans are much stronger supporters of a higher minimum wage, labor unions to strengthen workers' rights, a more progressive tax structure, higher taxes for high-income earners and corporations, affordable health coverage for everyone, government initiatives to decrease unemployment, and a stronger social welfare safety net for those facing adversity.[7]

PLUTOCRATS, THE PREDATORY CLASS, AND THE 1%

One might think that this popular vision of the good society would win out and Congress would enact policies to support it.[8] But that's not happening because tremendous wealth and political power go hand-in-hand in the United States today. As a result, a small number of individuals and groups have unprecedented sway over our daily lives and our collective destiny. They set the priorities of our elected officials.[9] They exert influence over the mainstream media regarding which narratives are promoted and which are obscured.[10] And, as we'll shortly see, through their psychological mind games they manipulate the public's understanding of what's happening, what's right, and what's possible.

This unhealthy and undemocratic arrangement is the defining feature of a plutocracy—a society and government controlled by the super-rich, directly and indirectly. With their massive economic and political resources, plutocrats pursue the further accumulation of wealth and power while undermining the common good. As plutocrats' fortunes multiply, the struggles and desperate circumstances faced by so many are ignored and grow worse. Almost 250 years ago, in 1776, economist and philosopher Adam Smith described it this way: "All for ourselves and nothing for other people, seems, in every age of the world, to have been the vile maxim of the masters of mankind."[11]

But "plutocrats" is just one term for these avaricious defenders of concentrated wealth and power. Other names also fit the bill. For example, economist James Galbraith has aptly described them as the "predatory class":

> Today, the signature of modern American capitalism is neither benign competition, nor class struggle, nor an inclusive middle-class utopia. Instead, predation has become the dominant feature—a system wherein the rich have come to feast on decaying systems built for the middle class. The predatory class is not the whole of the wealthy; it may be opposed by many others of similar wealth. But it is the defining feature, the leading force. And its agents are in full control of the government under which we live.[12]

The "1%" is another term that's resonated ever since Occupy Wall Street burst onto the scene in the fall of 2011, when tens of thousands of Americans protested economic inequality and corporate greed with demonstrations and encampments across the country.[13]

Whether they're called plutocrats, or the predatory class, or the 1%—and I'll be using them interchangeably—these people defend their empire and expand their reach through outsized influence over huge corporations, government institutions, and other organizations. Some of them have become household names, while others fly under the radar. Those with high profiles include Trump, the oil baron Koch brothers, the Walmart heirs, and the CEOs of some of Wall Street's largest banks and other Fortune 500 companies.[14] Also conspicuous are prominent politicians—many Republicans and some Democrats—who eagerly advance a plutocratic agenda. Trump's cabinet members have a combined net worth in excess of $10 billion;[15]

over half the members of Congress are millionaires.[16] As journalist and political analyst Chris Hayes wrote, "The 1 percent and the nation's governing class are more or less one and the same. If you are a member of the governing elite and aren't a millionaire, you're doing something wrong."[17]

Also supporting these plutocrats are groups such as the U.S. Chamber of Commerce, lobbying on behalf of big business, and the American Legislative Exchange Council, working behind the scenes to draft 1%-friendly model legislation for states and municipalities across the country. The network also includes right-wing "think tanks" that issue inequality-defending policy briefs, much to the satisfaction of their super-rich patrons. Billionaire Rupert Murdoch's Fox News cable TV channel and his *Wall Street Journal* are among the favorite media outlets of the predatory class. This is just a small sampling, as later chapters will show.[18]

But it's important to realize that members of today's plutocracy are *not* a monolithic group. Likewise, there's no need to posit some secret plot in which they all gather in smoke-filled rooms to conspire about how best to achieve their aims. The defense of extreme inequality arises from multiple corners. Some hold rigid ideological commitments—to "free markets," "traditional values," "small government," or "survival of the fittest"—that seemingly blind them to the tragic human costs of their convictions. Others relentlessly pursue personal wealth and power, devoid of any serious intellectual mooring or moral justification. And then there are those who, plutocrats by birth, lack self-reflection and simply conform to the expectations of their peers and upbringing.

To be clear, not all Americans with extraordinary wealth and power endorse the predatory class's self-aggrandizing values and priorities. Rather, some of them are deeply concerned about the welfare of those who are less fortunate, and some give generously of their time and resources in efforts to build a more equal and more just society.[19] The Patriotic Millionaires, for example, describe themselves as "high-net-worth Americans who are committed to building a more prosperous, stable and inclusive nation."[20] For them, this means a country where everyone shares equally in political power, wages are sufficient to enable full-time workers to support their families, and super-rich individuals and corporations contribute a greater share of our tax revenues. There are others much like them—all valuable allies in the pursuit of progressive change. So even though their wealth places such individuals in rarefied circles, they shouldn't be mistaken for the promoters of the pernicious mind games that are the focus of this book.

OUR FIVE CORE CONCERNS: SOFT TARGETS FOR MANIPULATION

Greed-driven plutocrats share one goal: the stifling of public outrage over extreme inequality. Through their deep-pocket efforts at obstruction, they aim to undermine the solidarity that's needed to counter their oversized influence and control.[21] As long as they're successful, a more decent society remains beyond our grasp.

But how exactly do the 1% prevent so many Americans from recognizing what's gone wrong, who's to blame, and what can be done to make things better? To a large degree, they rely on psychological persuasion. They inundate us with artfully crafted public relations campaigns. They seduce us with charismatic but deceitful spokespersons. And they prey upon us with manipulative appeals that are especially effective because they target the fundamental issues in our daily lives.

What are these key issues? That question has engaged me for much of the past 20 years in my work as a psychologist.[22] Through research and study, I've discovered that five issues consistently and profoundly shape the way we understand ourselves, our lives, and the world around us. They are *vulnerability*, *injustice*, *distrust*, *superiority*, and *helplessness*. Each of these is a core concern and the basis for one of the questions I mentioned earlier: Are we safe? Are we treated fairly? Who should we trust? Are we good enough? Can we control what happens to us?

Unfortunately, defenders of extreme wealth and power specialize in misleading and self-serving answers to these questions. In fact, their answers usually lead us away from the more equal and more humane society most of us desire. Let's now take a brief look at these five concerns. Later, in the chapters that follow, we'll examine the specific mind games that the 1% use to take advantage of them.

Vulnerability: Are We Safe?

Our concerns about vulnerability play a central role in how we see the world. Whether as passing thoughts or haunting worries, we wonder if we're safe, if the people we care about are in harm's way, and if there might be danger on the horizon. Right or wrong, our judgments on these matters go a long way in determining the choices we make and the actions we take. This focus on vulnerability isn't surprising. If our survival or well-being appears to be in doubt, if fear leaps to the forefront, other thoughts and feelings are quickly pushed aside.

Specific vulnerability concerns vary from one person or group to the next, in part because the range of possible threats is so broad. For some, life itself may hang in the balance: the homeless person on a frigid winter night, the cancer patient unable to afford urgent treatment, soldiers under fire on a battlefield. For others, the concerns are more about the daily struggle to get by: the low-wage worker with more bills to pay than money in the bank; the immigrant family confronting prejudice in their neighborhood; the high school graduates unable to afford college, or college graduates burdened with years of student debt.

Whatever our actual circumstances may be, when we think we're in jeopardy we look for ways to reduce that danger. Only when we think we're safe do we turn our attention elsewhere. However, we're not very good at assessing real risks or effective responses to them. As a result, often we make the mistake of either exaggerating threats or underestimating perils—especially when others mislead us to advance their own agenda.

Injustice: Are We Treated Fairly?

Concerns over just treatment are also a potent force in our lives. We regularly wonder whether particular circumstances or decisions are fair. Employees may doubt that they're being paid what they deserve, parents may worry that their children aren't receiving enough encouragement and recognition at school, public figures may have misgivings about whether they're being portrayed fairly by the media, and so on.

Cases of real or perceived mistreatment—from minor slights to profound abuses—stir anger and resentment, as well as an urge to right wrongs and bring accountability to those we hold responsible. At the same time, claims of injustice and calls for punitive or corrective measures can spur heated debate and disagreement. An action that one person or group considers an obvious instance of wrongdoing may be deemed legitimate by others. Similarly, what some see as a fair solution to a problem may be viewed by other stakeholders as yet a further miscarriage of justice.

Our perceptions about what's just and what's not are imperfect. That makes us potentially easy targets for skillful manipulation by those who have a selfish interest in shaping our views of right and wrong. We can be misled into believing that there's no injustice in our midst when in fact there is, or vice versa. We can also be misdirected into believing that innocent parties are the ones responsible for unjust conditions, thereby letting those who are actually guilty escape accountability.

Distrust: Who Should We Trust?

Consciously and unconsciously, we tend to divide the world into people and groups we find trustworthy and others we don't. Where we draw that line matters a lot. When we get it right, we avoid harm from those who have hostile intentions or are merely undependable. Appropriate levels of distrust are important in steering us away from bad decisions and costly outcomes. In much the same way, knowing who we can trust enables us to build valuable relationships that enhance the purpose in our lives and the effectiveness of our collective efforts.

We usually make these judgments with only limited information of uncertain reliability. Sometimes they're based on little more than fleeting interactions, rumors, or stereotypes. As a result, our conclusions about the trustworthiness of particular people, groups, and sources of information are frequently flawed and problematic. On the one hand, unwarranted suspicions can lead us to discount wise counsel, to reject promising opportunities, and to turn potential allies into adversaries. On the other hand, misplaced trust can have devastating consequences. Betrayal by people we believe have our best interests at heart is more than just emotionally painful. It can cost us our livelihood, our savings, our security, and the possibility of a brighter future.

It's regrettable, then, that our inclinations to either trust or distrust are soft targets for psychological manipulation— including by those who share neither our circumstances nor our priorities. The strategies used for this purpose take advantage of two natural tendencies: first, our penchant, all else being equal, to trust and give the benefit of the doubt to those who hold positions of authority; and second, our inclination to adopt a distrustful posture toward those we see as different, or those we've been taught to view as "outsiders."

Superiority: Are We Good Enough?

We're quick to compare ourselves to others, often in an effort to demonstrate that we're worthy of respect or admiration. Sometimes this desire is even stronger: We want confirmation that we're superior in some important way—perhaps in our accomplishments, or in our values, or in our contributions to society. In our efforts to bolster our own positive self-appraisal, we may direct attention toward what we consider worst about other people and groups, painting them in as negative a light as possible. At the extreme, some of those who see themselves as superior believe they're entitled to stand above the norms and rules that govern the lives of everyone else. Their narcissistic belief that they've earned or have been chosen for privileged status finds expression in displays of arrogance, harsh judgments of others, and overreaching in an effort to control scarce resources. These behaviors and the convictions underlying them can be sources of conflict with those subjected to humiliating and dehumanizing affronts.

The judgments we make about our own worth—and the positive or negative qualities of other people—are usually subjective and lack concrete evidence. As a result, these impressions are also susceptible to manipulation by self-interested parties. Consider how favorably we react to being flattered or singled out as special, particularly by those in positions of authority and esteem. These same individuals can persuade us to look down on others as undeserving of respect, and to view them with contempt and disgust instead.

Helplessness: Can We Control What Happens to Us?

Whether we're talking about individuals or groups, feelings of helplessness pose an obstacle to any undertaking. Those who lack confidence in their capabilities are more likely to give up and abandon their goals, and they don't bounce back as resiliently when their efforts prove unproductive. That's because believing we can't control important outcomes in our lives leads to resignation, which wrecks our motivation to work toward crucial personal or collective objectives.

In short, if we think our actions won't make any difference, we're inclined to do nothing. As a result, social change efforts are hampered when people feel that working together won't improve their circumstances. This notion—that our actions are futile and adversity can't be overcome—is something we fight hard to resist. But if we reach that demoralizing conclusion anyway, its effects can be paralyzing and very difficult to reverse.

Knowing that feelings of helplessness have a significant impact on the choices we make and the effort we're willing to expend, those with their own selfish agenda can take advantage of us by manipulating our perceptions of what's possible. For example, perceived helplessness—especially when it's widely shared—makes it easy for a small minority to control a much larger group. They're able to maintain an oppressive status quo because active resistance is absent and voices of opposition are silent.

THE 1%'S GAME PLAN AND THE CHALLENGES WE FACE

Our core concerns about vulnerability, injustice, distrust, superiority, and helplessness are psychologically powerful for multiple reasons. First, singly and in combination, they're essential lenses through which we interpret events, evaluate our circumstances, and decide what action, if any, to take. Second, the importance of these concerns extends from individuals to groups, and they therefore operate in a wide range of settings: interpersonal relationships; family relationships; work relationships; community relationships; and political relationships in local, national, and international spheres. Third, these concerns have the potential to undermine our capacity for careful and critical thinking because they're linked to hard-to-control emotions, including fear, anger, suspicion, contempt, and despair.

Given their power, it's not surprising that these five concerns figure so prominently in the propaganda campaigns of plutocrats who aim to discourage resistance to their agenda.

As examples, representatives of the 1% feed our vulnerability fears by pushing alarmist accounts of the perils associated with change. They twist our sense of injustice by insisting that their actions are designed to address wrongdoing and inequity. They promote confusion and doubt over who can be trusted in order to create suspicions and disorganization within the ranks of their opponents. They exploit notions of superiority by portraying the United States as a land of limitless opportunity where the cream always rises to the top. And they encourage feelings of helplessness by arguing that stark inequalities are the result of powerful forces beyond anyone's control.

Sometimes, the rich and powerful use their mind games to perpetuate an illegitimate status quo—for example, through voter suppression efforts, climate change denial, opposition to minimum wage increases, and draconian law-and-order policies. At other times, they use similar appeals to implement changes that expand their empire—for instance, through the privatization of public education, legislation that weakens workers' rights, corporate-friendly trade agreements, and deadly wars of aggression. When the 1% succeed in these efforts, few among us are spared the adverse consequences—especially those Americans already struggling to make ends meet and have their voices heard.

To be clear, there's nothing wrong with political appeals that highlight issues of vulnerability, injustice, distrust, superiority, or helplessness. After all, since these are core concerns it makes sense that they should be front and center when it comes to matters of public policy and the general welfare. What's deeply immoral, however, is that today's plutocrats exploit these concerns for the specific purpose of advancing their own narrow interests while bringing harm and suffering to so many.

Rather than use their enormous resources to help create a more equal and decent society, the 1% instead devote themselves to protecting and expanding their wealth and power—at the expense of those who don't live in their mansions, meet in their boardrooms, or vacation at their resorts. Moreover, when arguing their case, they conceal their true intentions with carefully crafted mind games that manipulate our perceptions, promote falsehoods and distortions, and prey upon our emotions and prejudices.

Trump's Presidential Campaign Mind Games

In the chapters ahead, we'll examine the 1%'s favorite mind games one by one, but it's important to recognize that these manipulative appeals are often used in combination for even greater effect. For example, plutocrats may defend a particular policy by arguing that it protects us from dire threats, combats current injustices, and reflects our country's highest values—and that critics are misguided and misinformed. More vividly, Trump's successful pursuit of the presidency provides an instructive case study of multiple mind games used to reach a single goal—the White House. It's worth briefly recalling several instances from the campaign trail, considering each issue in turn.[23]

First, Trump fed the public's worries about vulnerability. Describing himself as "the law and order candidate," he warned that "our very way of life" was at risk and insisted that only he could provide protection from a wide range of catastrophic threats.[24] Promising to build a "great wall" along our border with Mexico, he falsely claimed, "They're bringing drugs. They're bringing crime. They're rapists."[25] With similar over-the-top rhetoric, he railed against bringing Syrian refugees to the United States as "a personal invitation to ISIS members to come live here and try to destroy our country from within."[26] Trump also exploited fears in a different way: by issuing disturbing threats of his own. Responding to a protester at a rally, he told the crowd, "You know what they used to do to a guy like that in a place like this? They'd be carried out on a stretcher, folks."[27] And he had a warning for media representatives who criticized him: "We're going to open up libel laws, and we're going to have people sue you like you've never got sued before."[28]

Second, Trump portrayed his candidacy and platform as an effort to address injustices. When announcing his run, he lamented, "The U.S. has become a dumping ground for everybody else's problems."[29] Months later in his acceptance speech at the Republican National Convention, he feigned common cause with "the forgotten men and women of our country," promising "to fix the system so it works justly for each and every American."[30] Trump was also quick to cast himself as an aggrieved victim of injustice as well. Prior to his victory, he repeatedly claimed that the election was rigged against him, on one occasion saying, "They even want to try to rig the election at the polling booths...voter fraud is very, very common."[31] And he insisted that the media was mistreating him: "I get very, very unfair press having to do with women and many other things."[32]

Third, Trump preyed on issues of distrust. He characterized his political opponents as untrustworthy, for example referring to Republican Senator Ted Cruz of Texas as "Lyin' Ted" and to former Secretary of State Hillary Clinton as "Crooked Hillary." He cast doubt on the integrity of his media critics, arguing, "They are horrible human beings, they are dishonest. I've seen these so-called journalists flat-out lie."[33] Trump also encouraged the public's distrust of specific marginalized groups. He described the Black Lives Matter movement as "looking for trouble,"[34] and he placed Muslims under a cloud of suspicion, expressing potential support for special identification cards and a registry database.[35] Meanwhile, Trump presented himself as the only reliable truth-teller, one who shunned the deceptions of political correctness. When he accepted the Republican presidential nomination, he told attendees, "Here, at our convention, there will be no lies. We will honor the American people with the truth, and nothing else."[36]

Fourth, with his "Make America Great Again" motto, Trump aimed to instill a sense of superiority in his supporters. In part, he lifted them up by viciously belittling his adversaries, describing them as "disgusting," "total failures," "idiots," and "losers." Likewise, he claimed that current leaders had failed the American people and the U.S. flag that represents "equality, hope, and fairness...great courage and sacrifice."[37] Trump complained that Americans "have lived through one international humiliation after another"[38] and that "everyone is eating our lunch."[39] He also presented himself as a savior who would make sure the country and its citizens regained the stature they had lost. He claimed that his own accomplishments surpassed those of everyone else, boasting in one interview, "I'm the most successful person ever to run for the presidency, by far."[40] Trump also insisted that his name—and everything he does— is synonymous with top quality, on one occasion explaining, "Nobody can build a wall like me."[41]

Finally, targeting voters' concerns about helplessness, Trump extolled his capability, his expertise, and his doggedness regardless of the odds against him. He told one interviewer, "My life has been about winning."[42] In his acceptance speech for the Republican presidential nomination, he denounced "the system" and claimed, "Only I can fix it"; he concluded with "I'm with you, and I will fight for you, and I will win for you."[43] Memorably, he also told a crowd in Washington, D.C., "We will have so much winning if I get elected that you may get bored with winning."[44] Trump contrasted this purported track record of consistent success with the helplessness Americans would experience if his opponents prevailed. He warned of "uncontrolled immigration," "mass lawlessness," and "overwhelm[ed]...schools and hospitals,"[45] and he described prospects for immigrants to join the middle class as "almost impossible."[46] On Twitter, Trump tweeted, "Crime is out of control, and rapidly getting worse."[47] And he cautioned that efforts aimed at reforming gun laws would make Americans helpless to protect themselves: "You take the guns away from the good people, and the bad ones are going to have target practice."[48]

The Psychology of Persuasion

To understand why appeals like these can be so effective, it helps to know a bit more about the science of persuasion. Whenever we try to influence someone's attitudes, beliefs, or behaviors, we're engaging in persuasion. A parent may cajole a young child into eating vegetables. A teacher may exhort a student to buckle down. A friend may push for seeing one movie over another. A co-worker may encourage a colleague to try a different approach to complete a difficult assignment. Years of research—by psychologists such as Elliot Aronson, Robert Cialdini, and Anthony Pratkanis, among others—have gone a long way toward illuminating the key elements of effective persuasion.[49]

Of particular note, persuasion typically follows either of two different paths.[50] One route engages us in a careful, rational evaluation of the arguments presented. As listeners or readers, we review the evidence, assess which claims seem to make sense and which do not, and then draw our conclusions accordingly. With this route, we try to distinguish between strong arguments and weak arguments. It's an approach that has a lot to offer in getting it right. But it requires time, effort, and discernment—three elements that are often in short supply, especially when we're in a hurry, we're not very interested in the topic, or we lack important background knowledge and skills.

That's where the second persuasion route comes into play. With this path, our judgments are based on considerations quite different from the merits of the arguments themselves. One critical factor is the extent to which the message we hear taps into strong emotions, perhaps making us fearful, or angry, or optimistic. Emotional arousal can lead us to ignore the actual quality of the evidence being presented to us. For instance, if we're angry enough we may lose the capacity to think and see clearly—which is just what those offering weak arguments are hoping for.

In much the same way, certain characteristics of a speaker can heighten their credibility regardless of the claims being made. For example, we're more likely to believe someone who's presented as an expert—even if, unknown to us, this person has been paid to espouse a particular point of view. We're also more readily persuaded by an authority figure—a parent, teacher, boss, or leader of some sort—even if they have no expertise about the issue at hand. As well, we're inclined to accept the arguments offered by those we deem trustworthy and likeable because we tend to see such people as offering honest, objective appraisals unbiased by hidden motives—even when they're not.

In sum, there are a variety of reasons—both good and bad, both conscious and unconscious—why we might be persuaded by an appeal. In some situations, we're given the opportunity to consider carefully formulated arguments that are logical and based on solid evidence. At least as often, however, we find ourselves presented with arguments that have little to do with establishing the truth, despite any appearance to the contrary. The latter is the bailiwick of propaganda. Propagandists take advantage of our fallibility when it comes to figuring out what to believe and what not to believe. Consider the chaplain's insight in Joseph Heller's anti-war novel *Catch-22*, after he had mastered the technique of "protective rationalization":

> It was miraculous. It was almost no trick at all, he saw, to turn vice into virtue and slander into truth, impotence into abstinence, arrogance into humility, plunder into philanthropy, thievery into honor, blasphemy into wisdom, brutality into patriotism, and sadism into justice. Anybody could do it; it required no brains at all. It merely required no character.[51]

Further to this point, psychologist Melanie Green and her colleagues have shown that when it comes to persuasiveness, it doesn't necessarily matter whether we think we're hearing a fictional story or a fact-based account of real-world events. This means that an engaging narrative can change the way we think about things, regardless of whether it's labeled fact or fiction. These same researchers have also discovered that listeners who are absorbed by a story—when it "transports" them—don't even notice the inaccuracies it contains.[52]

So as far as changing opinions goes, making stuff up and packaging it into an emotionally gripping tale may get you a lot further than documenting facts and presenting them in a straightforward way. That's good news for storytellers, and nobody has more money to spend on creating elaborate tales than the predatory class. Moreover, defenders of extreme wealth and power are also by far the best equipped to make sure millions of people watch and hear these stories, over and over again.

Indeed, it's the mainstream media outlets—owned by a handful of mega-corporations—that help establish the news agenda in this country.[53] They decide what's newsworthy, what's worth knowing more about, and what's unimportant— and their choices usually favor the interests of the 1%. Even when Twitter and Facebook supersede them as direct sources of information, more traditional outlets still play a critical role in mediating how a lot of Americans interpret events by guiding our understanding of causes and consequences. For example, the mainstream media influences whether the public views drug abuse as a crime or an addiction, as deserving incarceration or treatment, and as a failure of the individual or society. Similarly, Black Lives Matter can be portrayed as a legitimate protest movement against violence or an anti-cop rallying cry.

A Battleground of Divergent Values

This book reflects a set of basic values. In simple terms, I believe political persuasion efforts that engage our five core concerns should serve to counter extreme inequality rather than preserve or extend it. These appeals should spur us to improve people's lives, not turn our backs on those who are struggling. And they should help us better understand how, together, we can make things better—for everyone. As we'll see, the mind games of the 1% do just the opposite.

That's why progress depends upon combating the destructive propaganda of today's self-aggrandizing plutocrats. It's a tall order, but unless we succeed, middle-class families will continue to face escalating healthcare and education costs and growing economic insecurity. And despite their resilience, those who are poor will have ever-dwindling hopes for a brighter future. The 1% have created a daunting environment for collective action by those who oppose their aims. But the rest of us have key resources of our own, including a compelling vision for our country—one in which danger, mistreatment, and crushed aspirations are no longer a routine part of so many lives.

The chapters that follow dissect the political mind games today's plutocrats rely on to exploit the public's concerns about issues of vulnerability, injustice, distrust, superiority, and helplessness. In each chapter, I'll examine four appeals used by the 1% to push their narrow agenda (the full list appears on the opposite page), and I'll highlight some of the underlying psychological factors that often make them effective. To debunk and counter these manipulative ploys, especially with a billionaire huckster in the White House, we need to better understand exactly how they work.

I finished writing *Political Mind Games* in November 2017, one year after the presidential election and a year before the crucial 2018 midterms. In many ways, Trump has now become the most frightening symptom of an entrenched system that prioritizes profits over people. But let's remember that America's plutocrats were using manipulative psychological appeals long before his demagogic campaign and unexpected victory, and they'll undoubtedly continue to do so long after he's gone. That's why I've chosen to offer readers an overarching framework that isn't limited to this particular political moment. And it's why the many examples I've included span a universe much larger than the mind games of Trump and his cronies alone. Let's get started.

THE MIND GAMES OF AMERICA'S PLUTOCRATS

VULNERABILITY

— *It's a Dangerous World* —
— *Change Is Dangerous* —
— *It's a False Alarm* —
— *We'll Make You Sorry* —

INJUSTICE

— *We're Fighting Injustice* —
— *No Injustice Here* —
— *Change Is Unjust* —
— *We're the Victims* —

DISTRUST

— *They're Devious and Dishonest* —
— *They're Different from Us* —
— *They're Misguided and Misinformed* —
— *Trust Us* —

SUPERIORITY

— *They're Losers* —
— *We've Earned It* —
— *Pursuing a Higher Purpose* —
— *They're Un-American* —

HELPLESSNESS

— *Change Is Impossible* —
— *We'll All Be Helpless* —
— *Don't Blame Us* —
— *Resistance Is Futile* —

2

VULNERABILITY MIND GAMES
EXPLOITING OUR FEARS AND INSECURITIES

"The greatest remedy for fear is to stand up and fight for your rights."

— HENRY A. WALLACE[1]

Our concerns about vulnerability are central to how we see the world around us. When our security is in jeopardy, nothing else matters as much. The mere prospect of danger can consume all of our focus and energy. Not surprisingly, then, the desire to ensure our own safety—and that of people we care about—is a powerful force in determining the policies we support and the actions we take.

That's why today's plutocrats work so hard to shape our perceptions of vulnerability for their own ends. The psychological mind games they employ for this purpose are often effective, even when the underlying arguments they offer have little merit. Although it's human nature to be attentive to possible threats, we're not very good at judging peril. As a result, we're susceptible to manipulation by those who skillfully misrepresent the dangers we face.

A memorable example of this gullibility was the panic that ensued when some listeners mistook an Orson Welles radio adaptation of *The War of the Worlds* for the real thing: a live account of Martian invaders landing in Grover's Mill, New Jersey. Fooled by the broadcast's air of authenticity, complete with "We interrupt our program" news bulletins, some frantically called the local police, others fled from their homes near the reported invasion site, and still others apparently fainted beside their radios. Within hours the hoax was revealed. But that autumn night in 1938 still stands as a reminder of just how impressionable—and off-target—we can be when it comes to figuring out whether or not we're safe.

Of course the 1% don't try to frighten us with warnings of invaders from outer space. Rather, they manipulate our concerns about potential threats much closer to home. In this chapter, we'll take a close look at four of the vulnerability mind games they use to shape our perceptions to their advantage: It's a Dangerous World, Change Is Dangerous, It's a False Alarm, and We'll Make You Sorry.

IT'S A DANGEROUS WORLD

Representatives of the 1% are adept at highlighting purported dangers that await if we fail to act upon their policy prescriptions. In many cases, they scare us and then offer an answer to our fears: Do exactly as we tell you. What they don't tell us is that their "fixes" will benefit big-money interests at the expense of those who are already disadvantaged.

We're soft targets for such tactics because, in our desire to avoid being unprepared when danger strikes, we're often quick to conjure catastrophe—the worst outcome imaginable—regardless of how unlikely it may be. In our personal lives, for example, we may worry that a headache is a symptom of an untreatable brain tumor, that a minor disagreement portends the end of a cherished relationship, or that one disappointing grade in school will require a change in career aspirations.

In this way, highly improbable—perhaps even impossible—negative outcomes can dominate our thinking, just because it would be so awful for them to happen. As William Shakespeare described it, "Present fears are less than horrible imaginings." Such catastrophizing—those horrible imaginings—can be very costly. We can miss out on valuable opportunities when we abandon careful analysis and concentrate solely on preparing for or avoiding nightmarish scenarios.

This tendency plays into the hands of influential marketers of fear. Indeed, our inclination to catastrophize typically becomes even stronger when authority figures are the ones forecasting doom. Dire warnings from high-level sources can short-circuit our critical thinking and propel us toward action—before we've examined the evidence or considered the consequences.

If a crisis environment exists, we're all the more responsive to forceful guidance about what must be done "for our own protection." This is true even when the recommended steps involve relinquishing rights and values we hold dear. Nazi propagandist Hermann Göring acknowledged this during the Nuremberg trials after World War II:

> Voice or no voice, the people can always be brought to the bidding of the leaders. That is easy. All you have to do is tell them they are being attacked and denounce the pacifists for lack of patriotism and exposing the country to danger. It works the same way in any country.[2]

Let's now further explore this It's a Dangerous World mind game by looking at some specific examples, including the Iraq War, the war on drugs, mass surveillance, and economic austerity.

Selling the Iraq War

Fearmongering has long been a staple in recipes for selling war to the American people.[3] A case in point was the White House's consistent use of the It's a Dangerous World mind game in the months leading up to the 2003 invasion of Iraq.

In August 2002, Vice President Dick Cheney told attendees at the national convention of the Veterans of Foreign Wars in Nashville, "There is no doubt that Saddam Hussein now has weapons of mass destruction. There is no doubt he is amassing them to use against our friends, against our allies, and against us."[4] Two months later, President George W. Bush presented this frightful image to an audience in Cincinnati:

> Knowing these realities, America must not ignore the threat gathering against us. Facing clear evidence of peril, we cannot wait for the final proof—the smoking gun—that could come in the form of a mushroom cloud.[5]

And Secretary of Defense Donald Rumsfeld was unequivocal at a December 2002 Department of Defense news briefing: "Any country on the face of the earth with an active intelligence program knows that Iraq has weapons of mass destruction."[6]

It didn't matter that these claims were all untrue; they were effective nonetheless. As White House officials had hoped, their warnings and alarmist predictions succeeded in persuading most Americans of two things: Iraq's dictator had weapons of mass destruction (WMD), and "preventive" military action was therefore necessary. Indeed, Bush knew he already had won over the public when he sat before the television cameras in the Oval Office on March 19, 2003, and announced that U.S. forces had invaded Iraq.[7]

After the invasion, when WMD stockpiles couldn't be found, the Bush administration shifted gears a bit. But it continued to feed the public's fears by linking the war in Iraq to the larger "global war on terror." Speaking at the National Lawyers Convention of the Federalist Society in Washington, D.C., in 2006, Cheney offered this analysis:

> On the morning of September 11th, we saw that the terrorists need to get only one break, need to be right only once, to carry out an attack. We have to be right every time to

stop them. So to adopt a purely defensive posture, to simply brace for attacks and react to them, is to play against lengthening odds, and to leave the nation permanently vulnerable.[8]

Debate over the correct course in Iraq intensified even more the following year—and the president again resorted to the It's a Dangerous World mind game. Bush warned of looming catastrophe with public statements like this: "If we do not defeat the terrorists and extremists in Iraq, they won't leave us alone—they will follow us to the United States of America. That's what makes this battle in the war on terror so incredibly important."[9] The fearmongering didn't stop when Bush left office. In a 2010 Veterans Day speech in St. Louis, General John Kelly—now retired and Donald Trump's chief of staff—insisted:

> Our enemy is savage, offers absolutely no quarter, and has a single focus, and that is either kill every one of us here at home or enslave us with a sick form of extremism that serves no God or purpose that decent men and women could ever grasp.[10]

Today it's clear that Iraq did not have an active WMD program.[11] Yet many Americans—including more than half of Republicans and Fox News viewers—continue to erroneously believe that such a program was found.[12] So too, in a 2011 poll almost half of Americans believed that Iraq either gave substantial support to al-Qaeda or was involved in the 9/11 terrorist attacks. Neither claim is true.[13] But the persistence of these false beliefs demonstrates the staying power of manipulative mind games designed to exploit our fears.

The enormous costs of the invasion and occupation of Iraq are now apparent. Thousands of U.S. soldiers and coalition allies were killed and many more suffered debilitating injuries; among the U.S. casualties, a disproportionate number were underprivileged youth.[14] At the same time, hundreds of thousands of Iraqi civilians died, and millions were driven from their homes.[15] To this toll we can add the emergence and growth of the brutal Islamic State (ISIS).[16] And our Iraq War expenditures—past, present, and future—will total trillions of dollars, a massive drain on crucial domestic programs for those in need.[17]

But despite this devastating scorecard, we shouldn't forget that the It's a Dangerous World mind game created its share of winners too—at least among the predatory class. Consider the executives and large shareholders in companies like Halliburton's former subsidiary Kellogg, Brown, and Root; General Dynamics; Lockheed Martin; and ExxonMobil, to name just a few. These corporations garnered huge war profits through no-bid defense contracts, oil sales, environmental cleanup, infrastructure repair, prison services, and private security.[18]

As former Congressional staff member Mike Lofgren has described it, "Being in favor of the Iraq War may have been objectively wrong, but it was an astute career move for many government operatives and contractors."[19] How true. Speaking to defense contractors at an August 2015 private event, Jeb Bush—who failed to gain the 2016 Republican nomination for his brother's old job—explained, "Taking out Saddam Hussein turned out to be a pretty good deal."[20]

Domestic Battles: Drug Wars and Mass Surveillance

Beyond ruinous military exploits, the It's a Dangerous World mind game is standard garb when it comes to camouflaging destructive domestic policies that serve only narrow interests. For example, according to our fearmongering president, Attorney General Jeff Sessions—the former Republican senator from Alabama dogged by accusations of racism—is "a great protector of the people."[21] But exactly which people does Trump have in mind as he and Sessions move to revive the country's discriminatory and discredited "war on drugs"? In pushing for mandatory minimum prison sentences for even low-level drug offenders, it seemingly doesn't matter to them

that this half-century, trillion-dollar war has failed misera-
bly—decimating communities, undercutting much-needed
addiction treatment programs, and fueling our country's epidemic of mass incarceration.[22]

That's not to say that the drug war hasn't had its share of
winners. On that list are various rich and powerful industries
(alcohol, tobacco, pharmaceuticals, and private prisons), those
who benefit from civil asset forfeiture laws allowing the seizure
of private property, and those who gain advantage from the
disenfranchisement of felons and ex-felons. But the public is
nowhere to be found among the beneficiaries. So, for decades,
distressing images have been used to frighten us and protect
the drug war from the scrutiny it deserves.

While president, Ronald Reagan told us that drugs were
"poisoning the blood of our children."[23] During his own White
House years, George W. Bush warned that drugs turn "play-
grounds into crime scenes."[24] And now we have the latest
rendition of the It's a Dangerous World mind game: Sessions
claiming that marijuana creates a "life-wrecking dependen-
cy"[25] little different from heroin and insisting that "families
will be broken up" and "children will be damaged" by pot
legalization.[26]

We've seen similar scare tactics—from leaders of both major
parties—in efforts to garner public support for another boon-
doggle: the controversial mass surveillance of Americans.[27]
They know that violating our basic constitutional rights
becomes more psychologically palatable if we're focused on the
prospect of violent death and destruction. After the Bush-era
revelations of warrantless wiretapping back in 2006, Senator
Pat Roberts, Republican of Kansas, then chair of the Senate
Intelligence Committee, offered this stark summary: "You have
no civil liberties if you are dead."[28] After the leaks by Edward
Snowden in mid-2013, President Barack Obama reassured
everyone that these surveillance programs "help us prevent
terrorist attacks."[29] And in late 2015, then-candidate Trump
expressed his support this way: "When you have the world

looking at us and would like to destroy us as quickly as possible, I err on the side of security."[30]

While it's-a-dangerous-world warnings may cow the public at large, others are cheered by such grim pronouncements. Handsomely paid private contractors like Booz Allen Hamilton (Snowden's former employer) earn billions of dollars each year from their work with the intelligence community.[31] It doesn't seem to matter that a 2013 analysis from a presidential task force concluded that meta-data collection has played no essential role in the prevention of even a single terrorist attack.[32] Indeed, keep-fear-alive business executives, with financial interests in an expansive surveillance state, continue to push for increasingly intrusive—and more expensive—spying operations.[33]

Austerity, for the 99%

Speaker of the House Paul Ryan has argued that it "will result in our children and our grandchildren experiencing a diminished future."[34] Admiral Mike Mullen, chairman of the Joint Chiefs of Staff under both Bush and Obama, has called it "the single, biggest threat to our national security."[35] Erskine Bowles, White House chief of staff under Bill Clinton, has warned that it's "a cancer that in time will destroy our country from within."[36] And Pete Peterson, billionaire founder of the private equity Blackstone Group, has described it as "a catastrophic threat to our security and economy."[37]

So what is this fearful creature that seemingly threatens our very survival, at least according to Republican and Democratic plutocrats alike? It's none other than government debt—the very same borrowing and spending that can promote economic growth, move us toward fuller employment, provide essential funding for social welfare programs and infrastructure repairs, and enhance the well-being of future generations.[38] Of course one-percenters have little interest in what helps the rest of us. They're stuck on finding ways to further feather their own nests, and economic austerity for the masses opens the golden door to lowering taxes and privatizing government services. That's why they repeatedly turn to the It's a Dangerous World mind game, agitating for an urgent reduction in the national debt through "belt-tightening" and "shared sacrifice." The adverse debt effects of Wall Street's greed and corruption go unmentioned.[39] Few sing this song better or louder than Peterson's "Fix the Debt" campaign. Launched in 2012, it brings together corporate titans, phony grassroots "astroturf" groups, and a pliable press to argue that budget deficits should be our foremost concern—more important than unemployment, poverty, or other sources of hardship and misery. In support of the austerity campaign's kickoff, billionaire and former Starbucks CEO Howard Schultz required his low-wage workers in the nation's capital to write "Come Together" on customers' cups.[40]

Making matters even worse, a common thread runs through the so-called solutions the 1% offer for their manufactured debt crisis: They're all designed to increase plutocratic wealth at the expense of those already burdened by financial insecurity. That's why we don't hear them calling for higher taxes on super-rich Americans and hugely profitable corporations—a simple way to help reduce the debt. Instead, Fix the Debt and other defenders of extreme inequality take aim at programs like Social Security, issuing dire forecasts about its solvency. And what kinds of reforms do they recommend? Shrinking the monthly checks senior citizens receive, reducing cost-of-living adjustments, and raising the retirement age for workers—all changes that would be especially harmful to lower-income individuals and families.[41]

Regrettably, the 1%'s It's a Dangerous World mind game has borne fruit. In regard to Social Security, two-thirds of Americans are now convinced that the current system has "major problems" or is in "a state of crisis."[42] These propaganda-generated fears belie the fact that Social Security isn't really in bad shape. Moreover, it would be even more secure if we merely raised the income cap on payroll taxes so that high earners pay at the same rate as those who earn less.[43] But that's the kind of equality-enhancing response considered out of bounds by fat cats with personal retirement accounts worth millions of dollars.[44] After all, their doomsday debt warnings and calls for austerity aren't really about advancing the common good. They're designed to accomplish something different: the further upward redistribution of wealth.

CHANGE IS DANGEROUS

With the Change Is Dangerous vulnerability mind game, today's plutocrats defend their agenda in a different way: by insisting that their opponents' proposals for change will endanger us all. Regardless of the benefits these alternatives could bring, the 1% argue that initiatives inconsistent with their own policy recommendations will have potentially catastrophic consequences for the country. This is true whether we're talking about tax increases for the wealthy (new investments stifled!), minimum wage hikes (forced layoffs!), curtailment of spying operations (terrorists everywhere!), new regulations to address climate change (U.S. businesses unable to compete!), reductions in mass incarceration (crime waves!), gun control (defenseless citizens!), or lower-cost imported medications from Canada (tainted drugs!).

Such appeals from self-interested one-percenters benefit from what psychologists call "status quo bias." We generally prefer to keep things the way they are rather than face the uncertainty of less familiar options. In part, this is because we usually experience losses more intensely than rewards. That's why winning $100 doesn't feel as good as losing $100 feels bad.[45] In much the same way, we tend to focus on how a proposed change could make things worse rather than better. Familiar expressions like "Better the devil you know than the devil you don't know" and "When in doubt, do nothing" capture the phenomenon well. This helps explain why patients are reluctant to change a medication they've been taking for years, even if their doctor tells them a newer one works better and has fewer side effects. Likewise, when it comes to elections, incumbents have an advantage over their challengers—even when they've disappointed their constituents. Preferences like these may be irrational, but that doesn't make them any less stubborn or potent.

Unfortunately, our status quo bias serves the interests of plutocrats and their Change Is Dangerous mind game. As a result of our psychological discomfort with change, we often view reformers more negatively than those who defend current arrangements. Research suggests multiple reasons for this. People tend to see reformers as extremists, while status quo supporters are seen as more moderate and reasonable in their stances. Also, those who are seeking change tend to be viewed as more selfish in their motivations than defenders of the status quo, especially when the former are of lower status than the latter.[46] Psychological tendencies like these can pose significant obstacles to the public's embrace of much-needed reforms.

Our natural skepticism about change also makes people more susceptible to faulty arguments from those who want current policies left alone. Status quo bias may lead us to be less discerning when a politician exaggerates the risks associated with new policy options, or when they offer flawed comparisons to historical cases where alarming predictions about change came true. Regardless of their intrinsic merit, arguments like these succeed when they create feelings of vulnerability and dread. But at such times, it's useful to remember that influential, entrenched interests also made dire forecasts when they opposed the abolition of slavery in the nineteenth century, resisted voting rights for women in the early 1900s, and condemned the civil rights movement in the 1960s.

Let's now take a closer look at how the predatory class uses the Change Is Dangerous mind game. Two important examples are their defense of the country's for-profit healthcare system and our bloated defense budget.

U.S. Healthcare: Caring for Profits Most of All

For decades, the 1% have blocked all attempts to meaningfully reform a broken healthcare system that prioritizes corporate profits over the needs of the frail and the ill.[47] Over this period and in various guises, the Change Is Dangerous mind game has been a central element in well-funded campaigns designed to stoke fears about the prospect of a government-financed system of national health insurance, what some call "Medicare for All."

Consider that in the early 1960s, in a radio address for the American Medical Association, Reagan decried socialized medicine, warning that if Medicare was enacted, "One of these days you and I are going to spend our sunset years telling our children and our children's children what it once was like in America when men were free."[48] In more recent years, Senator Rand Paul, Republican of Kentucky, has argued that healthcare as a right means "you believe in slavery."[49] Former U.S. Representative Tom Price, briefly Trump's Secretary of Health and Human Services, similarly cautioned, "as the government begins to define and control what constitutes health care, the rights and well-being of the American people will be compromised."[50]

Even though the 2010 Affordable Care Act—more familiarly known as "Obamacare"—extended health insurance to millions of Americans, moneyed interests made sure it didn't alter our underlying for-profit system, one that remains unnecessarily costly and inefficient.[51] From the outset, Obamacare was a grand bargain with the pharmaceutical, hospital, and insurance industries—all insisting that healthcare reform not stand in the way of ever-greater profits.[52] As a result, President Obama never pushed for popular options like Medicare for All, and today we continue to lack universal coverage.[53] These gaps in coverage—which are likely to grow larger under President Trump and a Republican Congress—take their greatest toll on lower socioeconomic groups, where infant mortality is higher and average life expectancy is lower than they are in many other countries.[54]

But Obamacare's faithfulness to industry interests has never stopped Republican politicians from condemning it anyway. In doing so, they've relied on psychologically seductive change-is-dangerous rhetoric to stir up panic over a range of imaginary perils: long waiting lines, a shortage of physicians, inferior care, and totalitarian control of our medical treatment. Former Alaska Governor Sarah Palin, John McCain's running mate in 2008, memorably ranted about fictitious "death panels" where heartless government administrators decide who receives life-saving treatment and who doesn't. She also warned of bureaucrats who deem "the sick, the elderly, and the disabled" unworthy of care.[55] With similar intent, Tea Party favorite Michele Bachmann, the former congresswoman from Minnesota, described Obamacare as "the crown jewel of socialism."[56]

These were far from isolated efforts aimed at portraying healthcare reform as the work of dangerous extremists. Representatives of the 1% have also funded the publication of purportedly scientific papers predicting the apocalypse if we abandon our for-profit healthcare system. They've established bogus grassroots groups to create the illusion of even greater populist outrage and fear over proposed changes.[57] And they used right-wing media personalities and anti-reform organizations to encourage the disruption of healthcare-focused town hall meetings.[58]

Every other major industrialized country has successfully adopted some form of a single, unified system in which health insurance is a nonprofit enterprise and everyone has coverage from birth until death.[59] In these systems, private insurance companies—staunch proponents of healthcare as a privilege rather than a human right—are eliminated, even where private doctors and private hospitals continue to provide patient care. But thanks to a heavy dose of change-is-dangerous propaganda, it's much different here in the United States.

Moreover, under Obamacare the enormously profitable insurance industry persists in finding ways to ruthlessly cut its own costs. Coverage is denied for life-saving medical procedures or medications. Deductibles are raised. Access to specialists is limited. Bureaucratic red tape is used to discourage patients from pursuing legitimate reimbursement claims.[60] As economist James Galbraith has pointed out, whenever controversy arises these companies fall back on their political clout and their "almost unlimited capacity to sow confusion among the general public over the basic economic facts."[61]

With the 2016 election, Republicans established full control over the House, Senate, and White House, making affordable healthcare for all an even more distant prospect. Indeed, recent proposals in Congress for repealing and replacing Obamacare would leave millions more without insurance. It's obvious to most Americans that this is the wrong direction to go in.[62] But healthcare industry executives and their plutocratic friends don't mind taking some heat: They're in line for windfall tax cuts and even greater profits if the plan ever becomes law.[63]

Defending a Bloated Defense Budget

We see the same Change Is Dangerous mind game at work in the 1%'s opposition to reductions in our bloated defense budget. Most Americans favor less military spending—which now exceeds a half-trillion dollars annually, more than half of the government's entire discretionary spending—over cuts to Social Security and Medicare.[64] But Congress, spurred by industry lobbyists and millions of dollars in campaign contributions, has reliably sided with the big-money interests that profit from defense spending. As a result, the massive post-9/11 funding for the "global war on terror" and its various spinoffs has come at the expense of domestic programs that could bolster employment, healthcare, and education.[65]

This isn't what the public wants, but members of the plutocracy—across the political spectrum, both within and outside of government—know how to keep us from finding firm footing. They take turns issuing frantic warnings about the heightened dangers on the horizon if the defense budget is cut. For instance, Howard McKeon, former chairman of the House Armed Services Committee, has argued, "Defense cuts...will weaken our nation, leave us vulnerable to attack and hasten in an unmistakable era of American decline."[66] General Peter Chiarelli, former Vice Chief of Staff of the U.S. Army, has advised, "If we get it wrong with defense, the consequences will be measured not just in treasure, but in blood."[67] Marion Blakey, former president and CEO of the defense-lobbying group Aerospace Industries Association (she now holds the same positions at Rolls-Royce North America), has warned, "Additional cuts...would tear through muscle and into the bone of America's national security."[68]

Such apocalyptic imagery can be psychologically potent, pushing us toward emotional rather than reasoned responses. But these change-is-dangerous appeals protect the predatory class far better than they protect our national security.[69] Let's remember that the U.S. defense budget exceeds that of the next seven largest countries combined.[70] It's also roughly twice as large as it was before the 9/11 attacks.[71] And who are the most direct beneficiaries of such outsized spending? Giant defense contractors and weapons builders. Lockheed Martin, Northrup Grumman, Boeing, General Dynamics, and Raytheon, among others, depend on war and terrorism fears to make hundreds of millions of dollars in annual profits. Indeed, Lockheed executive Bruce Tanner assured attendees at a December 2015 investors' conference that heightened conflict in Syria would bring increased demand for the company's planes and weapons.[72] Further support for the 1%'s narrow interests comes from their pot-of-gold pipeline, one that turns retired politicians and military officers into highly compensated board members and spokespersons for the defense industry.[73]

Those who defend concentrated wealth and power are ready with other tall tales if the public isn't persuaded by dire warnings that defense cuts will jeopardize our national security. One is the deceptive claim that reductions in military spending will weaken the economy and increase unemployment. For example, an analysis conducted on behalf of the Aerospace Industries Association estimated that one million jobs would be lost if military spending was reduced.[74] But independent economic studies argue otherwise. In fact, military funding is among the least efficient ways to create jobs. For the same number of fixed dollars, many more jobs could be created in underfunded areas like healthcare and education.[75]

But that doesn't matter to politicians beholden to plutocratic interests. They're steadfast in protecting defense outlays, and they target their budget cuts elsewhere—often at the programs that help people who are struggling to get by.[76] Perhaps they should recall General Dwight D. Eisenhower's words shortly after becoming our 34th president: "Every gun that is made, every warship launched, every rocket fired signifies, in the final sense, a theft from those who hunger and are not fed, those who are cold and are not clothed."[77]

IT'S A FALSE ALARM

With both the It's a Dangerous World and the Change Is Dangerous mind games, the 1% stoke our fears to achieve their aims. With the It's a False Alarm mind game, they adopt the opposite strategy instead, downplaying the real risks and costs to the common good that are associated with their self-serving priorities. Here, by their account, the dangers identified by others are either imaginary or greatly exaggerated. They dismiss these warnings of peril, hoping to keep the public in the dark about threats to our collective welfare. When plutocrats succeed in putting a convincing positive spin on current arrangements, opposition to their greed-driven agenda is stifled, and they can continue to reap the outsized rewards of extreme inequality.

We're susceptible to such ploys because, although we're prone to catastrophize and expect the worst under certain conditions, we take comfort in believing danger is far from our door. Disasters, accidents, and untimely deaths catch our attention on the daily news. But most of the time we much prefer to see the world as a place that's predominantly safe, where tragic outcomes are notable exceptions rather than common occurrences. It's this psychological preference that can make us so quick to fall for the It's a False Alarm mind game and assurances that everything's fine, especially when that "all clear" signal comes from someone who's considered an authority or expert.

In our personal lives, adopting a rosy perspective insulates us from nagging or overwhelming feelings of anxiety and the extreme discomfort they can bring. Indeed, from hour to hour and day to day, it's not unusual for people to block out painful realities, like the awareness of our own mortality or the prevalence of suffering in the world. Unless prompted otherwise, as a protective mechanism we'd rather go about our lives with a mindset typified by "see no evil, hear no evil," "don't worry, be happy," and "out of sight, out of mind."

Since plutocrats don't want us to recognize the dangerous and damaging consequences of the policies they promote, our anxiety-avoiding tendencies work to their advantage. When they assert that concerns are overblown and no cause for alarm, it can be music to our ears. And when they tell us to relax because they'll take care of whatever needs to be done, we're relieved to hear that too. Unfortunately, however, those assurances often help to lay the groundwork for their reckless pursuits—tax cuts, or industry deregulation, or overseas military adventures, to name just a few.

In examining the It's a False Alarm mind game more closely, we'll take a look at how the 1% rely on this third vulnerability appeal when they promote climate change confusion and when they prioritize corporate profits over public safety.

Climate Change: 1% Denials and Dismissals

The world's leading scientists long ago reached an over-whelming consensus: Climate change and global warming are happening; they're caused by human activity, especially the burning of fossil fuels; and the risks for our future and for the planet are devastating.[78] People already facing the hardships of poverty and poor health are among those who are most vulnerable to increasing temperatures, rising sea levels, and floods and droughts. But the adverse effects of climate change are likely to spare very few of us. As food and water supplies dwindle, conflict and violence will loom ever larger. International instability and economic losses will also increase, far exceeding the costs of tackling climate change directly.[79]

But other considerations take priority for the oil and gas industry. Their profits—hundreds of billions of dollars annually—will be jeopardized if we adopt new regulations that encourage greater reliance on renewable energy sources like solar power and wind.[80] That's why they turn to the It's a False Alarm mind game as part of a massive, multifaceted misinformation campaign. Their disingenuous appeals to the public include denials that climate change exists, assertions that scientists disagree about the facts, and assurances that there's no real crisis because we can make whatever adjustments may be necessary in the future.[81]

So even though the urgent need for environmental legislation is clear, wealthy climate change deniers and their cronies in Washington stymie these efforts. The newest entry on the scene is President Trump, who said, "I don't believe in climate change"[82] during his presidential campaign and then withdrew the United States from the international Paris climate accord shortly after taking office.[83] His pick to head the Environmental Protection Agency, former Oklahoma Attorney General Scott Pruitt, has close ties to the fossil fuel industry and to anti-regulation advocacy groups.[84] Pruitt has falsely claimed, "Scientists continue to disagree about the degree and extent of global warming and its connection to the actions of mankind."[85]

Then there's Republican Senator James Inhofe from Oklahoma, the former chair of the Senate Committee on Environment and Public Works. His largest campaign contributions come from energy industry giants, and he's been an influential obstructionist for a very long time. Bringing the It's a False Alarm mind game to the floor of the U.S. Senate, Inhofe once argued, "With all of the hysteria, all of the fear, all of the phony science, could it be that manmade global warming is the greatest hoax ever perpetrated on the American people? It sure sounds like it."[86] On another occasion he described the EPA as a "Gestapo bureaucracy."[87] All of these views are unsupported by any evidence, but they're far from insignificant in their consequences.

Right-wing think tanks and similar groups, with substantial funding from the fossil fuel industry and other plutocratic allies, also promote it's-a-false-alarm messages to reassure the public that all is well. These organizations present themselves and their spokespersons as credible sources of unbiased information about climate change. But that's a ruse. Their real aim is to confuse us by distorting or casting doubt on the clear scientific consensus about human-caused global warming. As one example, it's not unusual for writers, some with scholarly backgrounds, to receive financial support for publishing books and articles that contest the disturbing climate change reports issued by distinguished scientific bodies.[88]

Consider too the Heartland Institute, which claims to advance "pro-environment policies based on sound science and economics, not alarmism or ideology." That doesn't exactly fit with statements like this one from the organization's director of communications: "The people who still believe in man-made global warming are mostly on the radical fringe of society. This is why the most prominent advocates of global warming aren't scientists. They are murderers, tyrants, and madmen."[89] Taking it's-a-false-alarm appeals to even more absurd heights on a

Chicago highway billboard, Heartland equated people worried about climate change with terrorists like Ted Kaczynski, the Unabomber. The billboard paired Kaczynski's image with this message: "I still believe in Global Warming. Do you?"[90]

The Heartland Institute and similar groups have also been involved in bringing the It's a False Alarm mind game to the teaching of science in K-12 classrooms. In various states, teachers are forced to present the climate change denialist view as a scientifically valid position and global warming as a matter of controversy among scientists.[91] Describing obstacles encountered in these ongoing efforts to impose this alternative curriculum, a leaked Heartland fundraising document lamented that "Principals and teachers are heavily biased toward the alarmist perspective."[92] In one of its latest campaigns, Heartland is mailing free materials to over 200,000 public school science teachers—all designed to cast doubt on the human role in climate change.[93]

Finally, when other tactics fail to blunt our worries about a fraught environmental future, representatives of the 1% turn to yet another it's-a-false-alarm ploy. They argue that we can continue to rely on fossil fuels because any potential harm will be far less disruptive than people fear. In written comments to the EPA, the U.S. Chamber of Commerce—a lobbying group for big business—highlighted air conditioning as a way to make global warming more bearable.[94] Similarly, in 2012 ExxonMobil CEO Rex Tillerson—who once explained, "My philosophy is to make money"[95]—responded to concerns about rising sea levels with this: "We believe those consequences are manageable...We have spent our entire existence adapting, OK? So we will adapt to this."[96] Five years later, at his confirmation hearing as Trump's Secretary of State, Tillerson hadn't really changed his tune: "I don't see [climate change] as the imminent national security threat that perhaps others do."[97]

Corporate Profits, Whatever the Cost

When corporate giants deploy the It's a False Alarm mind game, obscuring the consequences of climate change is undoubtedly their most calamitous conquest. But they use the same psychological tactics in a wide range of other areas, insisting there's little to worry about as they aggressively pursue profits while giving short shrift to human welfare.

Our country's international trade deals, for instance, routinely prioritize the financial interests of multinational businesses over concerns about slave wages, human rights abuses, and environmental degradation. Consider the ill-fated Trans-Pacific Partnership, an agreement forged between the United States and eleven countries, including some with very ugly records when it comes to labor and civil rights. Had Trump not withdrawn the United States from the treaty upon taking office, the TPP likely would have depressed wages for American workers through the offshoring of U.S. jobs to partner countries where hourly minimum wages are much lower.[98] The deal also would have rewarded giant pharmaceutical companies by extending their patent protections on expensive life-saving drugs. And it would have enabled corporations to bring lawsuits in international tribunals against domestic laws that cut into their profits—even if those same laws served to protect consumers from contaminated food or substandard goods.[99]

Issues like these deserved acknowledgment and serious consideration. But the U.S. Coalition for TPP, which included familiar names like Apple, Facebook, ExxonMobil, Pfizer, and Walmart, was quick to downplay or disregard potential problems. The group assured the American public that the pact "will open markets for U.S. farmers, manufacturers and service providers, increase U.S. exports, and support American jobs." President Obama joined the it's-a-false-alarm chorus at that time, describing the worries of TPP critics as "pure speculation"[100] reflecting a "lack of knowledge."[101]

Another example where industry leaders dismiss legitimate public interest concerns is fracking, a controversial method for extracting oil and natural gas by pumping high-pressure fluids into rock formations deep underground. Currently, scientific debate swirls around the extent to which fracking poses widespread health risks. In specific cases, links have been found between the process and the contamination of local water supplies.[102] Researchers have also documented higher levels of health problems reported by residents living near these sites.[103] But such findings don't seem to matter so much to the American Petroleum Institute, an industry lobbying group that spends millions of dollars to block unwelcome restrictions.[104] The API's public relations campaign insists that fracking is entirely safe and characterizes concerns as merely "a barrage of politically based attacks attempting to tamper with scientific conclusions."[105]

Questions within the scientific community over the safety of glyphosate have produced the same type of It's a False Alarm mind game mischief from corporate honchos.[106] A research report from a World Health Organization task force has identified this herbicide, the primary ingredient in Monsanto's Roundup and other weed-killers, as "probably carcinogenic to humans."[107] Other scientific groups have questioned that conclusion. So it might seem as though the final verdict is still out. But that's not Monsanto's view. The agribusiness giant has called for a retraction of the critical WHO report, describing those findings as "junk science" while assuring the public that "Safety is the top priority for every person who works at Monsanto."[108]

It's worth noting here that there's an even more devious variation of the It's a False Alarm mind game. Rather than merely claiming that risks are overblown, sometimes corporations take steps to actually hide dangers from those who are imperiled. For decades, the Johns-Manville Corporation and other asbestos industry giants withheld information on the heightened risks of cancer and other diseases from their workers and customers alike.[109] For just as long, R. J. Reynolds and other tobacco companies concealed evidence from smokers of the addictive and cancer-causing effects of cigarettes.[110] Over many years, General Motors and other auto companies denied dangerous manufacturing defects, and in some cases tried to silence whistleblowers as well.[111] And finally, we shouldn't overlook the many cases where industry giants—Enron, WorldCom, Fannie Mae, and more—victimized employees and shareholders through fraudulent accounting practices.

WE'LL MAKE YOU SORRY

The fourth and final vulnerability appeal is the We'll Make You Sorry mind game. The 1% warn us—directly and indirectly, publicly and privately—that those who oppose them will pay a heavy price for doing so. Although they may prefer to use less heavy-handed tactics, the predatory class is not averse to threats and retaliation. After all, our country's history doesn't lack for examples where authorities cracked down on Americans seeking to improve their circumstances. Although such steps can jeopardize the plutocrats' public standing, much of the bullying that silences their adversaries undoubtedly transpires without the rest of us ever finding out about it.

Threats and retaliation alter the cost-benefit analysis of standing up to those in positions of power. Prospects of harm and humiliation heighten the personal stakes associated with acts of conscience and resistance, whether we're talking about protests, whistleblowing, or revelations of sexual harassment.[112] Depending on the situation, crossing the powerful can place one's job, family, relationships, and health at risk. So it's understandable that the downside may loom larger in our minds than the upside when we contemplate challenging entrenched authorities, especially if those in charge are known to be ruthless and unforgiving. Yet psychological research shows us that conformity and obedience are familiar responses even when the stakes are much lower.

Consider a series of famous conformity experiments conducted by psychologist Solomon Asch.[113] He gave volunteers a simple task: Look at a line and then find its match among three other lines of varying lengths. The correct choice was obvious, but there was a clever catch. Each research participant was part of a small group in which everyone else—all of them secretly working for the experimenter—offered their own answers first. One by one around the table, these confederates spoke aloud and gave the same wrong answer. In repeated trials of this experiment, Asch discovered that a substantial majority of the naïve participants also answered incorrectly at least some of the time. Rather than asserting the obvious truth, they instead opted to agree with the confederates' wrong choices, seemingly because they either doubted their own judgment or didn't want to stand out as different.

In related research, psychologist Stanley Milgram examined obedience to authority in a series of groundbreaking and highly controversial experiments.[114] His naïve volunteers were assigned the role of "teacher" and were instructed to give an electric shock to a "learner" whenever he made a mistake on a memory test. For this purpose, the teachers used a dial with interval markings that ranged from "Slight Shock" to "Danger: Severe Shock." They weren't told that the learner was a confederate of the researcher, and that he never actually received any shocks. But not knowing that his cries of pain and pleas for mercy were staged, many of the participants—themselves distraught over the situation—nevertheless obeyed the experimenter's insistent prodding. Step by step, they proceeded to administer the highest levels of electric shock. Findings like these from Asch and Milgram underscore aspects of individual psychology that represent significant hurdles to acting against the 1% and the established order they've created.

Let's now take a look at how the We'll Make You Sorry mind game is used to undermine worker activism, to pressure candidates running for public office, and to retaliate against whistleblowers and protesters.

Retaliation against Worker Activism

Workers who dare to organize—against poverty wages, or inhumane conditions—are routinely subjected to various we'll-make-you-sorry tactics. One harrowing example involved the temporary immigrant guest workers who peeled and packed crawfish at C.J.'s Seafood, a Walmart supplier in Louisiana. When these workers were assigned 16- to 24-hour shifts, were locked inside the plant, and were forced to live in overcrowded, dilapidated trailers on company property, some of them complained to their manager. He allegedly responded with threats of deportation and even worse: violence against their families living in Mexico.[115] Despite the risks, some of these workers went on strike anyway. Eventually, under pressure from growing negative publicity, Walmart suspended its contract with C.J.'s.[116]

This isn't to suggest that Walmart has a soft spot for low-wage employees. Indeed, just the opposite is true. Back in 2000, the company terminated its entire U.S. meatcutting operation after a handful of butchers at a single store voted to unionize.[117] In 2005, about 200 workers lost their jobs at a Canadian store after voting to form a union. Walmart simply closed the store, permanently.[118] Almost a decade later, Canada's Supreme Court ruled that the closure violated Quebec's labor code.[119] In the United States, dozens of Walmart workers have been fired or disciplined in recent years after participating in brief strikes protesting the retail giant's low-pay, low-benefits business model; company officials have denied any wrongdoing.[120] And in 2015, the retailing behemoth abruptly announced six-month closures of five U.S. stores, including one that was the epicenter of labor unrest, purportedly due to plumbing problems. Over 2,000 workers received just a few hours' advance notice; they were instructed to reapply for their old jobs whenever the stores reopened.[121]

Walmart is far from the only corporate titan that adopts ruthless practices aimed at quelling worker unrest and protecting profits. Efforts by employers to obstruct the unionization activities of their employees are notoriously widespread. In November 2017, for instance, billionaire Joe Ricketts, owner of the Chicago Cubs baseball team, shuttered two popular online local news sites—*Gothamist* and *DNAInfo*—following a vote by the staff to unionize. During the organizing effort, Ricketts had warned, "I believe unions promote a corrosive us-against-them dynamic that destroys the esprit de corps businesses need to succeed."[122]

In her own extensive research, labor scholar Kate Bronfenbrenner has found that it's not at all unusual for management to threaten plant closures, warn of wage and benefit cuts, and compel one-on-one anti-union meetings in which supervisors interrogate workers about where they and their co-workers stand on unionization efforts.[123] Even when these or other actions violate the law, management can expect that any adverse government ruling—months or years in the future—will be a small price to pay for successfully intimidating its workers.[124]

Electoral Dangers for Politicians and Judges

Candidates for public office—incumbents and challengers alike, in local and national races—are also familiar with the 1%'s We'll Make You Sorry mind game. They know that straying from the policy preferences of today's plutocrats can spell quick electoral defeat. The retaliatory risks of stepping out of line include the withholding of financial support, generous funding of their opponents' campaigns, and the reputational harm that comes from being the target of vicious attack ads. Wall Street banks, for instance, responded to Massachusetts Senator Elizabeth Warren's efforts to break them up by threatening to curtail contributions to Democratic candidates running for office in 2016.[125] Meanwhile, the Supreme Court's Citizen United decision, which allows unlimited independent spending on elections, has spurred the ever-growing influence of "super PACs" and other undisclosed sources of money. That's why conservative casino billionaire Sheldon Adelson referred to his wealth—his "pocket personality"—as the key reason he now has so many friends in the nation's capital.[126]

At the same time, when pressed to defend their close ties and fealty to big-money interests, politicians will go to improbable lengths to deny all impropriety. One high-profile example was the Democratic Party's 2016 presidential candidate, Hillary Clinton, the former U.S. Senator from New York and Secretary of State. Over a period of several years, she received millions of dollars in campaign contributions from Wall Street—and hundreds of thousands more for speeches given to Goldman Sachs and other investment firms. But during a primary debate against Bernie Sanders in Iowa, Clinton assured everyone that there was good reason for such remarkable generosity:

> I represented New York on 9/11 when we were attacked... We were attacked in downtown Manhattan where Wall Street is. I did spend a whole lot of time and effort helping them rebuild. That was good for New York. It was good for the economy. And it was a way to rebuke the terrorists who had attacked our country.[127]

In recent years, it's become clear that the sword of Damocles hangs over many judicial elections as well. With massive funding from the Koch brothers, Americans for Prosperity is among the political advocacy groups that have extended their reach to the campaigns of state-level judges.[128] As PBS's Bill Moyers put it during his show shortly before the 2012 elections, "In several states, partisan groups with funds from undisclosed sources are out to punish justices for rulings the partisans don't like."[129] Norm Ornstein, resident scholar at the American Enterprise Institute, has similarly argued:

> Imagine what happens when judges are deciding cases in which the stakes are high, and well-heeled individuals or corporations will be helped or damaged by the rulings. The judges know that an adverse decision now will trigger

a multimillion-dollar campaign against them the next time, both for retribution and to replace them with more friendly judges. Will that affect some rulings? Of course.[130]

Deep-pocketed conservative groups routinely set their sights on judges that the predatory class considers "too hard on businesses."[131] When their attack ads hit the airwaves, these candidates need their own campaign funds to counter the accusations. Regardless of the ultimate outcomes of political or judicial electoral contests, certain winners are guaranteed: The wealthy owners of the TV and radio stations that reap the windfall of expensive dueling ads, along with increased fees from other advertisers.[132] At a Morgan Stanley conference in early 2016, CBS CEO Les Moonves gushed about Trump's candidacy: "I've never seen anything like this, and this is going to be a very good year for us. Sorry. It's a terrible thing to say. But, bring it on, Donald. Keep going."[133]

Whistleblowers and Protesters

Potential whistleblowers worried about corporate corruption or illegal government activities also face threats and retaliation—including job loss, character assassination, and physical harm—aimed at cowing them into silence. In the lead-up to the 2008 financial meltdown, for example, employees who raised questions about suspect and fraudulent mortgage practices at the country's largest lenders and banks—Countrywide Financial, Wells Fargo, and Washington Mutual, among others—were reportedly harassed, muzzled, and fired.[134] General Motors made outcasts of employees who early on spoke up about ignition-switch safety issues that eventually led to the recall—after injuries and deaths—of millions of GM cars.[135] And Department of Veterans Affairs staff members who filed complaints about falsified records, excessive wait times, and inadequate care were subjected to transfers and suspensions by their supervisors.[136]

Street protests represent a different form of "whistleblowing" when they draw public and media attention to overlooked misconduct by those in positions of power. These too are frequently met with intimidation, and sometimes with violence. The threats and reprisals have a simple purpose. They're designed to sow concerns about personal vulnerability among would-be activists by increasing the real or perceived risks of involvement in displays of outrage and solidarity. Making examples of specific individuals can serve as compelling reminders of the looming dangers to a much broader audience of supporters.

This was clear during the anti-inequality demonstrations of Occupy Wall Street and its nationwide offshoots in 2011.[137] In New York City and beyond there were reports of unwarranted and aggressive surveillance and tracking of Occupy participants and allies—on behalf of corporate America and the 1%—by local and federal law enforcement and counter-terrorism agencies.[138] There were also widespread arrests of law-abiding demonstrators, with some subjected to brutal treatment by baton-wielding police dressed in riot gear.[139] In one incident that drew worldwide attention, a New York City police officer doused two women with pepper spray "as if he were spraying cockroaches."[140]

We saw similar intimidation tactics used against the Water Protectors engaged in acts of nonviolent civil resistance near the Standing Rock Sioux Reservation in North Dakota.[141] Members of Native American tribes, non-indigenous activists, and military veterans all sought to block construction of the final section of Energy Transfer Partners' $3.8 billion, thousand-mile Dakota Access Pipeline, built to carry fracked oil from North Dakota to Illinois. Militarized law enforcement personnel responded with attack dogs, tear gas, pepper spray, rubber bullets, percussion grenades, water cannons, aerial surveillance, and hundreds of arrests.[142]

SUMMING UP: THE PLUTOCRATS' VULNERABILITY MIND GAMES

As we've seen in this chapter, today's plutocrats rely on four vulnerability mind games to manipulate our fears for their own purposes. Let's review each of them.

The 1% use the It's a Dangerous World mind game to argue that their actions are necessary in order to keep everyone safe from ominous threats. They know that the public's support for any policy is strongly influenced by whether we think it will make the people we care about more or less secure. At the same time, they also recognize how readily we catastrophize. As a result, we're easy prey when it comes to their self-serving warnings that urge us to fall in line, take recommended precautions, and comply with all instructions, whatever they may be.

Members of the predatory class turn to change-is-dangerous appeals when they want to obstruct initiatives that could interfere with their ambitions. Despite a lack of evidence to support their claims, they insist that these unwelcome endeavors will place everyone in greater jeopardy. In much the same way as snake oil salesmen market worthless concoctions, the 1% take advantage of our emotions, especially our desire to protect those we love. In many cases the reforms they reject are exactly what's needed to tackle the scourge of extreme inequality. But that's the wrong goal as far as today's plutocrats are concerned.

With the It's a False Alarm mind game, the 1% defend their turf by arguing that worries about the adverse consequences of their policy priorities are overblown. Too often, we're quick to accept these comforting assurances from on high, failing to appreciate the extent to which peril characterizes the daily lives of so many Americans. Even more, we fail to recognize the extent to which responsibility for this precariousness rests at the feet of plutocrats who place the protection of their extraordinary wealth and power over what's best for the common good.

Finally, when stronger crackdowns against opponents seem necessary, the predatory class doesn't shy away from we'll-make-you-sorry appeals. The 1% command all kinds of resources they can put to use in punishing those who step out of line. Painful and potentially life-changing reprisals alter the stakes involved in individual acts of civil disobedience and sustained collective action.

It's clear that our worries about vulnerability are fertile ground for the manipulative mind games of those whose seek to preserve or extend their enormous wealth and power. The same is true for our second core concern—injustice—and that's where we'll turn our attention next.

3

INJUSTICE
MIND GAMES
HIJACKING OUR BELIEFS
ABOUT RIGHT AND WRONG

"The cry of the poor is not always just,
but if you don't listen to it,
you will never know what justice is."

— HOWARD ZINN[1]

The pursuit of justice is among the most potent drivers of human action. Recognizing the injustices in our midst can be a relentless force for progressive change. That's why today's plutocrats, committed to preserving their wealth and power above all else, use psychological mind games to influence the public's view of what's fair and what's not. Indeed, our sensitivity to injustice offers the 1% an attractive entryway for shaping our perceptions and advancing their own narrow agenda.

Whenever the predatory class succeeds at twisting our notions of what's just—for example, by promoting corporate school reform, opposing raises for low-wage workers, defending racial profiling, or suppressing voter turnout—it's a setback for achieving a more equal society. Unfortunately, their arguments often find a receptive audience. The public is eager to believe that those with great power are deeply concerned about the common good. The reality is quite different. The ploys of the 1% lead justice-seekers away from the truth or, at the very least, confuse them into a state of inaction.

Toward these ends, the 1%'s well-tuned propaganda machine runs non-stop. With help from a mainstream media that's sometimes spineless or complicit, their self-righteous tales as would-be defenders of justice gain broad dissemination. In this chapter, we'll explore four mind games that, regrettably, have proven effective at undermining the public's stubborn yet imperfect commitment to justice: We're Fighting Injustice, No Injustice Here, Change Is Unjust, and We're the Victims.

WE'RE FIGHTING INJUSTICE

Today's plutocrats don't always resist change and defend the status quo. Indeed, they become enthusiastic "reformers" if it serves their interests. They eagerly push new initiatives when they feel their privileged circumstances are in jeopardy, or when they're looking for ways to extend their influence even further. At such times, the 1% resort to the We're Fighting Injustice mind game, arguing that the steps they're taking are necessary to tackle widespread and outrageous inequities. Their claims are very misleading, however, especially since their purported corrective actions typically cause hardship for those who are already disadvantaged and struggling. But it seems the truth doesn't always matter as much as it should.

Defenders of extreme inequality know that presenting themselves as avengers of injustice is good politics and an easy way to advance their self-aggrandizing goals. That's because even though individuals or groups may disagree over what's just or unjust, there's general agreement that fairness ought to be a primary consideration in how people and institutions operate. As a result, in debates over policy alternatives, plutocrats gain the upper hand whenever they're successful in manipulating the public's concerns about right and wrong. Two key psychological dimensions of justice—distributive justice and procedural justice—are among the factors that heavily influence the perspectives of everyday Americans.[2]

Distributive justice focuses on allocation rules. For example, when resources are scarce, how should the proverbial pie be divided among multiple parties? Likewise, how do we determine whether people have received what they truly deserve? Psychologist Morton Deutsch identified three principles that are often applied when answering questions like these.[3] First, in some cases our perceptions of justice revolve around the principle of equity—the greatest rewards should go to those who have contributed the most to an effort's success. Second, in other cases the principle of equality prevails instead—equal outcomes for everyone is considered fairest, regardless of any differences in each person's relative contributions. And third, sometimes the guiding principle is one of need—here, justice requires that those with greater need receive more than the rest, even if they've contributed less. These three principles can lead to very different allocations, so the 1% work hard to guide our preferences.

Procedural justice, on the other hand, focuses on whether the rules that are used are implemented fairly. Especially relevant for our purposes are experiments that psychologist Tom Tyler and his colleagues have conducted in legal settings. These studies reveal that criminal defendants—regardless of the ultimate disposition of their cases—want to be treated with dignity and respect, and they want authorities to act with neutrality, objectivity, and consistency.[4] In short, even when we believe that punishment for our actions is appropriate, it still matters to us that the decision-makers act in an unbiased manner. If we think they're biased, we tend to view these authorities and the institutions they represent as illegitimate—and we're less likely to cooperate with them in the future. That's one of the reasons representatives of the 1% take such care to appear fair-minded while fleecing the public.

In exploring the We're Fighting Injustice mind game, we'll examine how members of the predatory class rely on these manipulative appeals in their pursuits of corporate "school reform" and voter suppression.

The Corporate School Reform Swindle

Many corporate "school reformers" are prime examples of plutocrats who take advantage of the We're Fighting Injustice mind game. They routinely adopt dramatic rhetoric designed to stoke our sense of grievance about the state of public education. But these efforts are far from benevolent. Turning our education system into a privately run, for-profit enterprise—one that's built on false promises of improving the learning, lives, and prospects of millions of underprivileged children—serves to further line their own pockets.

What these so-called reformers don't mention is that the K-12 education market is worth hundreds of billions of dollars annually. Corporate control of schools is a golden goose that could bring enormous profits to ownership groups and other well-heeled investors through for-profit charter schools, taxpayer-funded vouchers, textbook sales, standardized tests, real estate deals, tax credits, and more.[5] They're also slow to acknowledge something else: There's no compelling evidence that decimating our public education system would be a good thing—for most of us at least, including our children. Indeed, despite the hype, research studies show that, on average, charter schools and voucher programs fail to outperform public schools on key measures of educational achievement.[6]

Of course the underlying profit motive is obscured when billionaire voucher crusader Betsy DeVos—now Donald Trump's Secretary of Education—calls public schools a "dead end," or bemoans "America's broken education system," or warns of the plight of children "trapped by their zip code in a school that failed to meet their needs."[7] With comparable flair, back in 2010 Arne Duncan, then Barack Obama's Secretary of Education, called the premiere of the pro-charter school, anti-teachers' union film *Waiting for "Superman"* a "Rosa Parks moment."[8]

Similar emotional appeals have been offered by other high-profile advocates. Former Republican presidential candidate Mitt Romney told the 2012 Latino Coalition's Annual Economic Summit that the inadequate education of minority children is "the civil rights issue of our era and it's the greatest challenge of our time."[9] Republican Senator Ted Cruz of Texas chose 2015's School Choice Week to tell his Capitol Hill audience that "Dr. King stood at the Lincoln Memorial and promised justice for all of our children. School choice is the civil rights issue of the 21st century."[10] During his own campaign for the White House, Trump's website noted, "School choice is the civil rights issue of our time."

In their attempted takeover of public education, representatives of the 1% are quick to focus on underprivileged school children as innocent victims of injustices that thwart their dreams. In this they're undoubtedly correct. From pre-kindergarten through college, education in the United States is characterized by widespread inequities that bestow unwarranted advantages on the "haves" while holding back the "have-nots." Billionaire backers of the corporate assault want us to see teachers and their unions as the perpetrators. Teachers have been maligned as lazy, incompetent, and uncaring; unions are portrayed as inflexible obstructionists; and both are held responsible for shortfalls in student success.[11]

But the root causes of these profound injustices are actually far different from the corporate school reformers' self-serving diagnosis. Research shows that all school-based factors combined—including teacher performance—are simply no match against debilitating outside influences like poverty, broken homes, crime-ridden neighborhoods, unemployment, and inadequate nutrition and healthcare.[12] As Chris Hayes has put it, "We ask the education system to expiate the sins of the rest of the society and then condemn it as hopelessly broken when it doesn't prove up to the task."[13]

Not surprisingly, today's plutocrats downplay such findings because their priorities involve cutting education costs—including the salaries of experienced teachers and the retirement benefits that unions secure. That's how they plan to increase the profits flowing to privatizers and investors. So they have little interest in lasting solutions that require increased expenditures—for example, bolstering public schools through preschool programs, greater resources, and smaller classes, while simultaneously attacking concentrated poverty and racial segregation.[14] Indeed, the Trump administration aims to cut billions of dollars in public school funding, and DeVos isn't taking a stand for justice and civil rights when she dismantles protections that serve students with disabilities, students struggling with loan debt, and students victimized by sexual assault.[15]

Corporate reformers stick to their We're Fighting Injustice mind game for a simple reason: They want to distract us from well-documented strategies for improving education that run counter to their own moneymaking priorities. This isn't to say that all school reform supporters are driven by greed. Many parents are desperately looking for ways to level the playing field and provide their children with better educational opportunities. Unfortunately, however, these families are often manipulatively turned into the sympathetic public face of the privatization movement.

It would be tragic enough if this were all merely another heartless hoax that produces disappointment and disillusionment when outcomes fail to match the promises made. But it's worse than that. These efforts also decimate the teaching profession and drain crucial resources from the financially strapped public schools and communities that need them most. Education historian and privatization critic Diane Ravitch has explained the situation well:

> The privatization agenda excites the interest of edu-entrepreneurs, who see it as a golden opportunity to make money. But…it hurts public education not only by attacking

its effectiveness and legitimacy but by laying claim to its revenues. The money allocated to privately managed charters and vouchers represents a transfer of critical public resources to the private sector, causing the public schools to suffer budget cuts and loss of staffing and services as the private sector grows, without providing better education or better outcomes for the students who transfer to the private-sector schools.[16]

Voter Suppression

The 1% bring the same We're Fighting Injustice mind game to their anti-democratic voter suppression campaigns, which have become increasingly prominent in recent years. Over half of the states in the country—most of them controlled by Republican legislatures and governors—now require voters to present a government-issued photo ID or similar identification form at polling places.[17]

Such measures are unnecessarily restrictive. An independent national investigation of voter impersonation found only ten individual cases over an entire decade.[18] A separate analysis concluded that it's "more likely that an individual will be struck by lightning than that he will impersonate another voter at the polls."[19] Nevertheless, a poll conducted less than two months before the 2016 election demonstrated the 1%'s successful manipulation of public opinion: Nearly half of the respondents said they thought voter fraud takes place "very" or "somewhat" often.[20]

By framing these voter ID laws as an urgent response to the injustice of voter fraud, representatives of the plutocracy are able to disguise an unsavory goal: gaining electoral advantage by disenfranchising African Americans, Hispanic Americans, students, and low-income workers. These groups are logical targets because they're very unlikely to support the 1%'s inequality-boosting agenda. They're also less likely than most Americans to have valid photo IDs (because, for example, those who can't afford a car—or don't drive—don't have a driver's license).[21]

Transparent efforts to prevent Americans from voting would quickly be recognized as an outrageous abuse of power. That's why the 1% find their we're-fighting-injustice appeals—and the myth of rampant voter fraud—so useful. Over a decade ago, when he was the state's attorney general, Texas Governor Greg Abbott warned, "In Texas, an epidemic of voter fraud is harming the electoral process."[22] In a 2010 op-ed, James Woodruff II, a member of the Republican National Lawyers Association and the conservative Federalist Society, cautioned that "'one person, one vote' [is] becoming a myth and places the outcomes of elections in doubt as vote fraud pervades our election process."[23]

Similarly, Hans von Spakovsky of the right-wing Heritage Foundation has emphasized, "I believe in having fair elections, and I would never be willing to do anything that would encourage or allow cheating in an election."[24] John Fund of *National Review* has beat the drum on the need to "keep fraudsters away from polling places."[25] And Reince Priebus, former chairman of the Republican National Committee and briefly Trump's chief of staff, has argued that presentation of a photo ID card at the voting booth is "fair, reasonable, and just."[26]

The phantom injustice of voter fraud has even found its way into the official platform of the Republican Party. The 2012 platform stated, "Every time that a fraudulent vote is cast, it effectively cancels out a vote of a legitimate voter."[27] The 2016 platform endorsed legislation "to require proof of citizenship when registering to vote and secure photo ID when voting."[28] In the weeks leading up to the 2016 election, Trump repeatedly called upon his supporters to monitor polling places for signs of voter fraud. He told attendees at a Pennsylvania rally, "So, go and vote and then go check out areas because a lot of bad things happen, and we don't want to lose for that reason."[29]

There are also outfits like True the Vote, a Texas-based, Tea Party-affiliated group with wealthy conservative backers like the Koch brothers. True the Vote promotes itself as "regular citizens standing up for fair elections" and "the nation's largest nonpartisan, voters' rights and election integrity organization." But among its activities are reported instances of minority voter harassment and intimidation on Election Day.[30] The rest of the year, it offers trainings at local "Citizen Watchdog" events, such as the one founder Catherine Engelbrecht attended in Helena, Montana, shortly before Obama won re-election. The title of her keynote address that day was "Voter Fraud: The Plot to Undermine American Democracy."[31]

In 2016, after Trump won the election but lost the popular vote to Hillary Clinton by almost three million votes, Engelbrecht had this to say: "We believe millions of illegal votes were cast in this election."[32] Trump himself has continued to promote this evidence-free claim. He even created a Presidential Advisory Commission on Election Integrity, since disbanded, and stacked it with members who had long pushed for tighter voting restrictions under the guise of combating fraud.[33] One of the vice-chairs was Republican Kris Kobach, the Secretary of State of Kansas who, prior to the election, had insisted, "Even if it's just a handful of votes, it's still a huge injustice. Every time an alien votes, it effectively cancels out a vote of a U.S. citizen."[34]

But if there's a dangerous plot underway to cripple and corrupt our democratic institutions, it doesn't take the form of individuals impersonating other people at the voting booth. Rather, that plotting is happening at the meetings of this "commission," and those of groups like the influential corporate-funded American Legislative Exchange Council. As part of its portfolio, ALEC provides guidance and model legislation for state and local politicians looking to swing elections by suppressing voter turnout.[35]

It's important to recognize that ID laws aren't the only tactic here. There's a simultaneous push to require physical proof of citizenship, such as a birth certificate, for anyone who wants to register to vote. That requirement undercuts the effectiveness of low-income voter registration drives. Steps have also been taken to close polling places on or near campuses so that college students find it tougher to vote. Other laws have eliminated or reduced early voting periods and same-day registration, opportunities that have become increasingly popular among voters of color and lower-income voters.[36]

The bottom line is that all of these anti-democratic initiatives, which further marginalize individuals who already face fragile economic circumstances, need a persuasive cover story. So plutocrats employ their We're Fighting Injustice mind game and spin their tall tales of unchecked injustices threatening the integrity of the ballot box. With former Alabama Senator Jeff Sessions now serving as Trump's attorney general, voting rights are likely to be even further imperiled. Recall that Sessions referred to the Voting Rights Act as a "piece of intrusive legislation," and he described the NAACP and ACLU as "un-American."[37]

NO INJUSTICE HERE

When confronted with stark evidence of the hardships that characterize the lives of many Americans, the predatory class often takes a different tack and turns to a second injustice mind game. With the No Injustice Here mind game, plutocrats argue that even though current circumstances may be unfortunate for some people, that doesn't mean they're unjust. In so doing, they claim that the gulf between "haves" and "have-nots" isn't really a matter of injustice at all. Instead, so they insist, troubling disparities reflect bad luck or the shortcomings of those who are disadvantaged. If the 1% can sell this to the public, it helps them escape scrutiny of their own actions and policies—which actually form the foundation for today's extreme inequality.

These appeals frequently work because most of us find it comforting to believe that people get what they deserve and deserve what they get. Life seems less haphazard and unpredictable that way. Our own future feels more secure if those facing hard times are somehow responsible for their plight—for example, if their difficulties are the result of failing to work harder, or study longer, or save more, or develop stronger values. By this account, people who are worse off—whether it's financial woes, or poor health, or hostile treatment by others— are paying a reasonable price for their own ill-advised choices. As a result, their grievances are illegitimate and undeserving of redress, or so the 1% claim. The public's embrace of such arguments can stand in the way of real justice for the downtrodden. Not surprisingly, today's plutocrats are therefore quick to take advantage of our psychological preference to see the world as fair.

A rich history of psychological research has demonstrated the power and prevalence of our "belief in a just world." In one early experiment, Melvin Lerner and his colleagues had volunteers watch a student they were told was receiving electric shocks as part of a learning exercise (no shocks were actually delivered). Some of these volunteers were then given the opportunity to terminate the shocks, and just about all of them did so. But other participants were instead advised that there was nothing they could do to help the student escape the pain. Afterward, all of the volunteers were asked to rate the victim's likeability. Those who were unable to help gave him much more negative ratings. Their critical appraisals helped them feel that the situation wasn't as unjust as it seemed. In other words, through some psychological gymnastics they found a way to preserve their just-world beliefs.[38]

In other studies, researchers have used questionnaires to look at differences in the extent to which people believe the world is fair. This approach sheds light on exactly who tends to hold just-world beliefs and who doesn't. What these investigators have found is that people who strongly believe that the world is just are likely to be more conservative, more religious, and more authoritarian; they also tend to admire political leaders and existing social institutions; and they're more likely to view underprivileged groups negatively.[39] Of particular concern here, such beliefs contribute to preserving inequality and plutocratic rule because they dampen any urge to engage in the political activism necessary to produce meaningful change.[40]

In exploring the 1%'s No Injustice Here mind game, let's now take a closer look at how they use this appeal to cast blame on victims and to escape responsibility for their own wrongdoing.

Deserving of Their Plight?

Hurricane Katrina swept through the Gulf Coast in late August of 2005. The levee system designed to protect New Orleans was breached, causing massive flooding. Emergency evacuation warnings and rescue efforts were delayed, in large part due to administrative negligence and incompetence. As a result, many of the city's residents—especially those in the poorest, predominantly African American neighborhoods—were unable to escape the deluge. In a matter of days, over 1,800 lives were lost, tens of thousands of homes were destroyed, and stunning evidence of economic and racial inequality was apparent for all to see.

Yet comfortably removed from the flooding, representatives of the plutocracy were quickly out in force with no-injustice-here appeals, casting blame on those who were most afflicted. Former Republican Senator Rick Santorum of Pennsylvania called for tougher penalties when people fail to respond to a mandatory evacuation.[41] Bill O'Reilly, formerly of Fox News, argued that those left behind were "drug addicted" and "thugs," and he preached, "If you don't get educated, if you don't develop a skill, and force yourself to work hard, you'll most likely be poor. And sooner or later, you'll be standing on a symbolic rooftop waiting for help."[42] Some mainstream newscasts described Black survivors as "looters" for their desperate efforts to obtain survival items like food, clothing, and flashlights.[43] More than a year later, former Speaker of the House Newt Gingrich, a Republican congressman from Georgia, was still bemoaning the "failure of citizenship" displayed by the "uneducated" residents of New Orleans's Ninth Ward.[44]

In 2008, we witnessed a deluge of a different kind. The housing bubble burst and prices plummeted. Amid financial panic on Wall Street, defenders of extreme wealth and power—groups like the American Bankers Association, the Mortgage Bankers Association, and lobbyists for the big banks—condemned mortgage assistance programs that would have enabled more families to keep their homes.[45] One familiar victim-blaming, no-injustice-here appeal was the claim that foreclosure relief would reward personal irresponsibility. Consider John Tamny, an editor at *Forbes*, who wrote, "Far from deserving our sympathy, these people deserve our disgusted scorn."[46]

This callous stance ignored several basic realities. Unscrupulous mortgage brokers had scammed hundreds of thousands of homeowners with predatory lending schemes. Corrupt and reckless banks had received tens of billions of dollars in government bailouts. And the proposed mortgage assistance programs could have helped to stabilize the housing market and support the economic recovery for everyone.

The extension of unemployment insurance following nationwide layoffs was similarly portrayed as rewarding laziness. Former Republican Party presidential hopeful Senator Rand Paul of Kentucky insisted that extending benefits would encourage the jobless to "become part of this perpetual unemployed group in our economy."[47] The message from Richard Vedder of the American Enterprise Institute was much the same: "If you pay people to stay at home, many will do so."[48] But even if we ignore their heartlessness, these arguments still misrepresent key facts: Recipients must look for employment while receiving the insurance; those who lost their full-time jobs weren't the ones responsible for the nation's layoffs; there were far fewer jobs available than the number of job-seekers; and recipients of unemployment insurance tend to spend the modest benefits, which helps to stimulate the economy.[49]

The Massey Coal Mine Disaster

When they consider outright victim-blaming too much of a stretch, today's plutocrats use the No Injustice Here mind game in a different way: They argue that nobody can be held responsible when misfortune unexpectedly strikes. That was their self-serving stance on April 5, 2010, when 29 miners were killed by an explosion that ripped through Massey Energy's Upper Big Branch coal mine in West Virginia.[50] Under CEO Don Blankenship, Massey had a history of disregarding minimum safety standards, including proper underground ventilation. But millions of dollars in fines were apparently an acceptable cost of doing business for Massey.[51] Moreover, Blankenship was reportedly well known for protecting his company through large campaign contributions, including the $3 million he spent in support of a candidate running for the state's supreme court (that candidate was elected and later cast the deciding vote reversing a multimillion-dollar judgment against Massey in another matter).[52]

Immediately after the disaster, Massey spokespersons were quick to claim that the explosion was caused by a sudden gas leak, one that nobody could have anticipated or prevented. It was, by their account, one of those freakish and inexplicable "acts of God"—a case of rare tragedy rather than negligence that put workers at needless risk. Blankenship told listeners on a local radio show, "Any suspicion that the mine was improperly operated...would be unfounded."[53] The company also issued a press release with the assurance, "'Safety is Job 1' is not just a slogan...at Massey Energy, but a vow." And speaking at the National Press Club that July, Blankenship told his audience, "The physics of natural law and God trump whatever man tries to do."[54]

Sticking to their no-injustice-here claims, company representatives also disputed the conclusions of subsequent comprehensive investigations. An independent panel appointed by the governor of West Virginia reported in May 2011 that the explosion was "a failure of basic coal mine safety practices."[55] Six months later, the U.S. Department of Labor's Mine Safety and Health Administration identified Massey's corporate culture as "the root cause of the tragedy," a culture that "valued production over safety, and broke the law as they endangered the lives of their miners."[56] As United Mine Workers of America International president Cecil Roberts commented, "Until someone goes to jail for what happened at this mine, justice will not have been done."[57]

Instead, nine months after the blast, former Massey executives received millions of dollars in retirement packages when the company was sold to Alpha Natural Resources. Alpha later reached a financial settlement with the government: Each victim's family received a substantial payment, but the company was protected from prosecution. Six years after the deadly explosion, in April 2016 former CEO Blankenship was sentenced to a single year in prison after being found guilty on criminal charges for conspiracy to violate mine safety standards.[58] Meanwhile, efforts to strengthen federal mining regulations have been hampered by the coal industry's intense lobbying against safety bills and its campaign donations to regulation-opposing politicians, including Trump.[59] One miner, Tommy Davis, escaped the Massey explosion but his son, his brother, and his nephew were all killed. He hangs his son's work-shirt from a flagpole as a memorial.[60]

Accepting Mistreatment

Change efforts become much tougher when powerful status quo defenders use the No Injustice Here mind game to undercut the public's compassion for victims of unjust policies. But some of the most tragic consequences arise when the disadvantaged and oppressed come to believe that they don't really deserve better lives—when a woman thinks she doesn't deserve the same opportunities as her male counterparts in the workplace, or when a child raised in poverty thinks they don't deserve a chance at a college education, or when a homeless man thinks he doesn't deserve to be treated with respect.

It may seem surprising that people innocent of wrongdoing can be convinced that they deserve inferior treatment. But most of us are more impressionable than we realize. This is especially true when we're pushed to adopt a particular view—even an unfavorable one about ourselves—by powerful societal norms or by people in positions of influence. That's why, for example, some battered spouses or children accept claims of perpetrators that they deserved to be beaten. And that's why someone falsely accused of a crime may nonetheless confess when pressured to do so during an aggressive police interrogation.[61] So too, it can be hard to resist the constant drumming of supposed "truths" from authoritative members of the plutocracy, particularly when the mainstream media fail to offer alternative explanations for what's wrong and who's to blame.

Perceiving one's own mistreatment as somehow fair—as how things should be—is not only personally degrading. It also diminishes the capacity of an individual or a group to be an agent of change. In this way, the harm of the initial injustice is compounded when victims are persuaded by no-injustice-here appeals to accept their adverse circumstances without complaint.

CHANGE IS UNJUST

Today's plutocrats go to great lengths to draw attention away from a simple truth: Their privileged circumstances are built upon the daily misery and mistreatment of others. They'd rather avoid any public awareness that might spur outrage and a push for remedies they wouldn't like. But when they can't escape the spotlight, the 1% turn to the Change Is Unjust mind game, hoping to fend off unwelcome initiatives by arguing that these reforms will unfairly bring harm to many people. With this strategy, they aim to drive a wedge between current victims of injustice and those who sympathize with the victims' grievances. Defenders of extreme inequality are confident that broad-based solidarity will prove elusive if we're convinced that our own favorable circumstances will be jeopardized by changes designed to lighten the hardships of others.

One reason this mind game often works so well is that, psychologically, people tend to support and defend the political system in which they live, whatever it might be. As discussed earlier, we typically have a bias in favor of the way things are, and we find it reassuring to think that the world makes sense. But in their research on "system justification," psychologist John Jost and his colleagues have taken the study of this important phenomenon a step further. What they've found is that even those who suffer at the hands of an unjust system still find comfort in the belief that the status quo is legitimate. This is especially true when they think there's no realistic way to escape or alter their adverse circumstances anyway.[62]

Why would they feel this way? Because believing that society is fair—despite any evidence to the contrary—can be an effective coping mechanism. At least in the short term, adopting this perspective helps to reduce emotional discomfort and uncertainty—even though it can serve to reinforce extreme levels of inequality. Consistent with this view, some surveys have shown that people who are poor tend to feel greater satisfaction with their lives when they blame themselves rather than society's injustices for their poverty.[63] In much the same way, it's not unusual for those who are paid less than others for doing the same work—for example, women compared to men in many jobs—to feel that they somehow deserve the lower pay.[64]

There's another system-justifying tendency that also plays to the 1%'s advantage. Psychologically, people tend to endorse what are sometimes called complementary stereotypes. "Poor but happy" and "rich but unhappy" are two good examples. Accepting generalizations of this sort is problematic because they make it seem as though inequality actually has a silver lining for those who are worse off. Indeed, in a series of research studies, participants who first read brief stories about the "happy poor" and the "unhappy rich" tended to later express stronger support for the legitimacy and fairness of U.S. society.[65] In short, stereotypes like these can contribute to the preservation of unjust arrangements. More broadly, when we ourselves engage in system justification, plutocrats don't even need to break a sweat defending the policies that bestow such enormous rewards upon them.

In examining this third injustice appeal, let's consider the role played by change-is-unjust appeals in two specific contexts: the 1%'s defense of poverty wages and racial profiling.

Justifying Poverty Wages

Most Americans favor a minimum wage hike, but the 1% don't want resources to be allocated more equitably at their expense.[66] So they use the Change Is Unjust mind game to defend today's poverty wages, disingenuously arguing that wage hikes will unfairly hurt American workers and consumers—by forcing layoffs, shuttering small businesses, preventing teens and unskilled workers from getting the first jobs and training they need, and driving up prices. As it turns out, none of these claims is true. But that never stops plutocrats from telling self-serving tales.

Former Speaker of the House John Boehner, for example, once warned, "Why would we want to make it harder for small employers to hire people?" and "When you take away the first couple rungs on the economic ladder, you make it harder for people to get on the ladder."[67] *Wall Street Journal* editor Jason Riley told a Fox News audience that the minimum wage is "a proven job killer."[68] The Heritage Foundation's James Sherk and John Ligon predicted an increase to just $10.10 an hour would lead to hundreds of thousands of job losses.[69] And low-wage worker foe Andrew Puzder—former CEO of fast-food conglomerate CKE Restaurants and Trump's initial pick for Secretary of Labor—has argued, "Does it really help if Sally makes $3 more an hour if Suzie has no job?"[70] Puzder also described the fast-food workers he's hired at Hardee's as "the worst of the worst."[71]

Extensive research, however, tells a very different story. Modest increases in the minimum wage tend to have little or no effect on employment levels.[72] In fact, data suggest that those states that increased their minimum wage in recent years have produced greater job growth than those that didn't.[73] This makes sense when you consider that a pay raise gives low-wage workers more buying power, which in turn can stimulate the economy and create the need for more workers rather than layoffs. Wage hikes can also reduce turnover, thereby cutting costs and increasing efficiency.[74]

Employment data also contradict the 1%'s claim that minimum wage workers are primarily teens working their first part-time jobs, who will soon get raises and promotions if they're good employees. In fact, almost 90% of minimum wage workers are at least 20 years old. More than half of them work full time, not part time. Half are older than 30, and more than 25% have children of their own.[75] Such figures are even more sobering when we consider how many low-wage workers there are in the United States. In 2014 over 20 million people earned more than their state's minimum wage but less than the $10.10 per hour that Obama proposed that year as the new federal minimum wage standard.[76]

As for the cost of goods, conservative icon Rush Limbaugh has insisted that raising the minimum wage will impose unfair burdens on consumers. For instance, he's warned his radio audience that fast-food prices will skyrocket if wages are increased: "When you go in to buy a Big Mac or a Quarter Pounder, are you willing to pay double so that the people working there can get a raise?...If you're unwilling to pay higher prices, then shut up."[77] But again, such claims don't hold water. Scientific estimates suggest that a minimum wage of around $10 per hour would increase prices at McDonald's by about 10%, and a raise to $15 per hour would increase prices about

25%. That's somewhere between 40 cents and a dollar more for Limbaugh's Big Mac.[78]

The real bottom line is that when greed-driven plutocrats use the Change Is Unjust mind game to argue against wage hikes, they hope we'll overlook the fundamental injustice of working long hours every day and still not earning enough to provide for one's family.[79] This reality reflects a broken social contract, where workers don't get to share in the wealth created by their labor and their increased productivity. Instead, their standard of living falls.[80] Indeed, even if a higher minimum wage were to cause a small uptick in unemployment, that shouldn't be a deal breaker if, in exchange, many more Americans can earn a living wage and we're willing to provide assistance to those whose jobs disappear.[81]

Instead, we have a situation today where CEOs of S&P 500 firms earn roughly 300 times the salary of their average employees, and about 800 times the salary of minimum wage workers. These are enormous disparities. In fact, New York-based Wall Street employees received almost $24 billion in bonuses alone in 2016. That's more than one-and-a-half times the combined annual pay of the country's one million full-time minimum wage workers. It's also enough money to raise the wages of three million fast-food workers to $15 per hour.[82]

Defending Racial Profiling and Stop-and-Frisk

Under billionaire mayor Michael Bloomberg, the same Change Is Unjust mind game was a recurrent element of the 1%'s efforts to defend New York City's controversial anti-crime "stop-and-frisk" program. In certain quarters, it was celebrated for years as a remarkable success in protecting the city's residents, tourists, and businesses. Typical of the accolades was this tribute from Heather Mac Donald of the plutocracy-promoting Manhattan Institute: "New York's most vulnerable residents enjoy a freedom from assault unknown in any other big city, thanks to the N.Y.P.D.'s assertive style of policing."[83]

Despite the rave reviews, however, there was never any good evidence that the tactics worked.[84] Stops culminating in an arrest were very uncommon, and cases involving weapon possession were even rarer. That's actually not surprising, since many of the hundreds of thousands of stops each year were based on little more than a police officer's vague suspicions about an individual's "furtive movements"—along with pressure to meet certain quotas.[85] The program also had an even bigger problem: It overwhelmingly targeted young men of color. In 2011, for example, Black and Latino men under 25 years of age accounted for over 40% of all people stopped by the police, even though these two groups represented less than 5% of the city's residents. In many precincts, people of color accounted for 90% of all stops.[86]

But surrogates for the predatory class were always ready to run the Change Is Unjust mind game up the flagpole and oppose calls to curtail stop-and-frisk. Andrea Peyser of Rupert Murdoch's *New York Post*, for example, offered this over-the-top prediction: "It will end in buckets of blood on the city's streets."[87] That's imagery reminiscent of Batman's exile from Gotham City, with millions of decent and hardworking citizens unjustly placed in harm's way. Nevertheless, outrageous claims like this have a psychological purpose: In this case, to diminish the public's compassion for the minority youth who were being unfairly singled out, harassed, and humiliated by the police.[88]

These propaganda ploys seemingly hit a brick wall in August of 2013 when Judge Shira Scheindlin ruled that the city's implementation of stop-and-frisk was unconstitutional. She described the program's unwritten focus on targeting the "right people" as "indirect racial profiling."[89] Her decision reaffirmed the right of the less privileged to be free from unjust harassment—and to be treated with the same respect granted those who reside in the city's penthouses and corporate boardrooms.

But Mayor Bloomberg and New York City police commissioner Ray Kelly found high-profile platforms from which to defend stop-and-frisk and encourage the public to see itself as unjustly victimized by its curtailment. At a hastily arranged press conference, Bloomberg warned, "I worry for my kids, and I worry for your kids. I worry for you and I worry for me."[90] In a follow-up op-ed in the *Washington Post*, he argued, "Every American has a right to walk down the street without getting mugged or killed."[91] And on *Meet the Press*, Kelly predicted, "No question about it, violent crime will go up."[92] He was wrong. Over the next several months, with stop-and-frisks down almost 80%, the city's crime rate fell as well (and has continued to do so).[93] During the 2016 presidential campaign, such data didn't matter to Trump. He called for a return to old-style stop-and-frisk, baselessly offering the dog-whistle claim that it "had a tremendous impact on the safety of New York City. Tremendous beyond belief."[94]

It's worth noting that stop-and-frisk wasn't Bloomberg's and Kelly's sole use of racial profiling. The New York City Police Department also conducted an expansive secret surveillance program that spied on members of Muslim communities around the city, including at mosques, places of business, and college campuses. When the operation became public in 2012, Kelly was unapologetic and denied any wrongdoing, opting for a change-is-unjust appeal: "Not everybody is going to be happy with everything the police department does...But our primary mission, our primary goal is to keep this city safe, to save lives. That's what we're engaged in doing."[95]

Violating civil rights and perpetuating unwarranted, demeaning stereotypes were seemingly of little concern. Despite his profiling of minority communities, in some circles Kelly became a popular choice for Secretary of Homeland Security. John Avlon of *The Daily Beast*, a former speechwriter for Rudy Giuliani, described him as "a confidence-inspiring law-enforcement leader";[96] Democratic Senator Chuck Schumer, now the Senate's minority leader, pushed for his appointment, saying "New York's loss will be America's gain";[97] and President Obama was effusive as well: "Mr. Kelly might be very happy where he is, but if he's not I'd want to know about it, because obviously he'd be very well qualified for the job."[98] (Obama subsequently appointed Jeh Johnson instead.)

WE'RE THE VICTIMS

With this fourth injustice mind game, members of the predatory class exploit our sensitivity to injustice in a very different way. They shamelessly present themselves as victims unfairly maligned for their successes. When this turning of the tables is successful, the public's concern is directed away from those who are actually mistreated and disadvantaged. And when that happens, those with tremendous wealth and power face much less scrutiny and opposition in maintaining their privileged positions.

Even with their finely tuned propaganda machine, the 1%'s We're the Victims mind game—claiming that they're the ones being kicked around—might seem like a very hard sell. Yet this deceptive ploy can work surprisingly well because, psychologically, we're influenced by exactly how an issue is presented to us—that is, how it's "framed." As a result, we can be easy prey for an expert who wants to manipulate us into thinking one way and not another. Misdirection is the stock-in-trade of magicians who pull rabbits out of hats despite the close attention of skeptical audiences. In a similar manner, when we're encouraged to focus on a limited set of selected "facts" provided by those with a vested interest, we can lose sight of the broader context.

Psychologists who've studied framing effects have found that how information is presented to us strongly affects our subsequent judgments. The "anchoring effect" demonstrates that we tend to be biased by whatever information is most salient, even if it's entirely irrelevant to the decisions we're asked to make.[99] For instance, research experiments show that you're likely to think Mahatma Gandhi lived longer when asked, "Did he die before or after reaching the age of 140?" than if you're instead asked, "Did he die before or after turning 9 years old?" These two age anchors—140 and 9—affect our estimates even though we never would have imagined that he lived that long or died that young (Gandhi was 78 when he was assassinated). A similar phenomenon is at work when shoppers are enticed to buy a sale item. Paying $100 for a pair of jeans may seem like a bargain if the advertising highlights that they usually sell for twice that much.

A different and more consequential example of framing involves the well-documented agenda-setting role played by the mainstream media.[100] Research shows that we tend to consider an issue more important if it receives a lot of media attention. We're also inclined to adopt the media's perspective on the problem and potential solutions. So, for instance, poverty is more likely to become a high-priority concern for us if it receives substantial media coverage over time. The media also decide whether to frame poverty as a broad societal problem worthy of governmental intervention or less sympathetically, such as holding the poor solely responsible for their own circumstances.[101] This framing difference can be striking in its ramifications—and let's remember that the 1% exert considerable control over the most widely read and viewed media sources.[102]

In exploring the We're the Victims mind game, let's now take a detailed look at how the 1% use this injustice appeal in two different contexts: manipulating tax policies to their advantage and claiming innocence when confronted with evidence of prisoner abuse.

Taxes, Taxes, Taxes

The public understands that sufficient tax revenues are crucial to fund essential social services, including public education and programs that help the poor, the ill, and the elderly. So today's plutocrats often resort to the We're the Victims mind game when they're criticized for not paying enough taxes, whether through tax-avoidance schemes or lower rates applied to capital gains. Despite these reframing efforts, national polls have found that a substantial majority of Americans still feel that corporations and wealthy individuals don't pay their fair share in taxes. Conservative Republicans are the only ideological group that's "as bothered by the poor not paying their fair share of taxes as by the wealthy not paying their fair share."[103]

As the super-rich whine, it's worth remembering that the top income tax rates were once much higher than they are now. The highest marginal rate was nearly 70% when President Ronald Reagan first took office in 1981. Today it's below 40%. Yet today, when threatened with the prospect of paying more in taxes, many millionaires, billionaires, and Fortune 500 companies bemoan the purported injustice of the tax burdens placed upon them, complaining that they're being punished for hard work and success. The Koch brothers' Americans for Prosperity political advocacy group laments our "punitive tax structure."[104] Other plutocrats argue that too many Americans pay no income taxes at all. The *Wall Street Journal* has mocked these citizens, calling them "lucky duckies" despite their impoverishment.[105]

Former presidential candidate Mitt Romney expressed this Scrooge-like view at a 2012 fundraiser when he memorably said, "There are 47% who...are dependent upon government, who believe that they are victims, who believe the government has a responsibility to care for them, who believe that they are entitled to health care, to food, to housing, to you-name-it."[106] Rush Limbaugh has referred to these same people as "slovenly, lazy takers."[107] One-time leading House Republican Eric Cantor offered his own we're-the-victims appeal, explaining, "We also know that over 45% of the people in this country don't pay income taxes at all, and we have to question whether that's fair."[108] He went on to argue that by getting low-income workers to pay more taxes, rates can be lowered for everyone—including, of course, the fabulously wealthy.

But all these claims of injustice intentionally ignore basic facts. First, the low-wage workers described as "freeloaders" by the 1% are still subject to payroll, state, and local taxes, even when their earnings fall below the federal income tax threshold. Second, defenders of extreme inequality fail to acknowledge that for decades most of the benefits from increasing worker productivity have gone into the pockets of the country's CEOs and their well-connected friends. And third, despite complaints about over-taxation from top executives and company spokespersons, corporate profits as a percentage of the gross national product have reached their highest levels in almost a century. By comparison, employee compensation is at a multi-decade low, which is no coincidence.[109]

Moreover, major corporations and the super-rich exploit esoteric loopholes, overseas tax havens, and lax oversight to drastically reduce their tax burden.[110] In recent years, companies like General Electric, Boeing, and Verizon, among others, have received tax refunds from the IRS despite tens of billions of dollars in profits.[111] When Bernie Sanders criticized these corporations during his presidential campaign in 2016, GE's chairman dismissively responded, "We've never been a big hit with socialists."[112] Verizon's CEO followed up, accusing the Vermont senator of looking for "convenient villains for the economic distress felt by many of our citizens."[113] President Trump has also been part of the billionaires' we're-the-victims chorus, insisting, "We're the highest taxed nation in the world. Our businesses pay more taxes than any businesses in the world."[114]

Going a step further, some large U.S. companies strategically re-incorporate outside of the country—with no meaningful transfer of equipment or employees—for the sole purpose of reducing their taxes.[115] All the while, these firms continue to take advantage of the benefits the United States provides in terms of protecting their businesses and facilitating their growth and profits. The 1% argue that these tax loopholes are entirely legal. They neglect to mention the armies of high-powered lobbyists and attorneys they've hired to shape the relevant laws.

On a different front, today's plutocrats adopt the We're the Victims mind game when they portray the estate tax as a towering injustice. Republican leaders in Washington have long been especially fond of this ploy. Over a decade ago, before he retired to become a high-paid lobbyist, Republican Senator Jon Kyl of Arizona had this to say in a speech on the Senate floor: "It is an unfair, inefficient, economically unsound and, frankly, immoral tax."[116] In 2015, Republican Senator John Thune of South Dakota labeled the estate tax an "injustice" and a "nightmare,"[117] and Paul Ryan, then chairman of the House Ways and Means Committee, described the tax as "unfair and in conflict with the American Dream."[118] As Trump's chief economic adviser, former Goldman Sachs president Gary Cohn has joined in as well: "No one wants to see their children have to sell the family business to pay an unfair tax."[119]

Rhetorical flourishes like these from political leaders are designed to give us the wrong impression: that a considerable number of Americans are burdened by the estate tax. The truth is very different. Putting aside the suspect claim that a tax on accumulated wealth is somehow intrinsically unjust (without the tax, which in part supports various social programs, inequality would be even higher than it is already), currently only two out of every 1,000 people owe any federal estate taxes at all when they die.[120] And hardly any of them are the much-touted "family farmers" whom the plutocrats paint as victims when disguising their save-the-rich agenda.

Regrettably, however, the 1% have been very effective in misleading the public in order to garner opposition to the estate tax. Indeed, polling shows that a majority of Americans favor the repeal of the estate tax, and that they consider it the least fair of all federal taxes.[121] That's why the plutocrat-defending Heritage Foundation promotes the view that "Americans of all walks of life sense the deep injustice of federal death taxes."[122] But a recent experiment by a group of economists provides some encouragement. They found that people became much more supportive of the estate tax when they were provided with accurate information documenting both the extent of economic inequality today and the fact that only the very wealthiest Americans pay these taxes upon their death.[123] Of course, the public won't be receiving that information from the predatory class anytime soon. Indeed, in October 2017 Senate Republicans moved forward on a "Robin Hood in reverse" budget plan that would repeal the estate tax and provide multitrillion-dollar tax breaks for the 1%.[124]

Defending the Indefensible: Prisoner Abuse

The same We're the Victims mind game is familiar fare in the context of war, where claims of victimhood are promoted by perpetrators who've misused their extraordinary power. Among the memorable examples are the aggrieved pronouncements from top Bush administration officials—and their high-profile supporters—in response to evidence that prisoners in U.S. custody were abused and tortured during the "war on terror" and the invasion and occupation of Iraq.

At this point, it's well-documented that prisoner abuse was a regular occurrence at the detention center at Guantánamo Bay in Cuba and the Abu Ghraib prison in Iraq, as well as numerous CIA "black sites." Detainees at Guantánamo—most of whom were not al-Qaeda fighters[125]—were subjected to a wide range of brutal techniques, including physical beatings; painful stress positions; solitary confinement; sleep deprivation; exposure to extreme temperatures; harassment; and sexual, religious, and cultural humiliation.[126] The unauthorized release of horrific photos from Abu Ghraib in 2004 showed prisoners who were hooded, wired with electrodes, wearing a dog leash, threatened by growling dogs, forced to engage in sex acts, and piled naked on top of each other.[127]

Nevertheless, then-Secretary of Defense Donald Rumsfeld frequently portrayed criticisms and allegations of U.S. wrongdoing as unwarranted and unfair. When early reports first appeared in January 2002 suggesting that prisoners at Guantánamo were being mistreated, Rumsfeld took umbrage during a news briefing: "I haven't found a single scrap of any kind of information that suggests that anyone has been treated anything other than humanely—notwithstanding everything we have read and heard over the past three days."[128] His outrage was similarly on display in May 2004 during testimony before the Senate Armed Services Committee after the Abu Ghraib photos became public. On that occasion he angrily complained, "People are running around with digital cameras and taking these unbelievable photographs and then passing them off, against the law, to the media, to our surprise, when they had not even arrived in the Pentagon!"[129]

The following year, speaking at Johns Hopkins University in December 2005, Rumsfeld again turned to we're-the-victims appeals in condemning criticism he deemed unfair: "The worst about America and our military seems to so quickly be taken as truth by the press, and reported and spread around the world, often with little context and little scrutiny, let alone correction or accountability after the fact." And to applause from those assembled at the annual American Legion national convention in 2006, he lamented:

> Amnesty International refers to the military facility at Guantánamo Bay—which holds terrorists who have vowed to kill Americans and which is arguably the best run and most scrutinized detention facility in the history of warfare—as "the gulag of our times." It's inexcusable...America is not what's wrong with the world.[130]

Rumsfeld wasn't alone in attempting to misdirect the public's perceptions of injustice. For instance, during the hearing on the Abu Ghraib photos, Republican Senator James Inhofe aimed his outrage at two targets: "humanitarian do-gooders right now crawling all over these prisons looking for human rights violations while our troops, our heroes, are fighting and dying," and "the press and the politicians and the political agendas that are being served by this."[131] When Democratic Senator Dick Durbin of Illinois compared the abusive interrogations of Guantánamo detainees to Nazi horrors and Soviet gulags,[132] he was condemned by the White House ("reprehensible" and "beyond belief"[133]), by Senate colleagues ("deplorable"[134]), and by right-wing bloggers ("treacherous"[135]).

But despite repeated denials and we're-the-victims appeals, torture allegations leveled against the Bush administration were true. George W. Bush, Cheney, and others were not the victims of unjust and false accusations. Rumsfeld himself was personally responsible for the authorization of cruel, inhuman, and degrading interrogation techniques. Indeed, in 2008 a bipartisan Senate Armed Services Committee report concluded that decisions by Rumsfeld and other senior officials "conveyed the message that physical pressures and degradation were appropriate treatment for detainees in U.S. military custody."[136]

SUMMING UP: THE PLUTOCRATS' INJUSTICE MIND GAMES

In this chapter we've explored four mind games used by the 1% to confuse the public about what's fair and what's not. Before turning to our third core concern, distrust, let's review each of them.

With the We're Fighting Injustice mind game, today's plutocrats argue that their initiatives are a necessary corrective to the unjust actions of others. This ploy is designed to misappropriate and misdirect the outrage that injustice arouses—and it's nothing new. Over 2,400 years ago, Plato observed, "The highest reach of injustice is: to be deemed just when you are not."[137] That wolf-in-sheep's-clothing disguise is pretty much exactly what contemporary defenders of extreme inequality wear as they ply us with tall tales about their justice-seeking exploits.

At other times, the 1% turn to deceptive no-injustice-here appeals. When they do so, they deny the existence of real injustices, portraying them instead as instances of mere misfortune or as the natural consequence of the victims' own poor decisions. The predatory class hopes that the public will be fooled into accepting these alternative explanations for the country's unconscionable disparities in wealth, power, and life prospects. When this strategy succeeds, it discourages collective action by defusing the passion that's associated with the pursuit of justice and the righting of wrongs.

With the Change Is Unjust mind game, today's plutocrats adopt a somewhat different tack, warning that even greater injustices will befall us if we support the grievances of those who are struggling. But here too, their goal is essentially the same: to give us pause by raising concerns as to whether efforts to help the disadvantaged might create conditions that are worse rather than better. Planting these seeds of doubt can be enough to frighten or perplex us into passivity, which serves to obstruct the formation of coalitions committed to challenging the 1%'s agenda.

Finally, when they use their we're-the-victims appeals, the 1% brazenly complain of being mistreated themselves. With these claims, they aim to encourage uncertainty and disagreement among the public over issues of right and wrong and victim and perpetrator. This is, of course, a manipulative diversion from a basic reality: Extreme inequality persists thanks to injustices that work to the advantage of "haves" over "have-nots." Indeed, we've reached the point where life, liberty, and the pursuit of happiness, in their fullest forms, are becoming the private reserve of today's greed-driven plutocrats.

As with vulnerability earlier, we can now see just how often our injustice concerns are targeted and manipulated in order to advance the interests of a privileged few. In the next chapter, we'll find the same predatory artifices prevail in a third psychological domain: distrust.

4

DISTRUST
MIND GAMES
MISDIRECTING OUR DOUBTS
AND SUSPICIONS

"We have to distrust each other.
It's our only defense against betrayal."

— TENNESSEE WILLIAMS[1]

For better or worse, we tend to divide the world into those we believe we can trust and those we can't. Exactly where that line is drawn creates either bridges or barriers to working with others toward mutually beneficial goals. At times, our suspicions may be warranted. But these doubts can also be manipulated or based on misinformation or biases that lead us to overlook our common interests or shared fate.

As we'll see, the various distrust mind games that today's plutocrats use primarily involve two overarching strategies. First, they seek to create distance between those who are most disadvantaged by their policies and the broader public whose support is needed to produce real change. The goal is to fray any positive connection—whether it's sympathy, compassion, outrage, or a sense of solidarity. This tactic is evident, for example, in attempts to raise doubts about the character of those who are poor or unemployed.

Second, plutocrats try to disrupt the formation of coalitions among those who, because they suffer from similarly adverse circumstances, might logically work together in the pursuit of change. For instance, defenders of extreme inequality sow distrust as a wedge between racial, ethnic, or religious groups. In combination, these two strategies keep the moat around the 1%'s castle both wide and deep. Here are the four distrust mind games we'll examine in this chapter: They're Devious and Dishonest, They're Different from Us, They're Misguided and Misinformed, and Trust Us.

THEY'RE DEVIOUS AND DISHONEST

In 1964, J. Edgar Hoover called a press conference and told the American people that Martin Luther King Jr. was the "most notorious liar in the country." In doing so, the FBI director was employing a distrust appeal that's common fare for the 1%. Plutocrats routinely assert that those who oppose their goals are dishonest and lack integrity. In this way, they aim to undercut the public's concern for people who are struggling by arguing that their claims of adversity are exaggerations or fabrications. We're told that these people are treacherous, that they spread lies for personal gain, that they have ulterior motives, and that only the most gullible among us would fall for their deceptions. When this discrediting propaganda works, the public turns away from—or even worse, turns against—the actual victims of the predatory class's self-aggrandizing policies.

When representatives of the 1% warn us that there are sinister deceivers and tricksters in our midst, they're tapping into our lifelong sensitivity to issues of trust and betrayal. These psychological concerns begin during infancy, when we're entirely dependent on others for our protection and for the satisfaction of our most basic needs. They continue into early childhood. Parents are familiar with "stranger anxiety," the temporary distress that young children experience when first encountering a new face. As we grow older, our fears change and we become more discerning, but we can still err in trusting too readily or not trusting enough.

Psychologists have long studied the factors that go into determining how we size up and feel about another person. What they've found is that it's our perceptions of the other's "warmth"—including their trustworthiness—that carry the most weight.[2] From an evolutionary perspective, this makes a lot of sense. After all, our welfare—indeed, our survival—can depend upon quick and accurate judgments about whether someone is friend or foe. Perhaps these same self-protective inclinations are why negative impressions are harder to change than positive ones—and why a bad reputation seems easy to acquire and hard to lose, while the opposite applies to a good reputation. For many of us, it's also the case that feelings of distrust can be stubborn and difficult to overcome, whereas trust may prove to be surprisingly fragile.

We can add another relevant research finding to this mix: a phenomenon called "negativity dominance."[3] Across a wide range of issues, "bad" things carry more psychological heft than "good" things. Financial losses usually cause more distress than the pleasure we derive from comparable-sized gains. Successful relationships typically depend upon a much higher proportion of pleasant compared to unpleasant interactions. Negative emotions often overwhelm positive ones. Greater weight is given to negative characteristics than positive ones when forming impressions of people. Regarding this last point, researchers have found that it takes multiple favorable adjectives to cancel out the impact of a single unfavorable adjective when we're given a description of another person. Putting all these psychological tendencies together, it's not surprising that being told someone is devious and dishonest can have a powerful and lasting influence on us—and the 1% use this to their advantage.

In taking a closer look at the They're Devious and Dishonest mind game, we'll first examine the role played by this appeal in President Donald Trump's "fake news" rants. Then we'll look at plutocratic efforts to turn the public against racial justice advocates and low-wage workers, and to gain support for military aggression.

Donald Trump's "Fake News"

At his first news conference as president of the United States, Trump lashed out at the purported untrustworthiness of the press:

> The press has become so dishonest that if we don't talk about, we are doing a tremendous disservice to the American people. Tremendous disservice. We have to talk to find out what's going on, because the press honestly is out of control. The level of dishonesty is out of control.[4]

Incensed by critical coverage during the election campaign and by negative appraisals of his early days in office, Trump's nationally televised attack was really just a single shot in what's been an ongoing barrage. Throughout, he's used the They're Devious and Dishonest mind game as a weapon designed to turn Americans—and especially his devout supporters—against the major news outlets. Aside from predictable exceptions like the fawning Fox News network, the president has belligerently sought to discredit reporting and reporters from the mainstream media. He's portrayed their stories as "fake news" intended to impede his own tireless efforts to "Make America Great Again."

Trump has been prolific on Twitter with his they're-devious-and-dishonest appeals. Here are several examples from just his first six months in the White House:

Just leaving Florida. Big crowds of enthusiastic supporters lining the road that the FAKE NEWS media refuses to
mention. Very dishonest![5]

The FAKE NEWS media (failing @nytimes, @NBCNews,
@ABC, @CBS, @CNN) is not my enemy, it is the enemy
of the American People![6]

FAKE NEWS media knowingly doesn't tell the truth. A
great danger to our country. The failing @nytimes has
become a joke. Likewise @CNN. Sad![7]

The Fake News Media works hard at disparaging &
demeaning my use of social media because they don't want
America to hear the real story![8]

The Fake News Media has never been so wrong or so dirty.
Purposely incorrect stories and phony sources to meet
their agenda of hate. Sad![9]

With all of its phony unnamed sources & highly slanted &
even fraudulent reporting, #Fake News is DISTORTING
DEMOCRACY in our country![10]

The president's allegations about pervasive media dishonesty
have proven to be both overwrought and false. Where actual
evidence has been brought to bear in evaluating his claims,
Trump and his surrogates have consistently been on the
wrong side of the truth.[11] Such instances are far too many to
fully recount, but they've included the size of the crowd at his
inauguration, the claim that millions of undocumented immigrants voted unlawfully in the November election (and thereby
cost him the popular vote), concerns raised about qualifica-
tions and conflicts of interest involving senior staff and cabinet
appointees, and his taking credit for various accomplishments
of the Obama administration.

On one occasion, adviser Kellyanne Conway even went so
far as to argue that the president's shaky position was based
on a set of "alternative facts." That's obviously an absurd

defense for his fabrications, yet the White House's they're-devious-and-dishonest ploys have succeeded in promoting public skepticism about accurate and reliable media reports. One measure of their effectiveness comes from a national poll conducted 100 days into Trump's term. Respondents were asked, "What do you think is a bigger problem—mainstream news organizations producing false stories or the Trump administration making false claims?" Fully 80% of Trump voters identified the media as the bigger problem, while only 3% held the opposite view. In the sample overall, the breakdown was 40% and 43%, respectively.[12] While the media are not without fault, the president's campaign to demonize them as untrustworthy has regrettably borne fruit.

One additional lesson here is that we shouldn't expect Trump's ardent supporters to abandon him simply because he pursues policies that hurt rather than help them. Especially if they're surrounded by like-minded devotees who fall for this distrust mind game, many will instead embrace his "alternative facts" and his false claims about "fake news." In part, this is because, psychologically, the desire for consistency in our beliefs and actions leads us to interpret the world in whatever ways most readily reduce any dissonance we feel. That's why misplaced political loyalties can persist without the adherents even recognizing how far they've gone astray.

The Real Race Hustlers

Some one-percenters have adopted the same They're Devious and Dishonest mind game to disparage those who draw attention to ongoing racial injustices in the United States. Here are some of the facts these defenders of extreme inequality hope to hide from the public.[13] African Americans suffer from poverty at rates almost three times that of their white counterparts,[14] and the median wealth of white households is twenty times greater.[15] In our criminal justice system, African Americans are far more likely to be the targets of "stop-and-frisk" operations,[16] are disproportionately arrested and prosecuted for minor offenses,[17] and are given longer prison sentences for comparable crimes.[18] In comparison to predominantly white schools, "minority majority" schools are underfunded and overcrowded, and levels of segregation in education today are little different from what they were prior to the Supreme Court's landmark *Brown v. Board of Education* ruling that overturned "separate but equal" in 1954.[19]

In short, the ugly and not-so-distant history of slavery, of post-emancipation Jim Crow laws and lynchings, and of legalized discrimination and segregation still casts a long shadow.[20] But such overwhelming evidence is of little concern to the likes of Bill O'Reilly and his former colleagues at Fox News. They've frequently used they're-devious-and-dishonest appeals to denounce outspoken change advocates as untrustworthy "race hustlers."

In early 2014, for example, Wisconsin congressman Paul Ryan—now Speaker of the House—offered the tired but ever-popular claim of the predatory class that poverty reflects an inner city "culture problem."[21] California congresswoman Barbara Lee, a Democrat who was also the lone vote against the open-ended use of military force following the 9/11 attacks, condemned Ryan's statement as a thinly veiled racial attack. "Instead of demonizing 'culture,' and blaming Black men for their poverty, Mr. Ryan should step up and produce some legitimate proposals on how to tackle poverty and racial discrimination in America," she said.[22] In response, O'Reilly impugned the integrity of Lee and her fellow reformers: "They don't want to solve the problem. These race hustlers make a big living, and they get voted into office, by portraying their constituents as victims."[23] A few days later he added to his attack: "Not only is she a pinhead, a race hustler, she's a liar."[24]

Similar efforts to smear racial justice activists as dishonest have been prominent in other plutocratic circles following nationwide protests over the killing of unarmed African American individuals by police officers—in Ferguson,

Missouri; New York City; Cleveland, Ohio; North Charleston, South Carolina; Balch Springs, Texas; and far beyond. Conservative author and pundit Dinesh D'Souza, for example, described the outrage as spurred on by those who've "perfected the art of manufacturing racial resentment even when there really shouldn't be any."[25] In much the same way, the Heritage Foundation's Hans von Spakovsky lamented, "We should be more concerned about the violence, looting and arson in Ferguson, as well as the false narrative being pushed across the country that black Americans are routinely treated unfairly in the criminal justice system."[26] False narratives are indeed a very serious problem—and here again we see that one-percenters are masters at creating them.

Deceitful Corporate Giants

The hardships faced by workers with neither a decent paycheck nor job security are certainly no mirage either. The links between declining real wages, shrinking labor unions, a fragile and dwindling middle class, and worsening income inequality are clear.[27] Consider that the average hourly wages of employees at giant retail and fast-food chains place these workers under or perilously close to the official poverty line. In fact, while their CEOs take home millions annually in salaries and bonuses, companies like Walmart and McDonald's pay many of their workers so little that U.S. taxpayers are left to fund billions of dollars in food stamps and other public assistance for their employees.[28]

Nevertheless, huge and highly profitable corporations use the They're Devious and Dishonest mind game to discredit workers who are seeking better pay, benefits, or job security. In recent years, for example, Walmart workers organized nationwide protests about poverty wages on Black Friday—the busy shopping day after Thanksgiving. Walmart management has responded with statements characterizing their claims as mere smoke and mirrors, insisting that most of the company's employees have high levels of job satisfaction. Of course, the fact that Walmart has reportedly fired or disciplined dozens of workers who participated in one-day strikes around the country makes it hard to take the company's argument seriously.[29]

Corporate low-wage giants don't rely solely on their own public relations offices to encourage the public's distrust of protesting workers. They also pay front groups to lend a hand. Worker Center Watch, for instance, has described its own efforts as "dedicated to exposing the often disingenuous and potentially nefarious actions of labor activist worker centers." Along with spinning tales of "professional protestors" and "shakedowns of non-union businesses," this big-business defender portrays labor activism as a plot to "replace the capitalist system that built this country with a socialist system that penalizes risk takers."[30] That's quite an absurd accusation against workers who are merely organizing to earn a living wage and respect at work.

Truth, the First Casualty of War

Building support for aggressive military action is another venue in which representatives of the plutocracy call upon the They're Devious and Dishonest mind game. Recall how the White House promoted the March 2003 invasion of Iraq as a necessary response to the treachery of one of our "axis of evil" enemies. Iraqi president Saddam Hussein was certainly a brutal dictator, but he had nothing to do with the terrorist attacks of September 11, 2001. Nevertheless, the Bush administration used those horrific attacks as an opportunity to push for long-desired regime change. They obscured their own subterfuge by focusing the public's attention on the duplicity of Hussein instead.

In August 2002, at a meeting of the Veterans of Foreign Wars in Nashville, Vice President Dick Cheney told the audience, "Saddam has perfected the game of shoot and retreat, and is very skilled in the art of denial and deception."[31] Several weeks later, speaking in the Rose Garden less than six months before the invasion, President George W. Bush also warned about Hussein's duplicity: "They buy time with hollow promises. They move incriminating evidence to stay ahead of inspectors. They concede just enough...to escape punishment, and then violate every pledge when the attention of the world is turned away."[32] He continued with the same distrust ploy in his January 2003 State of the Union address: "The dictator of Iraq is not disarming. To the contrary, he is deceiving."[33]

After the invasion, similar suspicion-raising appeals warned Americans that we shouldn't be tricked into modifying or abandoning the war effort. During an October 2006 press conference, for instance, Bush urged us not to be taken in by others' efforts to manipulate and deceive: "We must not fall prey to the sophisticated propaganda by the enemy, who is trying to undermine our confidence and make us believe that our presence in Iraq is the cause of all its problems."[34]

Yet throughout, the Bush administration—in various ways and through multiple spokespersons—based its arguments for war on disingenuous claims. That campaign included numerous misrepresentations of fact, most notably assertions that Hussein possessed weapons of mass destruction and that he was collaborating with al-Qaeda.[35] Ultimately, the Iraq War cost the lives of several thousand U.S. soldiers and hundreds of thousands of Iraqi civilians. But it was a boon to certain members of the 1%, including U.S. defense contractors and oil companies.

Similar they're-devious-and-dishonest appeals were employed in efforts to advance the broader "global war on terror," in which Iraq was presented as a key battlefield. Consider the false statements made by the White House in defending its treatment of prisoners at the Guantánamo Bay detention center. In the earliest days, Cheney appeared on Fox News and described the detainees as "the worst of a very bad lot. They are very dangerous. They are devoted to killing millions of

Americans."[36] Defense Secretary Donald Rumsfeld argued that they were "among the most dangerous, best trained, vicious killers on the face of the earth."[37] Several years later—and despite growing evidence of detainee abuse[38]—Rumsfeld was still pushing this distrust ploy in a speech to the Council on Foreign Relations: "They're trained to lie. They're trained to allege that they've been tortured. They're trained to put out misinformation, and they're very good at it."[39]

But as noted earlier, reports from government and independent agencies have established that prisoners held at Guantánamo Bay, CIA "black sites," and other facilities were indeed tortured and treated inhumanely by U.S. personnel.[40] Moreover, most of those subjected to indefinite detention—a violation of international law—had no meaningful connection to the 9/11 attacks or to any terrorist activities.[41] Indeed, according to Lawrence Wilkerson, former Secretary of State Colin Powell's chief of staff, the "vast majority" were innocent, there was no evidence against them, but they were held nonetheless because of the political fallout and embarrassment that would result if they were released.[42]

THEY'RE DIFFERENT FROM US

With this second distrust mind game, defenders of extreme inequality promote a simple, manipulative message: Those who oppose the 1%'s policies are very different from the American public at large. When this ploy works, heightened suspicions of these "other people" make us less likely to support their hard-fought and deserving efforts. In choosing to stand aside, our passivity instead serves the selfish ambitions of the rich and powerful.

The psychological dynamics of the They're Different from Us mind game are clear. When we're persuaded that someone isn't part of our group, it adversely affects how we judge and behave toward them. In their research, social psychologists have found that individuals perceived as fellow ingroup members have several advantages over those who are viewed as belonging to an outgroup: We think of ingroup members as more trustworthy, we hold them in higher regard, and we're more willing to share scarce resources with them.[43]

But what accounts for our positive stance toward people we consider part of our ingroup? In large measure, this positive bias results from our belief that these individuals have a lot in common with us. Even if we've never met them, we tend to think that their values, attitudes, and life experiences are probably similar to our own. This applies to a wide range of groups, including those based on race, ethnicity, religion, or nationality.

Favoritism of this sort is pervasive. Indeed, it's easy to manufacture artificially in the psychology lab—even among people who don't share much in common at all. In what are called minimal group experiments, research participants are assigned to one of two groups, either randomly or based on some trivial consideration, such as a preference for the paintings of one artist over another. Despite the weak basis for these bonds, members of each arbitrary group soon start treating one another better than they do members of the other group.[44]

The bottom line is that there's a lot riding on whether or not we view other people as members of our ingroup. If we don't see them that way, there's a greater chance that we'll consider them potential adversaries rather than allies. Not surprisingly, such divisiveness within the 99% is exactly what the predatory class wants.

In exploring they're-different-from-us appeals, let's now take a closer look at how the 1% advance their agenda by preying on prejudices and by sowing division among their opponents.

Preying on Prejudice

The They're Different from Us mind game is a favorite tool of plutocrats because they can use it to stifle broad-based opposition by exploiting the public's misguided prejudices. Solidarity with and among disadvantaged groups is jeopardized whenever differences based on irrelevant characteristics like race are emphasized and exaggerated. That's why the 1% highlight these differences and simultaneously downplay important similarities in circumstances and aspirations. It's an effective way to generate distrust and to fragment groups that might otherwise form a united resistance to their agenda. When opposition coalitions fail to materialize, defenders of extreme wealth and power are the undeserving beneficiaries.

To be clear, these tactics don't require that all plutocrats hold explicitly racist views about African Americans, Hispanics, Muslims, or other groups. But even when they don't, they can still take advantage of the fact that racism—and other forms of bigotry—continues to divide individuals and groups whose collective futures could be brighter if unwarranted suspicions gave way to constructive engagement. Law professor Ian Haney López has described this approach as strategic racism: "purposeful efforts to use racial animus as leverage to gain material wealth, political power, or heightened social standing."[45] Journalist Naomi Klein has similarly noted, "White supremacy, misogyny, homophobia, and transphobia have been the elite's most potent defenses against genuine democracy."[46]

As one example, consider how distrustful racial biases among the public indirectly add to the revenue stream for companies—telemarketing, food supply, agriculture—that rely on the availability of cheap and abundant prison labor.[47] As research by psychologists Rebecca Hetey and Jennifer Eberhardt shows, white Americans are stronger supporters of mass incarceration—including lengthy sentences for minor nonviolent offenses—when they believe that African Americans are the ones disproportionately affected by these draconian policies.[48] In this way, racist attitudes reduce the public's opposition to mass incarceration. That's good news for businesses eager to find workers they can pay much less than the minimum wage.

So too, anti-immigrant sentiment is a boon to private prison corporations and their executives. They rake in fortunes because many of us accept misrepresentations claiming that men, women, and even children caught at the border are dangerous and must therefore be held indefinitely in detention facilities.[49] Feeding this distorted view are comments from high-profile one-percenters like Trump, who had this to say of Mexican immigrants when he announced his 2016 presidential run: "They're bringing drugs. They're bringing crime. They're rapists."[50]

In a similar way, defense and homeland security contractors land enormous paydays because enough Americans have been persuaded to adopt a suspicious, "they're different" view in which all Muslims are seen as potential terrorists. For his part, at various times Trump has expressed support for the profiling of Muslims—including identification cards and a national database of Muslims in the United States[51]—as well as a "total and complete shutdown" of Muslims immigrating to or visiting the United States.[52]

When the 1% encourage prejudice or merely fail to use their influence to reduce it, they're prioritizing the preservation of their tremendous material advantages over the creation of a more decent society. Even more, their strategic efforts to cultivate distrust can spur disadvantaged groups to start blaming each other for their plight, rather than directing their sights at the real source of their travails: the plutocrats themselves.

Divide and Conquer: Union-Busting

Representatives of the predatory class also rely on the They're Different from Us mind game to foster unwarranted competition—and a false sense of incompatible goals—among natural allies who are ultimately destined to sink or swim together. In their effort to halt opposition coalitions before they even form, the 1% promote a zero-sum, dog-eat-dog worldview. Any potential gains for one struggling group are portrayed as the inevitable source of worsening conditions for another group. If seeds of distrust are successfully planted, two groups are much less likely to join forces.

The anti-labor actions of Wisconsin Governor Scott Walker, a Republican, and his wealthy allies are an illustrative case. Shortly after he was elected in 2010, Walker set out to turn the public against the state's unionized government employees. As a start, in a speech to the Milwaukee Press Club, he touched on issues of inequality with this divisive message: "We can no longer live in a society where the public employees are 'the haves' and taxpayers who foot the bills are 'the have-nots.'"[53]

With support from the Koch brothers, the American Legislative Exchange Council, and other union-busting devotees, Walker made his next move the following year. In a private conversation with a prospective billionaire donor, the governor explained, "The first step is we're going to deal with collective bargaining for all public employee unions, because you use divide and conquer."[54] Sure enough, Walker's "budget repair bill" left private sector unions untouched but hammered public sector unions, sharply curtailing bargaining rights over wage increases, working conditions, and benefits for most state employees, including teachers and nurses.

Although they represent public employees too, the firefighter and police unions—traditionally more supportive of Republican candidates—were exempted from the new regulations, further fraying labor's unity. Then in 2015, having significantly weakened public sector unions, the governor took aim at private sector unions too, signing into law a so-called right-to-work bill that undercut their ability to collect dues from members.

What's been the net result of this duplicitous campaign? Wisconsin's public and private sector unions alike have fallen on hard times, foiled in part by the divide-and-conquer strategy of Walker and his super-rich backers. All the while, the governor's union-busting had little effect on reducing the state's budget shortfalls, which arose from tax breaks and other concessions to the 1%. Other Republican governors now consider Walker's they're-different-from-us ploys as a model for their own anti-labor crusades.

Creating False Divisions: Teachers and Protesters

Here's another way that the 1% use they're-different-from-us appeals: They paint their opponents as having values and priorities that diverge sharply from those of most Americans. This strategy shows up in a wide range of areas. Consider how corporate "school reformers"—eager to line their own pockets—try to persuade parents that public school teachers can't be trusted. They argue that the teachers' motives and agenda don't align with what's best for their students. According to greed-driven proponents of privatization, many teachers have little commitment to educating our children because all they really care about are personal matters like salary, benefits, and job security.

Representatives of the plutocracy never offer serious evidence to support these broad claims. But they know their manipulative campaign can bear fruit nonetheless, simply by raising doubts. When it succeeds, parents and the public no longer see teachers as community members who share our goals for children. Instead, they're viewed as outgroup members and adversaries who should be treated with suspicion. This divide is counterproductive, of course—and it's demoralizing to the people who've devoted themselves to a teaching career, a career that already fails to bestow upon them the respect and appreciation they deserve.[55]

In a similar manner, defenders of extreme inequality were quick to describe the thousands of Occupy Wall Street participants—who called for an end to corporate control of our democracy—as dangerously out of sync with the rest of the country. Right-wing talk show hosts were overwrought and vicious in their condemnations. Glenn Beck warned, "If you're wealthy, they will kill you for what you have."[56] Rush Limbaugh referred to the protesters as a "parade of human debris."[57] While campaigning to be president, multimillionaire Mitt Romney likened the Occupy movement to class warfare. An anti-Occupy film directed by Steve Bannon, briefly Trump's chief strategist in the White House, premiered at the 2012 Republican National Convention. It argued that the goal of Occupy Wall Street was to spread anarchy and destroy the American government.[58]

These and other gross distortions cast the movement as a fringe group with priorities far different from those of the average American. In reality, however, the values of most Occupy supporters reflected the economic frustrations that characterize the American people more broadly, as well as the widely shared belief that protecting the common good is more important than expanding the wealth and power of the fortunate few. One need only watch videos of Wall Street executives drinking champagne from a balcony above the demonstrators to recognize who's truly different and out of touch.[59]

THEY'RE MISGUIDED AND MISINFORMED

When the 1% worry that attacking their adversaries as deceivers or deviants might backfire, they turn to a third distrust mind game in their quiver. With the They're Misguided and Misinformed mind game, plutocrats instead depict their opponents as naively wrongheaded—arguing that they lack an adequate education, or suffer from unrecognized biases, or are the victims of others' intentional misinformation.

Much as a savvy trial attorney works cautiously to undermine an otherwise sympathetic witness in the eyes of the jury, this appeal is used when the public holds a positive view of those who face adverse circumstances. So, we're told that the misguided don't understand the real causes of the problems they seek to fix, and that their proposed remedies will only make matters worse for everyone. When these negative characterizations by the predatory class stick, the public becomes less likely to mobilize for greater equality because we doubt the credibility of those who are calling for change.

Not surprisingly, appearing credible is a highly prized commodity for anyone who hopes to have influence. Indeed, psychological research has long demonstrated that greater credibility leads to greater attitude change in a target audience. Psychologists and other scholars have also figured out which personal characteristics tend to make a speaker more or less believable. The two most important factors? Perceived expertise and perceived trustworthiness.[60]

Expertise is often conveyed through in-depth knowledge, which may come from either extensive study or firsthand experience. Imagine, for instance, a presentation on the dangerous impairments associated with driving while drunk. A distinguished scientist who's devoted their career to this area of study is likely to be very persuasive. But there's a good chance that we'll also be influenced by an alcoholic who describes the fatal accident they caused while behind the wheel. Some researchers have focused on courtroom settings in their studies of expertise, sometimes relying on mock juries for this purpose. Among their findings, experts from more prestigious universities were considered more persuasive than those from less well-known schools—even when their testimony was identical.[61]

Turning from expertise to trustworthiness, our perceptions are typically linked to judgments about a speaker's honesty, integrity, character, and likeability. If we think someone has these characteristics, then we're more likely to be persuaded by what they tell us. In part, that's because we have confidence that such an individual's message isn't self-serving. In courtroom studies, for example, highly paid "hired guns" were deemed less believable by jurors than experts who were paid less, due to concerns over possible bias. Of course, we don't always have enough information to make correct judgments; it's always possible for us to mistakenly bestow expert or trustworthy status on those who don't deserve it. Likewise, we may fail to give a person the credit they deserve. Unfortunately, undermining the credibility of their adversaries is a strategy that today's plutocrats carry out with considerable proficiency.

In discussing the They're Misguided and Misinformed mind game, we'll examine the role played by this appeal in a few specific contexts, including the 1%'s efforts to discredit Occupy Wall Street, to marginalize dissent against overreaching government policies, and to defend for-profit prisons.

Discrediting Occupy Wall Street

The They're Misguided and Misinformed mind game was a key part of the campaign used by the 1% to delegitimize the Occupy Wall Street movement. At first, defenders of extreme wealth and power ignored the predominantly youthful protesters at Zuccotti Park in New York City and other sites that sprung up around the country. But when the movement's "We Are the 99%" message condemning corporate greed and the focus on profits over people began to resonate with more and more Americans, representatives of the predatory class took notice and moved quickly to disparage them.

Before he eventually shut down the encampment, New York's billionaire mayor Michael Bloomberg claimed that it was a mistake for the demonstrators to protest against Wall Street workers "struggling to make ends meet," and that to hold the banks responsible for the worldwide recession was to "blame the wrong people."[62] Trump appeared on the TV show *Fox & Friends* and said, "Nobody knows why they're protesting but they're having a good time...A lot of them are down there for dating purposes."[63] And spokespersons for think tanks funded by plutocrats were quick to join the chorus. The Heritage Foundation's Rory Cooper argued that the Occupy movement suffered from an "emptiness of ideas and solutions,"[64] while the Cato Institute's Roger Pilon characterized their efforts as a "mindless" approach to public affairs.[65]

But despite such dismissive and self-serving appraisals from the 1%, Occupy protestors succeeded in revealing the gaping economic divide in the United States, and they inspired a critical national conversation about extreme inequality that's ongoing today. Just as importantly, these protesters were right in directing outrage toward the country's huge financial institutions. Banks' avaricious leaders and their corrupt practices cost millions of people their livelihoods, their homes, and their life savings. All the while, these "too big to fail" banks and their directors have escaped the financial devastation that befell so many others, and they've largely eluded criminal prosecution as well.

Marginalizing Dissent against Government Policies

Those with political power—who are so often beholden to the 1%—also use they're-misguided-and-misinformed appeals in their efforts to marginalize those who disagree with controversial government policies and actions. Here too the goal is to encourage the public to view critics as unreliable and therefore not worth taking seriously. We see this ploy from Republicans and Democrats alike.

Consider some of the tactics used by the Bush administration to discredit those opposed to the Patriot Act and the dismantling of Americans' civil rights in the name of fighting terrorism. Shortly after the 9/11 attacks, at a time when doubts were being raised about new Justice Department initiatives, then-Attorney General John Ashcroft told the Senate Judiciary Committee, "To those who scare peace-loving people with phantoms of lost liberty, my message is this: Your tactics only aid terrorists for they erode our national unity and diminish our resolve. They give ammunition to America's enemies."[66] It may have been effective rhetoric, but history shows that those who were worried about abuses of government power—including invasions of privacy and discriminatory profiling of Muslims—were neither misguided nor mistaken.

In a similar fashion, Bush White House political adviser Karl Rove characterized anti-war critics as naïve and unreliable. In June 2005, with U.S. forces bogged down in Iraq and that country in shambles, he mockingly told the Conservative Party of New York State, "Conservatives saw the savagery of 9/11 in the attacks and prepared for war; liberals saw the savagery of the 9/11 attacks and wanted to prepare indictments and offer therapy and understanding for our attackers."[67] A year later, in remarks to New Hampshire Republican Party officials, Rove had this to say about Democrats: "They are ready to give the green light to go to war, but when it gets tough, and when it gets difficult, they fall back on that party's old pattern of cutting and running."[68] Despite Rove's dismissiveness, it's apparent that concerns about military aggression in Iraq and Afghanistan were well justified, even if the public failed to heed those warnings.

But this ploy doesn't belong to one political party alone. At times, President Barack Obama also resorted to characterizing serious critics as misinformed, irresponsible, and not worthy of the public's trust. For example, the leaks from whistleblower Edward Snowden revealed that the National Security Agency engaged in surveillance activities on a massive and previously unrecognized scale. These operations have collected the call information, emails, text messages, and contact lists of millions of regular Americans; they've also involved extensive spying on citizens, embassies, and world leaders overseas, including some of our closest allies.[69]

Nevertheless, Obama defended these programs and encouraged the public's skepticism of the disturbing revelations. In June 2013 remarks, he condemned the release of information "willy-nilly without regard to risks"; he ridiculed any notion of an Orwellian Big Brother program "run amok"; and he misleadingly assured everyone that "nobody is listening to your phone calls."[70] Two months later, at a White House press conference, Obama warned that the unfolding debate was "very passionate but not always fully informed"; he discounted "the impression that somehow we're out there willy-nilly just sucking in information on everybody and doing what we please with it"; and, despite its irrelevance, he insisted that those who work for the intelligence community "love this country and believe in our values. They're patriots."[71]

Overall, Obama's efforts to characterize NSA critics as misinformed misrepresented the underlying reality.[72] It's also worth noting that the Obama administration was extraordinarily secretive and consistently withheld information about national security policies, including by using feeble "state secrets" claims in legal proceedings. At the same time, spying is very big business. In recent years, major telecommunications companies like AT&T have received hundreds of millions of dollars for their partnership in the NSA's clandestine operations.[73] These words from Google CEO Eric Schmidt about his company's practices, back in 2009, are worrisome too: "If you have something that you don't want anyone to know, maybe you shouldn't be doing it in the first place."[74]

Defending For-Profit Prisons

Representatives of the 1% regularly resort to the They're Misguided and Misinformed mind game when defending specific industries or companies, especially those that raise public policy concerns. One example is the flourishing private prison industry, dominated by CoreCivic (the artful 2016 rebranding of Corrections Corporation of America) and the GEO Group. Banks including Wells Fargo, Bank of America, and JP Morgan Chase have provided the debt financing essential for these companies' rapid growth.[75]

It's easy to understand the strong arguments against a system of for-profit incarceration. Such arrangements create perverse financial incentives that encourage—rather than counter—mass incarceration. These companies are most successful for their shareholders when prisons are full, when sentences are long, and when probation and parole are unlikely. They can further increase their profits by relying on inexperienced and inadequately trained staff; reducing other expenses, such as costs associated with security, rehabilitation programming, and prisoner healthcare; and aggressively promoting new business opportunities, such as detention facilities for undocumented immigrants that grow in size and number as immigration reform efforts are blocked.[76]

But without offering any convincing evidence, proponents of private prisons like to assert that they save money for governments at the local, state, and federal levels, while also providing significant economic benefits to the surrounding communities. At the same time, these companies have gone to federal court in efforts to withhold information from the public about their government contracts.[77] When placed on the defensive about their suspect assurances, their spokespersons have argued that opposing analysts shouldn't be trusted because they're the ones who are misinformed and blinded by ideological biases.

For instance, in response to a critical report from the ACLU,[78] a CoreCivic public affairs director told NPR, "This stale report does not enter the realm of credible discussion. It's an exceedingly thin old mix of dated news, willful bias and unfounded opinion. It's being advanced by a familiar cast of industry critics and is blind to our industry's many benefits."[79] Similarly, GEO executive Pablo Paez said of allegations regarding the company's immigrant detention centers, "These allegations reflect a misunderstanding of our company's services and are based on inaccurate or incomplete reports."[80]

But a 2016 Department of Justice report indicated otherwise. It found that for-profit prisons were more likely to improperly place prisoners in isolation, and that they tended to have higher rates of safety and security incidents.[81] Despite these troubling realities, at a town hall meeting in March 2016, Trump made this evidence-free assertion: "I do think we can do a lot of privatizations and private prisons. It seems to work a lot better."[82] Not surprisingly, the day after his election these stocks soared on Wall Street.[83]

TRUST US

The three distrust mind games described thus far all involve strategies the 1% use to undermine the credibility of their opponents. But defenders of extreme inequality also advance their agenda by promoting themselves as especially deserving of the public's trust. That's where the Trust Us mind game comes in. With this appeal, they paint a contrast between their own purported trustworthiness on the one hand and the supposedly questionable character, motives, and competence of their adversaries on the other. In this effort, today's plutocrats benefit from their favorable circumstances and resources. Our society bestows tremendous stature upon those who've achieved wealth and power. Helping to further establish their narrative, the 1% control much of what we read about them in the mainstream media.

Despite the plutocrats' assurances, however, psychological research raises serious doubts about their claims of heightened honesty and integrity. In a series of illuminating studies, social psychologist Paul Piff and his colleagues compared the actions of people they categorized as either "upper class" or "lower class" in a variety of different situations.[84] In general, these researchers found that the former were more likely to behave in a dishonest and unethical manner than the latter.

For example, using the age, model, and appearance of cars as a proxy for drivers' wealth and social status, one study found that those driving more expensive vehicles were more likely to cut off pedestrians and other cars in the crosswalk at a busy intersection. In another study, the researchers first encouraged the participants to view themselves as either high or low in social rank. Later, those with the instilled elite mindset took more candy from a jar they were told had treats intended for children in a lab nearby. A third study involved a hypothetical salary negotiation in which the participants played the role of a prospective employer. Those who rated themselves higher on social class were more likely to deceptively withhold important information from the job applicant. And in a fourth study based on the computerized rolling of dice, the participants who identified themselves as members of the elite cheated more often in order to receive a modest cash prize.

In seeking an explanation for this pattern, these researchers concluded that a sense of entitlement and more favorable attitudes toward greed—an apt description of the 1%—played key roles. Many Americans probably wouldn't be surprised by their findings. In a national poll, 55% of the respondents said that "rich people" are more likely to be greedy than the average person, and only 9% said that the opposite was true. Similarly, 34% said that the rich are less likely to be honest than the average person, while only 12% considered them more likely to be honest.[85]

In examining the Trust Us mind game, we'll take a close look at how the 1% use this appeal to promote false yet seductive images of family and reciprocity, while behind the scenes corporate honchos are still placing profits above all else.

We Are Family

At a shareholders' meeting in Fayetteville, Arkansas, Walmart's then-president Mike Duke offered this to the boisterous crowd: "We aren't just associates and customers in our stores. We're people who grew up together, worship together, and live on the same streets. We're friends and neighbors. At Walmart, we are family and community."[86] Upon reflection, that's a rather peculiar family portrait—one that includes the poverty-wage cashier and multimillionaire CEO side by side. But the feel-good rhetoric of "we are family" is a tactic that large corporations use to burnish their trustworthiness bona fides.

Despite the jarring inequalities among "family members," when skillfully executed this trust-us ploy creates a deceptive yet psychologically comforting sense of ingroup closeness, similarity, and shared commitment—which management can then exploit to its own advantage. Usually at the very top of that wish list is saving money on wages by restraining workers' efforts to unionize. The message from above goes something like this: "We're on your side; we understand what matters to you; you can trust us to do the right thing; we'll take care of you and yours." If the employees believe it, then unionization can seem unnecessary, disruptive, and risky. After all, as the boss explains it, why bring unwelcome outsiders into a happy home, where all they'll do is create conflict and destroy the peace?

However, the corporate family envisioned by Walmart and other high-profit, low-wage giants fits the "strict father model" described by cognitive scientist George Lakoff.[87] This particular notion of family means a workplace dominated by harsh paternalism. Those in charge call all the shots and mete out rewards and punishment as they deem appropriate. Employees who complain or step out of line are subject to quick discipline and "tough love." It's also notable that these employers aren't telling their workers—their "children"—things like "You can have the keys to the car," or "I'm writing you into my will," or "If you get sick, I'll care for you for as long as it takes." In matters like these, the much-celebrated family suddenly dissolves. It's replaced by the stark, lopsided, dollars-and-cents relationship between wealthy employer and impoverished employee.

Trust Us Because We Trust You

Here's another variation of the Trust Us mind game. Plutocrats insist that since *they* trust *us*, it's only right that we return the favor and demonstrate our faith in *them*. With this ploy, the

1% rely on the psychological power of two phenomena: flattery and reciprocity.

First, it feels good to think that we're respected and appreciated by those who possess tremendous wealth and power. So, politicians pushing the predatory class's low-tax agenda will argue that the government should keep its hands out of our pockets because "we the people" know best how to spend our hard-earned money. Similarly, industries pushing for deregulation to bolster profits will argue that American consumers are smart enough to make their own judgments when it comes to product safety or the relative merits of environmental conservation versus cheaper store prices. In short, we tend to develop a favorable impression of those who say nice things about us—even when they have ulterior motives.

Second, because reciprocity is a natural component of most relationships, we're inclined to trust those who have expressed trust in us. This is true for spouses, for worker and boss, for customer and salesperson, and in many other situations. Today's plutocrats get this, so they're eager to suggest that their agenda actually reflects their confidence in the American people. In turn, they argue that we should be comfortable placing our trust in their leadership and vision for the country. All too frequently that's exactly what we do.

One might imagine that retaining the public's trust would require some evidence that the 1% are promoting the common good. In other words, fool me once, shame on you; fool me again and again and again, certainly shame on me. Yet plutocrats are a resourceful bunch. Their skillful use of the mind games described in this book are a large part of the reason we're slow to recognize their duplicity.

Flawed Ethics and Corporate Corruption

Let's consider the extent of that duplicity a bit further. "If our clients believe that we don't deserve their trust, we cannot survive."[88] So said Goldman Sachs CEO Lloyd Blankfein—who's described himself as a "big fat cat, plutocrat kind of guy"[89]—during a 2010 Senate hearing. In that hearing, he and his colleagues defiantly denied any wrongdoing by the investment banking giant during the financial crisis.[90] But Blankfein's awkward homage to trustworthiness rang hollow for many. After all, just before the housing collapse a few years earlier, Goldman had recommended and sold to its clients billions of dollars of deceptively valued securities tied to risky home mortgages. Goldman never told the buyers that it was working to unload those toxic assets from its own accounts or that the firm was simultaneously making huge bets that these securities would soon plummet in value, as in fact they did.[91]

Even when confronted with damning evidence, a spokesperson still argued that the company "had no obligation to disclose how it was managing its risk."[92] It took six years for Goldman Sachs to join the likes of JP Morgan Chase, Citibank, Bank of America, and Morgan Stanley in reaching a multibillion-dollar settlement with the government. That kind of penalty sounds impressive, until one realizes that it's dwarfed by Goldman's annual profits. At the same time, continuing the norm of impunity for members of the plutocracy, no individual executives were held responsible for defrauding investors.[93]

The entire financial meltdown might have been avoided if a 1%-friendly Congress hadn't been so quick to accept other disingenuous claims of trustworthiness from the big banks. Let's not forget that prior to the market's collapse, wealthy industry representatives and their political allies in both parties had successfully argued that government oversight and regulation were no longer needed—because keeping their operations free from corruption was supposedly in the banks' own self-interest.[94]

This particular example of misplaced trust in corporate executives is only the tip of the iceberg. A more comprehensive list would be far too long to review here. But that hall of shame—and shamelessness—includes the fraud perpetrated by Enron officials who artificially propped up the company's stock price; shortly thereafter thousands of unsuspecting employees lost their retirement savings when Enron collapsed. General Motors turned a blind eye to manufacturing defects and then, despite the heightened risk of driver injury and death, engaged in a years-long cover-up until the magnitude of the problems became too great to hide.[95] R. J. Reynolds and other tobacco companies spent decades withholding scientific evidence and misleading the public about the harmful effects of smoking.[96] Some of today's largest for-profit colleges and training institutes lure students into expensive programs with deceptive advertising, offer false assurances of future employment, and then saddle them with lifetimes of debt.[97] And the hard-sell tactics used to promote Trump University—such as founder Donald Trump's assurance "I can turn anyone into a successful real estate investor, including you"—deserve mention as well.[98]

Cases like these—and many others, including those where corruption still remains hidden today—all point to the same reality. Far too often, the deceitful protection of personal wealth and corporate profits is prioritized over our collective welfare.[99] Quite simply, behind the Trust Us mind game, the extensive track record of egregious violations of the public trust by corporate titans puts the lie to any claim that members of the predatory class are exemplars of trustworthiness or integrity.

SUMMING UP: THE PLUTOCRATS' DISTRUST MIND GAMES

In this chapter, we've explored four distrust mind games that today's plutocrats routinely rely on to advance their inequality-boosting agenda. Before turning to our fourth core psychological concern, superiority, let's review each of them.

The 1%'s They're Devious and Dishonest mind game is used to paint opponents as treacherous, devious, and evil in their intent. Through this message, the public is encouraged to be suspicious and unsympathetic toward those who are facing difficult or insurmountable hardships. If we're persuaded by this discrediting propaganda, we're more likely to turn our backs on the actual victims of the self-aggrandizing policies promoted by the predatory class.

If today's plutocrats believe the public will view such extreme accusations with skepticism, they turn to they're-different-from-us appeals instead. Their adversaries are portrayed as people who are deviant and out of step with what most Americans want—and therefore unworthy of our trust. This strategy can lead potential allies to see each other as enemies instead. When that happens, coalitions that might otherwise develop between individuals and groups opposed to the 1% are squelched or destroyed.

At other times, defenders of extreme wealth and power opt for the They're Misguided and Misinformed mind game. Here they spur us to distrust their critics by arguing that they're sadly misinformed and unreliable, and that their poor judgment makes their contrary views unworthy of serious consideration. When this ploy is successful, the public tends to disregard important voices of dissent because they're seen as not credible. As a result, crucial opportunities for tackling inequality and advancing the common good are lost.

Finally, members of the predatory class use trust-us appeals to promote themselves as paragons of integrity. They know that their efforts and policies will be much harder for others to counter if most Americans view them as trustworthy in word and deed. The weight of evidence doesn't support that image, but the reality doesn't matter if we fail to recognize the 1%'s devious misrepresentations, hollow promises, and corrupt enterprises.

These mind games are all strategies of manipulation by which today's plutocrats turn our concerns about distrust to their advantage. They do much the same with our psychological concerns about superiority, as the next chapter will show.

5

SUPERIORITY MIND GAMES
ENTICING US WITH PRAISE AND PRETENSIONS

"They smashed up things and creatures and then retreated back into their money or their vast carelessness or whatever it was that kept them together, and let other people clean up the mess they had made."

— F. SCOTT FITZGERALD[1]

The positive and negative judgments we form about ourselves are often based on comparisons with others. That's part of how we make sense of the world around us, and how we understand our place in it. When we make these judgments, we hope to find that we measure up well. The yardstick can be nearly anything: for example, our intelligence, professional success, community stature, or the quality of our relationships. These comparisons can also revolve around more abstract notions like moral values, "chosenness," and future destiny.[2]

To reinforce our positive self-appraisals, we sometimes intentionally focus attention on the worst characteristics of other people or other groups. After all, if they're inferior, then we're definitely superior. This perspective is especially perni-cious when taken to extremes. Others may be viewed as less than human, as undeserving of even meager expressions of respect and decency. History has taught us the awful repercus-sions that such levels of contempt can bring.

Our uncertain self-evaluations—driven by the desire to be "better" or at least "good enough"—are going on all the time, consciously and unconsciously. As a result, they're prime tar-gets for the manipulative appeals of today's plutocrats, who seize the opportunity to turn our hopes and doubts to their advantage. In this chapter, we'll take a close look at four of their favorite superiority mind games: They're Losers, We've Earned It, Pursuing a Higher Purpose, and They're Un-American.

THEY'RE LOSERS

The 1% frequently cast those who are struggling with hard-ship as simply inferior to everyone else. When viewed in this way, extreme inequality becomes a natural and inevitable out-growth of differences among people in their dispositions and talents. The purported inferiority of the downtrodden takes a variety of forms: weak character, low intelligence, lack of will-power, or some other deficit. The predatory class promotes the view that those left behind are casualties of their own short-comings, rather than victims of a deeply flawed system that institutionalizes preordained "winners" and "losers."

In part, the They're Losers mind game takes advantage of our misguided inclination to explain other people's behav-ior on the basis of their presumed character traits instead of the situation in which they find themselves. Psychologists call this the "fundamental attribution error."[3] For example, in an instant we decide that a driver who cuts us off in traffic is an obnoxious jerk—and not that his visibility may have been obscured. We're more likely to see a teen with behavioral prob-lems in school as having a poor attitude, rather than thinking they have a disruptive home environment that interferes with focus and preparation. And we may be inclined to imagine that someone who's unemployed is lazy or unmotivated, rather than that they've applied for dozens of jobs without success. These everyday biases are easy targets for the 1%.

Numerous psychology experiments have also demonstrated just how hard it can be for us to break this habit of thought, one that favors dispositional over situational explanations for others' behavior. In one set of studies, research participants were told that they'd be listening to someone who'd been instructed to read a speech that either supported or opposed a particular policy. It was made clear to them that the speech did not reflect the speaker's personal views—rather, reading it aloud was a requirement imposed by the researcher. Nevertheless, study participants tended to conclude that the speaker actually subscribed to the position they advocated. In other words, even when we're told otherwise, we still mistakenly discount the situation when it comes to assessing another person's behavior.[4]

It's important to note that the fundamental attribution error typically operates only when we're critically evaluating someone else's actions—not our own shortcomings. Indeed, we usually give ourselves the benefit of the doubt. When we do something good, we see it as evidence of who we truly are; and when we do something bad, we blame it on our circumstances instead. We deem a rude stranger to be someone of poor character, but we attribute our own less-than-courteous behavior to being under stress at work, having just received some worrisome news, or some similar situational justification.

In exploring the They're Losers mind game further, let's now examine the role played by this appeal in specific contexts, including how today's plutocrats promote illusions of upward mobility and encourage us to feel contempt and disgust toward those who are disadvantaged.

Illusions of Upward Mobility

Research shows that close to half of the children (43%) who grow up in families in the lowest fifth of the income ladder in the United States remain at that very bottom rung as adults.

Moreover, fully 70% never make it to the middle rung, and only 6% move into the top fifth over the course of their entire lives.[5] That's why Nobel Prize-winning economist Joseph Stiglitz has described equal opportunity as a national myth: "The life prospects of an American are more dependent on the income and education of his parents than in almost any other advanced country for which there is data."[6] The nonpartisan Congressional Research Service has reached a similar conclusion: "The United States is a comparatively immobile society, that is, where one starts in the income distribution influences where one ends up to a greater degree than in several advanced economies."[7]

Despite the evidence, however, a familiar version of the They're Losers mind game is the predatory class's beguiling claim that the United States is a land of remarkable opportunity for everyone. If we believe this is true, then it naturally follows that people get what they deserve, and where we stand on the ladder of economic success is up to each of us. With sufficient talent or effort, we're supposedly free to climb as high as we want, so those who spend a lifetime at the bottom are responsible for their own unfortunate circumstances. In a *Wall Street Journal* op-ed, a senior fellow at the right-wing Heartland Institute offered a typical articulation of this bogus argument: "Most Americans will move up and down the income ladder over the course of their lives, reflecting little to none of the class stratification and inheritance concerns warned about by inequality mavens."[8]

In a similar vein, today's plutocrats love to promote rags-to-riches stories to convince us that the ravages of poverty, unemployment, and homelessness are almost exclusively the plight of those unwilling to work hard. By their account, failing to obtain a college education is the student's fault, being laid off from a job is the worker's fault, and suffering a debilitating illness that forces a family into bankruptcy may even be the fault of the sick parent. These arguments that blame the victim are nothing new for the 1%. Depending on the situation, only their specific targets change.[9]

Yet even the fictional protagonists in Horatio Alger's popular tales from over a century ago—usually young boys who escaped poverty to become upstanding members of the middle class—were often as dependent on good luck as persistence. The same is certainly true today. But if the They're Losers mind game persuades us that success is a choice, then it becomes less heartless to condemn and even criminalize aspects of poverty and all who fall into its clutches.[10]

Consider, for instance, the nearly 600,000 men, women, and children in this country—including many military veterans—who are homeless on a typical winter night. Increasingly, they're treated as criminals for sleeping in public, deserving of scorn rather than succor. In some cities, you can be arrested for sharing food with someone who's homeless.[11] In much the same way, those who are poor are arrested at staggering rates for minor infractions like unpaid parking tickets—and then they're incarcerated because they don't have the money to pay the fines levied against them. There's also the double standard by which those of limited means are singled out for paternalistic and demeaning oversight when it comes to government programs. This includes drug testing before receiving welfare payments and tight restrictions on what can be purchased with food stamps.[12]

It's important to recognize that victim-blaming appeals sometimes take more subtle forms. They don't always directly call out and denigrate those who are deemed to be falling short. Indeed, even messages designed to uplift and motivate can simultaneously communicate something very different. During a Hillary for America rally in the last week of the 2016 election campaign, President Barack Obama said this: "If you are willing to contribute, if you are willing to work hard, if you do the right thing, you can put your shoulder to the wheel of history. You can make a difference. You can live out your dreams."[13] This kind of statement—highlighting personal responsibility and ignoring the country's extreme inequality and the 1%'s concerted efforts to preserve it—indirectly casts blame at the feet of those who fail to flourish.

Who Stole the Ladder?

In their indictment of the less fortunate, defenders of extreme inequality rarely acknowledge the central role that they themselves play in blocking upward mobility and pushing so many into dire straits.[14] For example, despite substantial increases in worker productivity over the past few decades, income growth has been concentrated at the very top of the economic ladder.[15] Over this period, the income share of the top 1% has nearly doubled, while the income share of the bottom 90% has declined.[16] In short, the rewards of economic growth have gone into the pockets of CEOs and corporate shareholders, rather than into paychecks for workers.

The predatory class also works against improving the standard of living for average Americans. Union-busting certainly fits that bill. But there are also various international trade agreements, written in secret with strong corporate representation all along the way. These treaties prioritize profits for huge companies over domestic wages, international human rights, and environmental protections. Meanwhile, if the federal minimum wage had merely kept pace with inflation, that wage today would be over $20 per hour, rather than the current $7.25.[17]

But such statistics don't fully capture the ruthlessness displayed by the 1% when they run roughshod over those working to achieve the American Dream. The case of the "Hyatt 100" is emblematic. In the summer of 2009, three Boston-area hotels in the international chain instructed their housekeepers to train some "temps" to ensure adequate coverage whenever they took vacations. What the long-time employees weren't told, however, was that they were actually training their own permanent, less expensive replacements.

As soon as the training was finished, the current staff members were all laid off in a "cost-cutting" move. The new trainees—from an outsourcing agency in Georgia—were then hired, at minimum wage and with no benefits. The total savings from discarding 100 hardworking employees was roughly

$1.5 million annually. To put that figure in context, it's just one-fifth of the annual salary of Hyatt's CEO. Five years later, in an agreement to end an ongoing boycott call by the labor union UNITE HERE, Hyatt paid a settlement that averaged a modest $10,000 to each of the laid-off housekeepers.

Encouraging Contempt and Disgust

The ultimate goal of the They're Losers mind game is to undercut the public's concern by encouraging us to view the disadvantaged with contempt and disgust. Negative reactions of that sort lead to avoidance rather than engagement, which is just what today's plutocrats are hoping for. That's why they so often use demeaning and dehumanizing language in describing those who are struggling to get by.

Stuart Varney of the Fox Business Network, for instance, offered these mean-spirited comments about those who are poor: "Many of them have things. What they lack is the richness of spirit."[18] When describing low-wage workers, conservative radio host Neal Boortz once told his listeners, "I want you to think for a moment...of how incompetent, how ignorant, how worthless is an adult that can't earn more than the minimum wage."[19] Similarly, when discussing the bankruptcy of the city of Detroit, Dan Mitchell, formerly at the libertarian Cato Institute, conjured up images of pigs feeding: "When you have a very bad ratio of people who produce compared to all the people who have their snouts in the public trough, then you wind up with a financial disaster."[20] Steve Bannon, formerly of Breitbart News Network and for several months a senior adviser in the Trump White House, called the Occupy Wall Street protestors "the greasiest, dirtiest people you will ever see,"[21] and former Republican Speaker of the House Newt Gingrich told them they should "go get a job right after you take a bath."[22] Gingrich also said to an audience at Harvard University that poor children should work after-hours as janitors at their schools.[23]

Sometimes these verbal assaults are simultaneously couched as life lessons for the rest of us. That was Bill O'Reilly's approach in his admonition to his Fox News audience after Hurricane Katrina back in 2005:

> So every American kid should be required to watch videotape of the poor in New Orleans and see how they suffered because they couldn't get out of town. And then every teacher should tell the students, if you refuse to learn, if you refuse to work hard, if you become addicted, if you live a "gangsta" life, you will be poor and powerless just like many of those in New Orleans.

Such "educational" commentary from the 1% combines false gestures of compassion with the callous condemnation of those who deserve a better fate. In O'Reilly's case, it's remarkable to think that poverty can somehow be considered a legitimate basis for failing to rescue New Orleans's most at-risk residents.

WE'VE EARNED IT

With the We've Earned It mind game, today's plutocrats try to legitimize their stature by claiming that their extraordinary wealth and power reflect the magnitude of the contributions they've made to society. By the 1%'s telling, unique talents, remarkable insights, and tireless work—all confirmed by the infallible operations of our "free markets"—have proven them to be the most deserving among us by far. They assert they're entitled to privileged lives beyond society's norms and rules. All of the standard conventions, including consequences for one's actions, seemingly apply only to others.

In certain ways, this attitude is reminiscent of Garrison Keillor's long-running public radio show, *A Prairie Home Companion*. He ended each segment by describing his fictional hometown of Lake Wobegon as a place "where all the women are strong, all the men are good looking, and all the children are above average." It's a reminder that plutocrats aren't unique in overvaluing themselves. Indeed, psychologists have found that this phenomenon is quite prevalent in the United States and other countries where individualism is highly prized. In these places, most people tend to think they're better than others are—in matters such as virtue, intelligence, competence, popularity, and compassion—even though statistically we just can't all be above average.[24]

In psychology, such misjudgments are called the "illusory superiority effect," and most of the time they're harmless. In fact, inflated positive self-appraisals can sometimes play a healthy role in nurturing our self-esteem and protecting us from depression. But as some members of the 1% demonstrate with regularity, an exaggerated sense of self-importance and privilege can instead reflect something much darker: a seemingly unquenchable thirst to win and dominate. This latter profile fits what psychologist Jim Sidanius and his colleagues describe as a "social dominance orientation."

These researchers have identified consistent differences in the extent to which individuals share the predatory class's view that inequality is a good thing and that social policies should be designed to enhance, rather than constrain, hierarchies among groups.[25] Across a variety of situations, they found that people who score high on surveys measuring social dominance orientation tend to be much more comfortable employing cutthroat or Machiavellian strategies for getting ahead—to the point of oppressing those they see as weak and inferior. Even when not overtly hostile, these individuals tend to support the preservation of status differences between groups and they oppose initiatives aimed at reducing inequalities, such as the expansion of civil rights, gay rights, and affirmative action based on race, ethnicity, or gender.[26] Some, such as the "alt-right," adopt explicitly racist ideologies.[27]

In examining the We've Earned It mind game further, let's now take a detailed look at how the 1% use this appeal to argue that they deserve praise rather than criticism, how they take advantage of their elevated status, and what the data show about their claims of extraordinary generosity.

So Terribly Misunderstood?

As the We've Earned It mind game highlights, today's plutocrats insist that their massive wealth and financial success
should garner adulation, not criticism or condemnation. They
see themselves as victims of exploitation, since in their eyes
everyone else mooches off their accomplishments. Indeed,
this is a central premise in the ideology of one of their heroes,
author Ayn Rand, who wrote:

> The man at the top of the intellectual pyramid contributes
> the most to all those below him, but gets nothing except
> his material payment, receiving no intellectual bonus
> from others to add to the value of his time. The man at the
> bottom who, left to himself, would starve in his hopeless
> ineptitude, contributes nothing to those above him, but
> receives the bonus of all of their brains.[28]

When the public fails to embrace this worldview, the 1% react
with their own special brand of indignant outrage. Consider
hedge fund billionaire Stephen Schwarzman, the chairman of
the Blackstone Group. Back in 2010, when the Obama White
House considered a plan that would eliminate a tax loophole
favorable to him and his hedge fund cronies, Schwarzman
compared such a step to "when Hitler invaded Poland."[29] And
then there's billionaire venture capitalist Tom Perkins, before
his death in 2016 the proud owner of the world's largest private
yacht ("I just wanted the biggest boat").[30] In a January 2014
letter to the *Wall Street Journal*, Perkins wrote: "I would call
attention to the parallels of fascist Nazi Germany to its war on
its 'one percent,' namely its Jews, to the progressive war on the
American one percent, namely the 'rich.'"[31]

Almost as brazen were the comments of fellow plutocrats
who came to Perkins's defense. The *Wall Street Journal* editorial board was quick to support his thesis, if not his precise
parallels, arguing that criticisms of Perkins were a reflection
of liberal intolerance.[32] Fellow billionaire Sam Zell told a
Bloomberg News interviewer that Perkins was right: "The 1%

are being pummeled because it's politically convenient to do so. The problem is that the world and this country should not talk about envy of the 1%. It should talk about emulating the 1%. The 1% work harder."[33] Billionaire private equity investor Wilbur Ross, now Donald Trump's Secretary of Commerce, chimed in as well, saying, "I agree that the 1 percent is being picked on for political reasons."[34]

In a subsequent TV appearance, Perkins offered his own unsurprising policy suggestion: "I think the solution is less interference, lower taxes, let the rich do what the rich do."[35] His recommendation echoed the perspective of Goldman Sachs CEO Lloyd Blankfein who, at the height of the Great Recession, had responded this way to the question of whether it's possible to make too much money:

> Is it possible to be too successful? I don't want people in this firm to think that they have accomplished as much for themselves as they can and go on vacation. As the guardian of the interests of the shareholders and, by the way, for the purposes of society, I'd like them to continue to do what they are doing. I don't want to put a cap on their ambition. It's hard for me to argue for a cap on their compensation.[36]

Blankfein went on to explain that he and his fellow bankers were just "doing God's work." Around the same time, a Goldman international adviser, participating in a panel discussion on the place of morality in the marketplace, told an audience at London's St. Paul's Cathedral, "We have to tolerate the inequality as a way to achieve greater prosperity and opportunity for all."[37]

Sometimes the 1%'s astounding sense of superiority and entitlement leaks through less intentionally. Public statements made by executives of BP (formerly British Petroleum) after the deadly Deepwater Horizon explosion and massive oil spill in the Gulf of Mexico in April 2010 are a case in point. Eleven workers died in the blast, and the environmental disaster impacted thousands of residents and workers along the Gulf Coast, as well as marine wildlife and flora.

Yet when BP CEO Tony Hayward tried to offer a public apology the following month, he couldn't help turning the focus to his own personal travails: "We're sorry for the massive disruption it's caused to their lives...There's no one who wants this thing over more than I do. I'd like my life back."[38] Two weeks later at the White House, BP Chairman Carl-Henric Svanberg's attempt to defend his company included this arrogant assurance: "I hear comments sometimes that large oil companies are greedy companies or don't care. But that is not the case indeed. We care about the small people."[39]

Taking Advantage of Their "Entitlement"

In contrast to all of the "small people," today's plutocrats are accustomed to having things their way. At the same time, they don't feel particularly fortunate in this regard, because by their account they deserve all the privileges they receive. Their special treatment is especially apparent when we consider the corrupting influence of wealth on "equal justice under law," the hallowed words engraved atop the Supreme Court Building in Washington, D.C.

The Sentencing Project, a research and advocacy organization promoting reform of our justice system with a focus on racial disparities, has described the problem this way: "The United States in effect operates two distinct criminal justice systems: one for wealthy people and another for poor people and minorities."[40] That unequal treatment runs the gamut from the likelihood of arrest and prosecution to the leniency offered in sentencing. Attorney and author Glenn Greenwald has provided a thorough analysis of the disturbing phenomenon of 1% impunity in the criminal justice context, including this:

> Prosecutions, courtrooms, and prisons, it's hinted—and sometimes even explicitly stated—are for the rabble, like the street-side drug peddlers we occasionally glimpse from our car windows, not for the political and financial leaders who manage our nation and fuel our prosperity.[41]

Journalist Matt Taibbi has summarized several of the unwarranted allowances provided to Wall Street's white-collar criminals this way:

> Which defendant gets put in jail, and which one gets away with a fine? Which offender ends up with a criminal record, and which one gets to settle with the state without admitting wrongdoing? Which thief will pay restitution out of his own pocket, and which one will be allowed to have the company he works for pay the tab? Which neighborhoods have thousands of police roaming the streets, and which ones don't have any at all?[42]

Typical of this reality, millionaire tax cheats have developed a broad repertoire of arguments—based on the We've Earned It mind game—for why they should receive a light sentence or no sentence at all after being caught, prosecuted, and found guilty (all rarities in their own right). The 1%'s farfetched leniency appeals that some judges have found persuasive include the following: They've already suffered sufficient public humiliation for their misdeeds; although they cheated, they've also been generous in their charitable donations; the fines they paid were sufficiently punitive; and their status as "job creators" made it unwise to remove them from the community and put them behind bars.[43]

Not Quite So Remarkable After All

But are the 1% truly society's indispensable saviors, as they'd like us to believe? No, they're not, and let's review some of the evidence. First, despite their recurrent claims—for example, Trump's presidential debate assurance that, with his proposed tax cuts, "the wealthy are going to create tremendous jobs"[44]— research shows that the plutocrats among us are not in fact miracle-working job creators.[45] That's because trickle-down economics doesn't work. This is clear from years of data showing that, over the past several decades, the tax cuts bestowed upon the wealthy simply have not led to the employment growth they've promised. But what's more, there's not even simple logic behind this job-creator propaganda.

Indeed, public policy scholar and former Secretary of Labor Robert Reich has called this tale one of the biggest right-wing lies about inequality.[46] And wealthy entrepreneur Nick Hanauer has pointed out, "When workers have more money, businesses have more customers. Which makes middle-class consumers—not rich businesspeople—the true job creators...A thriving middle class is the source of growth and prosperity in capitalist economies."[47] Hanauer also notes that the enormous salaries of Wall Street executives and securities traders are not an accurate reflection of either the true value of their work or the importance of these positions to society. Rather, they're the result of bargaining power and status advantages that teachers, firefighters, homebuilders, and low-wage workers lack.

Second, the 1% aren't more generous than the rest of us—despite the occasional high-profile displays of benevolence that grab media attention. The actual data on this front are mixed, but some research suggests exactly the opposite pattern may apply when it comes to proportional giving. For example, a 2012 analysis of tax records by the *Chronicle of Philanthropy* showed that middle-class Americans gave a much larger percentage (7.6%) of their discretionary income to charity than did wealthier individuals (4.2%) (lower-income Americans were not included in this particular analysis).[48] And where the rich were concentrated in high-wealth neighborhoods, their generosity diminished even further.

According to the *Chronicle*, these disparities became even starker in the years immediately after the Great Recession. During this period, the wealthy cut back on their charitable giving while those in lower income brackets stepped up their percentage donations.[49] In explaining this general pattern of differential giving, psychologist Paul Piff has suggested that wealth appears to have an insulating and desensitizing effect: "Simply seeing someone in need at the grocery store—or looking down the street at a neighbor's modest house—can serve as basic psychological reminders of the needs of other people."[50] For those in predatory class enclaves, it's instead "out of sight, out of mind."

Third, considerable psychological research supports the view that "upper-class" individuals fall short of their "lower-class" counterparts in certain basic skills necessary for building positive connections with other people. A range of studies have shown that members of the upper class tend to be less compassionate in their approach toward others, reflecting a troubling lack of empathy. In one experiment, lower-income participants were substantially more willing to take on extra work to help out a distressed research partner than were the upper-income participants.[51] In another study, lower-class participants demonstrated a stronger compassion-related physiological response than did their upper-class counterparts after watching a video of children suffering from cancer. In a third study, the lower-class participants in a stressful interview process showed greater sensitivity and compassion toward their competitors than did the upper-class interviewees.[52] And in an experiment with four-year-old children, those from less wealthy homes behaved more altruistically than those from wealthier homes, donating more of their prize tokens to children they were told were hospitalized.[53]

A related series of studies found that individuals from a lower social class were significantly better than upper-class research participants at judging the emotions being portrayed when they were presented with photos of human faces.[54] The researchers suggested that this enhanced ability may reflect the reality that those who are less well off must rely more on accurately reading their social environment, because they're more dependent on interpersonal relationships and collaborative efforts in their daily lives. On the other hand, individuals with extensive material resources—like the 1%—are more likely to find close relationships, especially with people of lesser means, quite unnecessary in their goal-oriented pursuits, and their perspective-taking abilities may suffer as a result.

When it comes to tackling today's extreme inequality, the relative lack of compassion and the poor "emotional intelligence" of plutocrats don't bode well for the rest of us. As Hanauer has described the problem, "Some capitalists actually don't care about other people, their communities, or the future...When Walmart or McDonald's or any other guy like me pays workers the minimum wage, that's our way of saying, 'I would pay you less, except then I'd go to prison.'"[55]

PURSUING A HIGHER PURPOSE

With this third superiority mind game, today's plutocrats present themselves and their own agenda as an affirmation of what's truly special about the United States. They argue that their preferred policies reflect deep moral purpose and the cherished principles that lift this country above all others. In so doing, they aim to draw broad public support while simultaneously condemning their critics as unappreciative, unpatriotic, and out of touch with their fellow Americans. When this effort succeeds, extreme social and economic inequality are discounted as the small imperfections that come with the pursuit of collective greatness. The 1% use uplifting language—words like "opportunity" and "democracy"—to suggest common purpose, when in fact the predatory class primarily seeks to preserve its own enormous wealth and power.

Plutocrats using the Pursuing a Higher Purpose mind game take advantage of a basic fact: We're social animals. Our core sense of who we are is tied up in the emotional bonds we form with others. This is easy to understand with our immediate family; after all, they're people with whom we've shared experiences over the course of a lifetime. What's more surprising is that we also feel such strong attachments toward much larger groups—for example, our national, religious, or ethnic group—even though we know only a very small percentage of its members personally and we may not really share all that much in common with many of them.[56] Nevertheless, what psychologists call "group identification" creates a deep well from which the 1% draw to advance their own narrow ambitions.

Research shows that there are multiple dimensions to our personal identification with a group. These include feelings that the group is important; that we should be committed to its welfare; that it is superior to other groups; and that we should respect the group's norms, symbols, and leaders.[57] It's this psychology of group identification that gives us a feeling of personal pride when "our group"—or one of its members—succeeds, despite the fact that we had nothing to do with the accomplishment. That's the case when we take pleasure in the victory of our hometown sports team or an Olympic medalist, or when we feel special because a famous movie star, author, or politician went to the same high school we did.

In situations like these, we're "basking in reflected glory"—another common phenomenon psychologists have investigated.[58] For instance, in one study Robert Cialdini and his colleagues carefully observed college students on the days after a big football game. They found that clothes with the school's colors and emblem were much more prevalent after victories than defeats. But they also discovered that students were more likely to use the pronoun "we" after a win and the pronoun "they" after a loss when discussing the game. This suggests another psychological tendency—"cutting off reflected failure"—that operates in the opposite direction. To protect our self-esteem and reputation, we try to disassociate ourselves from a group or from individual group members who've become a source of shame and embarrassment. These too are inclinations that the 1% manipulate to serve their interests.

In discussing the Pursuing a Higher Purpose mind game, we'll examine how today's plutocrats advance their narrow agenda by promoting seductive ideas like "American exceptionalism," "freedom," and the "right to work."

American Exceptionalism

Our political leaders, whose priorities routinely reflect the 1%'s agenda, often use the Pursuing a Higher Purpose mind game when discussing U.S. foreign policy. They argue that the United States has a special destiny to fulfill as a uniquely moral actor in the global sphere. This appeal to American exceptionalism isn't solely the province of Republicans, conservatives, and defense hawks. It spans party affiliation and ideology alike.

Consider these Democratic Party entries. President Obama's official National Security Strategy document, released in February 2015, emphasized:

> Strong and sustained American leadership is essential to a rules-based international order that promotes global security and prosperity as well as the dignity and human rights of all peoples. The question is never whether America should lead, but how we lead.[59]

While running for president, Hillary Clinton offered much the same message in a June 2016 campaign speech on national security:

> If America doesn't lead, we leave a vacuum—and that will either cause chaos, or other countries will rush in to fill the void. Then they'll be the ones making the decisions about your lives and jobs and safety—and trust me, the choices they make will not be to our benefit.[60]

At the Democratic National Convention in Philadelphia in July 2016, retired Marine Corps general John Allen took to the stage and—amid chants of "USA! USA!"—shouted to the assembled delegates, "The free people of the world look to America as the last best hope for peace and liberty for all humankind. For we are...the greatest country on this planet!"[61]

In each of these instances, the patriotic sentiment is understandable and unsurprising. But the underlying arrogance and sense of entitlement still pose serious obstacles when it comes to supporting international norms, cooperation, and partnership. Former longtime Congressional staffer Mike Lofgren has summarized mainstream Washington's troubling worldview this way: "Any foreign action perceived to conflict with America's grandiose conception of its destiny is automatically deemed hostile."[62] Recent history highlights the costs and limitations associated with the unilateral use of our "shock and awe" military power.

There are other reasons that global moral leadership can be an ill-fitting mantle for the United States. If we take another look at Obama's National Security Strategy document, we see that it also includes this assertion: "America's growing economic strength is the foundation of our national security."[63] This stance is nothing new. But blurring the lines between national security and economic dominance makes greed-driven plutocrats the primary drivers and beneficiaries of key foreign policy decisions. By contrast, the vast majority of Americans are relegated to absorbing the risks and burdens of foolhardy, overreaching, or immoral choices that prioritize corporate profits.

One arena where the Pursuing a Higher Purpose mind game is sorely tested is our country's standing as the largest international seller of major weapons in the world—with ongoing efforts to promote even bigger markets for U.S. arms companies.[64] At the State Department it's considered "economic statecraft." As one representative explained the rationale, "When we deem that cooperating with an ally or partner in the security sector will advance our national security, we advocate tirelessly on behalf of U.S. companies abroad, and I think I have the frequent flyer miles to prove it."[65] Yet much of the tens of billions of dollars in arms sent overseas annually go to the very same countries that the U.S. government legitimately criticizes for serious human rights abuses.[66]

As a case in point, corporate titans like Boeing and Lockheed have increased their weapons sales to Saudi Arabia and other Middle Eastern countries run by repressive autocrats.[67] Indeed, in its January 2016 report, professional services giant

Deloitte noted that heightened tensions and turmoil, including the growing threat posed by the Islamic State (ISIS), provide defense contractors with a fortuitous opportunity "to sell
more equipment and military weapons systems."[68] It's worth
noting that some of those weapons have undoubtedly found
their way into ISIS's hands.

Profiteering to the tune of American exceptionalism isn't
limited to the defense industry. Pharmaceutical companies
take advantage of trade deals to protect their huge profits—
despite potentially dire public health consequences in developing countries.[69] Over a decade ago, drug manufacturers,
supported by the U.S. government, filed an intellectual property lawsuit against the government of South Africa. Why? To
prevent Nelson Mandela's government from obtaining more
affordable medicines for the country's deadly HIV epidemic.[70]
International public outrage eventually led the drug companies
to drop that suit, but not much has really changed.[71] As part
of the now-defunct Trans-Pacific Partnership deal, the United
States continued to push pricing agreements that would benefit Big Pharma—at the expense of worldwide public health—by
blocking easier access to less expensive generic drugs.[72]

Freedom, for the 1%

Representatives of the 1% also use the Pursuing a Higher
Purpose mind game when they turn to the rhetorical power of
"freedom" to advance their less-than-lofty agenda.[73] Appeals
to freedom have special resonance in this country, as national
polls make clear. In a values survey, respondents cited "freedom of speech" and "freedom of religion" as the two "superior
values" that most distinguished the United States from other
countries. It should be noted, however, that four-fifths of the
participants in the survey felt that the executives at Wall Street
banks did not share their values—they viewed these bankers as
driven by greed and self-interest.[74]

In another poll, over three-quarters of Americans rated the United States as either "above average" or "best" in regard to "individual freedoms" when compared to other modern, industrialized countries.[75] But at the same time, only about one-third gave such positive assessments to our economic and healthcare systems. The results from both of these polls confirm two points: the centrality of freedom in the American psyche and the extent to which the public has doubts about whether defenders of extreme wealth and power truly share their commitments.

But despite the public's skepticism about their motivations, today's plutocrats sing the freedom refrain and take advantage of the positive feelings it evokes whenever they can, applying it to issues ranging from taxes to education to healthcare. Attorney and author Ian Millhiser has described their intensive marketing of "freedom" this way:

> In today's America, the Koch brothers pour millions into organizations with names like "FreedomWorks." The Club For Growth touts its plan to privatize Social Security and slash taxes on the rich as "economic freedom." Sen. Ted Cruz's (R-TX) weekly audio program, where he touts his plans to deny health care to millions of Americans, is named "Freedom Minute." Rep. Paul Ryan (R-WI), with his plans to voucherize Medicare and cut food stamps, contrasts "freedom" with "the supervision and sanctimony of the central planners." Sen. Rand Paul (R-KY) turns Dr. King's dream on its head, declaring that segregated neighborhoods and whites-only lunch counters are "the hard part about believing in freedom."[76]

What should be apparent is that plutocrats prefer to be free to pursue their ambitions in ways that actually diminish opportunities and well-being for anyone who doesn't receive their blessing. Big-money interests tout the wonders of so-called free markets, but they rarely even whisper about a troubling reality: The vast economic rewards they celebrate are bestowed upon very few, while the crushing human costs that accompany unfettered markets are felt most directly by those who are already struggling.

Of course, crucial markets aren't truly "free" in the first place. While many government regulations protect consumers, others directly benefit the predatory class through subsidies (for example, government-funded research used by drug companies), monopoly arrangements (the casino industry), and corporate tax loopholes (overseas tax havens).[77] As Robert Reich has noted:

> Freedom has little meaning without reference to power. Those who claim to be on the side of freedom while ignoring the growing imbalance of economic and political power in America and other advanced economies are not in fact on the side of freedom. They are on the side of those with power.[78]

"Right to Work" (for Less)

One increasingly prominent arena for false freedom propaganda is the promotion of "right to work" laws. These state-level legislative efforts are aimed at undermining labor unions and the protections and benefits they provide workers. When successful, big business gains even greater control over the lives and livelihoods of average Americans. But that's not the way members of the predatory class tell it. They resort to the Pursuing a Higher Purpose mind game, as though the Statue of Liberty herself had become a spokesperson for union-busting.

With funding from the Koch brothers, the Walton family, and other billionaires, the National Right to Work Legal Defense Foundation claims to defend "individual freedom" and "the right of all Americans to be free of compulsory unionism abuses."[79] Similarly, in 2015, when Wisconsin Governor Scott Walker signed into law the "Freedom to Work" legislation, he disingenuously argued that it "puts power back in the hands of Wisconsin workers" by giving them the "freedom to choose."[80] Meanwhile, think tanks like the conservative

Heritage Foundation publish papers emphasizing how right-to-work laws "expand personal freedom" and prohibit "coercive schemes."[81] Yet all of this grand talk about freedom by defenders of extreme wealth and power boils down to just one thing: their cherished freedom to pay workers less.

In states where right-to-work legislation has not been enacted, workers represented by a union can be required to contribute a modest amount each month to help sustain the union's work negotiating on their behalf and pursuing workplace grievances when they arise. But where right-to-work laws have been adopted, these fees are no longer mandatory, so workers can garner the benefits of union representation without actually having to pay for them. That's an arrangement with the potential to cripple unions by denying them the financial resources they need to defend workers' rights, in which case all workers ultimately suffer.

Indeed, in right-to-work states union and non-union workers alike receive, on average, lower wages and fewer benefits than workers in states that have not adopted these laws.[82] So right-to-work "freedoms" are a very bad deal for workers. The real beneficiaries are the 1%, who further increase their freedom to exploit everyone else. As for President Trump, he told the South Carolina Radio Network, "My position on right to work is 100 percent."[83] Following state-level Republican victories in the November 2016 election, this anti-worker push is accelerating.[84]

THEY'RE UN-AMERICAN

With this final superiority appeal, the They're Un-American mind game, defenders of extreme inequality portray their adversaries as disgruntled and unappreciative critics of the United States and the values and traditions the country holds dear. At the same time, they promote themselves and their agenda as perfectly aligned with the interests and aspirations of the American people. In doing so, they take particular advantage of the public's respect and deference toward long-established leaders and institutions, regardless of how corrupt they may actually be.

The 1% benefit whenever members of the public give undue or uncritical support to those in positions of power. "Right-wing authoritarianism" is a psychological mindset that leads to just this kind of behavior. Overall, it's characterized by the tendency to condemn anyone who questions established authority. Based on his research, psychologist Bob Altemeyer has identified three specific markers.[85] The first is "authoritarian submission," which involves strict obedience toward the designated leaders of a group. The second is "authoritarian aggression," which takes the form of extreme hostility toward those who appear to fall short of the group's rigid standards. The third marker is "conventionalism," which revolves around dutifully honoring and observing the group's traditions and norms.

Right-wing authoritarians—like today's neo-Nazi, white supremacist "alt-right"—consider group boundaries to be sacrosanct. As a result, they value conformity and fear diversity. To them, clear and firm borders protect those inside the circle from those who are outside and don't belong. Not surprisingly, research links this psychological profile to ugly prejudices—for example, against people of color, immigrants, those who are unemployed, and people with physical disabilities. The specific prejudices aren't necessarily fixed. That's because these individuals submissively look to their leaders to tell them which groups to despise at any particular time. So, when the leadership targets a new group, right-wing authoritarians change course and follow along.

A related psychological mindset is "blind patriotism." This ideology involves the rigid and staunch conviction that one's country is never wrong in its actions or policies, that allegiance to the country must be unquestioning and absolute, and that criticism of the country cannot be tolerated.[86] As one might expect, "blind patriots" tend to be right-wing authoritarians as well. They're also more likely to uncritically endorse military aggression (for example, the U.S. invasion of Iraq in 2003), in part because they favor the harsh and punitive treatment of adversaries. The 1% don't have to be right-wing authoritarians or blind patriots themselves to reap rewards by gaining support from the segment of the public who are.

In examining the They're Un-American mind game, let's now take a look at how today's plutocrats use this ploy to promote culture wars and to marginalize Blacks and Muslims in the United States.

Weapons of Mass Distraction: The "Culture Wars"

The interests of the 1% are most readily advanced when the public is distracted from the realities of extreme economic inequality. So, time and again, they foment "culture wars" by portraying their adversaries as disrespectful of our country's venerated traditions and accomplishments. With the They're Un-American mind game, plutocrats aim to place certain views and lifestyles beyond acceptable mainstream boundaries, characterizing them as foreign, unpatriotic, or dangerous.

In one recurring version of this ploy, the predatory class identifies those who pursue change as "liberal elitists" rather than "regular Americans." Consider a famous—or infamous— political attack ad from the 2004 presidential campaign. With former Vermont Governor Howard Dean gaining traction in Iowa, the right-wing, anti-tax Club for Growth targeted him with a TV spot in which a middle-aged couple respond to an interviewer's question this way: "Howard Dean should take his tax-hiking, government-expanding, latte-drinking, sushi-eating, Volvo-driving, New York Times-reading, body-piercing, Hollywood-loving left-wing freak show back to Vermont, where it belongs."[87] The tax hikes that Dean was proposing would actually have benefited almost all Iowans—but not the plutocrats. So defenders of extreme inequality buried him under an avalanche of adjectives designed to cast him as a "freak" who didn't measure up as a real American.

Journalist and historian Thomas Frank has argued that these kinds of culture war divides serve as a vehicle for Republican leaders, who are typically closely aligned with the predatory class, to "speak on behalf of the forgotten man without causing any problems for their core big-business constituency." According to Frank, the propaganda of high-profile conservatives presents:

> A way of talking about life in which we are all victims of a haughty overclass—"liberals"—that makes our movies, publishes our newspapers, teaches our children, and hands down judgments from the bench. These liberals generally tell us how to go about our lives, without any consideration for our values or traditions.[88]

In a similar vein, writer Paul Waldman has described the superiority narrative that representatives of the plutocracy use to discredit liberals this way:

> After an era of decadence and weakness, strong and righteous Americans stood up for right against wrong. Despite the impediment of liberal apologists and appeasers, they defeated totalitarian communism, then turned their attention to releasing Americans from the shackles of big government and restoring respect for the family. Empowering entrepreneurs and liberating citizens, they cut onerous taxes and regulations, enabling Americans to live freer lives. But at every turn they are hindered by powerful liberal elitists who want to take Americans' money, waste it on programs for the lazy and the sinful, banish God from the nation and tell us all how to live our lives.[89]

We witnessed an even more virulent form of this authoritarian intolerance and aggression in the bluster of Trump on the campaign trail. To enthusiastic cheers, he offered vague policy prescriptions that ignored civil liberties and humanitarian protections for anyone he deemed outside his narrow vision for the country. His promises to "make America great again"— by "bombing the hell out of ISIS," strengthening the military so "no one will mess with us," building a wall "that Mexico will pay for," and shutting out "Muslims entering the United States"—were reminiscent of dangerous demagogues from earlier eras. Consistent with this mindset, Trump described those who disagreed with him as "disgusting," as "losers," and as "idiots." After a year in the White House, he hadn't really changed his tune.

Fox News: Defending Plutocrats and "Real Americans"

Plutocratic defenders also use the They're Un-American mind game to argue that people who don't fit the "right" profile are extremists who fail to appreciate this country's greatness. Such propaganda is standard fare on Fox News, one jewel in billionaire Rupert Murdoch's right-wing media empire (the *Wall Street Journal* is another). Despite its long-time, now discarded "fair and balanced" motto, the network serves as a megaphone for the GOP and the 1%. Hosts often act as bullies, turning their followers' wrath on those they characterize as undesirables. Two prominent examples are the assaults on the Black Lives Matter movement and Muslim Americans.

What is Black Lives Matter? Alicia Garza, Patrisse Cullors, and Opal Tometi, the three women who launched the movement after the killing of teenager Trayvon Martin by George Zimmerman back in 2012, describe it as:

> An ideological and political intervention in a world where Black lives are systematically and intentionally targeted for demise. It is an affirmation of Black folks' contributions to this society, our humanity, and our resilience in the face of deadly oppression.[90]

According to a national poll conducted in early 2016, twice as many Americans support the movement as the number who oppose it. Not surprisingly, however, white Republicans (the predominant viewers of Fox News) are the group that expressed the strongest opposition.[91]

Every movement for social change frightens those who benefit most from the status quo. That's why, on multiple occasions, Fox's Bill O'Reilly demonized the supporters of Black Lives Matter, telling his TV audience that they're "the radical left, the real fringe nuts that run around the country saying crazy things";[92] that the activists themselves use "Gestapo tactics," want to "tear down the country," and are interested only in "condemning white society";[93] that they're "a hate group" that he's personally "going to put...out of business";[94] that the group is "killing Americans";[95] and that they're "essentially a hate America group."[96] During an appearance on O'Reilly's former show while campaigning for the Republican Party nomination, Trump said, "I think they're trouble. I think they're looking for trouble...And I think it's a disgrace that they're getting away with it."[97]

Others on the network have relied on similar talking points. Sean Hannity, for example, compared Black Lives Matter to the Ku Klux Klan.[98] A regular guest on *Fox and Friends* denied that police brutality exists and described the movement as "subversive" and "garbage."[99] Another described it as "a terrorist group."[100] Former New York City mayor Rudy Giuliani appeared on the network to argue that the movement is "inherently racist" and "puts a target on the back of police."[101]

In mid-2016, a coalition of groups linked to the Black Lives Matter movement released a multifaceted, comprehensive platform of specific demands and policy recommendations.[102] Highlights include criminal justice reforms, including an end to the death penalty; decriminalization of drug offenses; the demilitarization of local police forces and community oversight in cases of police misconduct; greater investments in education, jobs, and health services; and a federal commission to study reparations for past and continuing harms suffered by descendants of slaves. Are measures like these really "un-American"?

At other times, Fox News has used the They're Un-American mind game to target American Muslims, painting them as extremists who don't respect the country's laws and traditions. These claims diverge sharply from reality. Muslim and non-Muslim Americans share much in common. Over half of the respondents in a survey of Muslim Americans said that most Muslims who move to the United States want to "adopt American customs and ways of life."[103] Nearly half did report that they think of themselves as Muslims first, rather than Americans—but this prioritizing of religious identity is much higher for another group of Americans: white evangelical Christians. And in terms of religious observance, American Muslims' devoutness is comparable to that of their Christian counterparts. Finally, a report about the same survey's findings noted, "Opposition to violence is broadly shared by all segments of the Muslim American population."[104]

But Islamophobia sells well at Fox News, so it's seemingly always on the menu. For example, a decade ago Minnesota's Keith Ellison became the first Muslim ever elected to the U.S. Congress. Consistent with his faith, Ellison planned to use the Quran—rather than the Christian Bible—for his swearing-in ceremony (as it turns out, he used a Quran that had belonged to none other than Thomas Jefferson). This choice spurred outrage from familiar right-wing "culture warriors" like Fox's Hannity, who raised the specter that Ellison would "embolden Islamic extremists and make new ones." Hannity even asked a guest whether it should be acceptable for someone "to choose... Hitler's *Mein Kampf*, which is the Nazi bible."[105]

Other Fox News personalities have regularly pushed an Islamophobia narrative as well, including promoting concerns that most or all American Muslims practice sharia law, and that the country is at risk of having its entire legal system replaced if Muslims gain power. Stuart Varney defended 2016 Republican presidential candidate Ben Carson's statement— that he "absolutely would not agree with a Muslim being elected president of the United States"—by falsely claiming, "Under Islam, church and state are combined. They are one. There is no separation."[106]

Similarly, Glenn Beck welcomed a guest who warned that sharia law is "the biggest threat to our constitutional rights over the next 25 years."[107] And Brian Kilmeade insisted, "Not all Muslims are terrorists, but all terrorists are Muslims." He also suggested that Americans have a right "to look at moderate Muslims and say, 'Show me you're not one of them.'"[108] Unfortunately, these and other outrageous claims resonate with the Fox News audience. A survey found that "trust in Fox News" was correlated with negative attitudes about Muslims and a heightened concern over a Muslim extremist agenda.[109]

SUMMING UP: THE PLUTOCRATS' SUPERIORITY MIND GAMES

Although these four superiority mind games of today's plutocrats are deeply flawed, resisting them can be daunting nonetheless. Let's review each in turn.

With the They're Losers mind game, the 1% try to win our allegiance by casting the most disadvantaged in America as inferior to the rest of us. Commending us for qualities that others supposedly lack, they encourage the public's psychological distance from decent people who deserve our concern and solidarity. By boosting our own sense of self-worth, they likewise aim to discourage us from recognizing that today's massive concentrations of wealth and power reflect ruthless exploitation and unconscionable disregard of the needy. If we make the mistake of aligning ourselves with the plutocrats rather than those facing hardship, we become unwitting shields and disposable pawns in preserving a destructive status quo.

When they turn to we've-earned-it appeals, the 1% fraudulently argue that they've earned all of their extraordinary wealth and power through grit, determination, and fair play—and that they deserve praise rather than criticism for their actions and choices. In making these claims, it hardly matters whether individual members of the predatory class are witting pretenders or are truly blind to their considerable shortcomings and undeserved advantages. Either way, these assertions of superiority go hand in hand with the pursuit of ever more dominant positions. As long as we let their distorted, self-glorifying narratives go uncontested, extreme inequality will remain a disturbing fixture of American society.

With their Pursuing a Higher Purpose mind game, today's plutocrats insist that their efforts embrace and protect the values cherished by most Americans. But by prioritizing big-money interests over all else, the 1% subvert the transcendent vision of the United States as a nation of equal opportunity, where people from all walks of life join together in pursuing the greater good. Despite this glaring contradiction, the appeal retains its persuasive power if we fail to question its legitimacy. Unfortunately, that's a mistake especially easy to make when the predatory class packages its greed-driven agenda in ways designed to tap into our sense of pride over our country's accomplishments and influence in the world.

Finally, the 1%'s they're-un-American appeals stoke intolerance by presenting critics as inauthentic and unpatriotic Americans whose views and preferences undermine the country's greatness. Here too, this propaganda is self-serving. Today's plutocrats recognize that their unparalleled dominance will be jeopardized if unwelcome change-seekers draw sufficient support from the broad public. So they condemn those individuals and groups that refuse to silently accept hardship and mistreatment, characterizing them as ungrateful outsiders who fail to appreciate all that's good about the United States.

It should be clear that our concerns about superiority are soft targets for mind games aimed at defending extreme inequality for the benefit of the 1%. There's one more core psychological concern that governs our lives—helplessness—and that's where we'll turn next.

6

HELPLESSNESS MIND GAMES
MANIPULATING OUR PERCEPTIONS OF WHAT'S POSSIBLE

"For, while the tale of how we suffer, and how we are delighted, and how we may triumph is never new, it always must be heard. There isn't any other tale to tell; it's the only light we've got in all this darkness."

— JAMES BALDWIN[1]

Control over what happens in our lives is tremendously important to us, and we strive to resist feelings of helplessness. But if we come to believe that our actions are futile, that to persevere is a waste of time and energy, sooner or later we stop trying. This sense of resignation can overwhelm the commitment and motivation necessary to achieve our goals. Even more, once feelings of helplessness settle in, they can be very hard to dislodge.

This isn't only true for individuals. Groups too can feel powerless to improve their circumstances, either because their members think they lack certain capabilities and resources or because they see the larger system as rigged against them. Either way, a shared perception of helplessness represents a significant hurdle because effective political mobilization depends upon believing there's some reasonable likelihood of success. Those who participate must think that their efforts are capable of righting the wrongs they see.

In short, perceived helplessness undermines individual and collective action alike. We can experience, witness, or learn about the most glaring injustices, but if we think there's nothing we can do about them, we turn our energies elsewhere.[2] These tendencies are well recognized by today's plutocrats, who craft psychological appeals that use our perceptions about helplessness to their own advantage.

In this chapter, we'll take a close look at four of the helplessness mind games they use: Change Is Impossible, We'll All Be Helpless, Don't Blame Us, and Resistance Is Futile.

CHANGE IS IMPOSSIBLE

With the Change Is Impossible mind game, the 1% claim that nothing can be done to fix extreme inequality, even if we'd like to do so. Such assertions about inexorable forces beyond everyone's control benefit the wealthy and powerful who wish to maintain the status quo. We just have to accept that certain problems can't be solved, they argue. This is an old refrain that never goes out of style. In 1991, economist Albert Hirschman criticized the "futility thesis." This argument is used to obstruct progressive change by warning that "attempts at social transformation will be unavailing" and that they "will simply fail to 'make a dent.'"[3] Of course acceptance of current conditions comes much easier for plutocrats with fat bank accounts and luxurious mansions.

This first helplessness mind game is related to a broader area of longstanding interest to psychologists: how people explain the causes for their successes and failures. One important distinction in this context is the difference between *internal* versus *external* attributions.[4] With an internal attribution, we hold ourselves responsible for whether things go well or go poorly—a work assignment, or a difficult conversation, or an athletic competition, or a fundraising appeal. If we instead make an external attribution in these situations, we believe the factors determining whether the outcome is favorable or not are beyond our control. Our judgments aren't necessarily correct. We can have control without realizing it, and we can think we have control when we don't. Still, regardless of their accuracy, these attributions affect how we approach future challenges.

Psychologists also make a second distinction, between *stable* and *unstable* attributions. One example of a stable internal attribution for success or failure is a person's ability. We often think of intelligence or skill as something that's relatively stable and doesn't change much over time. So, for instance, if someone consistently beats me at chess, I may reasonably conclude that they're better at the game than I am. In contrast, effort is an internal attribution that's considered unstable. When you attribute an outcome—like a lost chess match—to how hard you tried, you're still taking responsibility for the defeat, but you're also predicting that a different result is possible if you try harder the next time around.

The same stability distinction can be made in reference to external attributions as well. Here, a common stable external attribution is the inherent difficulty of a particular challenge or assignment. For instance, certain surgical procedures or athletic feats are demanding and formidable regardless of how many times a skilled doctor or athlete has attempted them. On the other hand, a very different kind of external attribution—an unstable one—is luck. When we believe we've won or lost because we were lucky or unlucky, we're thinking that the outcome could be different the next time around even if we approach the situation exactly the same way again. Overall, the combination of internal versus external and stable versus unstable attributions goes a long way in determining how we respond to setbacks and whether we believe our future can be brighter. Today's plutocrats use this knowledge in pursuing their goals.

In examining the Change Is Impossible mind game further, let's now explore the role played by this appeal in a few specific contexts, including the defense of globalization and escalating healthcare costs.

Unfettered Globalization

Members of the plutocracy use the strategic opportunities presented by globalization to ruthlessly squeeze more profits out of the developing world's impoverished workforce. At the same time, they block efforts to improve job security for American workers, using threats of overseas outsourcing as a cudgel to limit wages, benefits, and bargaining power. If they were worried about anyone below their executive suites, they'd take meaningful steps to prevent or minimize globalization's damage. But they're not.[5] Instead they rely on the Change Is Impossible mind game to preserve the status quo.

Nobel laureate Joseph Stiglitz is among the economists who've publicly rejected the plutocrats' tales about helplessness in the face of globalization. Here's his description of how they advance their own narrow interests:

> The rules of economic globalization are likewise designed to benefit the rich: they encourage competition among countries for business, which drives down taxes on corporations, weakens health and environmental protections, and undermines what used to be viewed as the "core" labor rights, which include the right to collective bargaining. Imagine what the world might look like if the rules

were designed instead to encourage competition among countries for workers. Governments would compete in providing economic security, low taxes on ordinary wage earners, good education, and a clean environment—things workers care about. But the top 1 percent don't need to care.[6]

Back in 1999, the United Nations Human Development Programme warned of the inequality-boosting downside of globalization dominated by corporate interests:

> The new rules of globalization—and the players writing them—focus on integrating global markets, neglecting the needs of people that markets cannot meet. The process is concentrating power and marginalizing the poor, both countries and people.[7]

But that same year, defenders of the plutocratic order, like Thomas Friedman of the *New York Times*, preferred to ridicule the thousands of demonstrators who gathered in Seattle to oppose the big business agenda of the World Trade Organization. Friedman mocked them for thinking that the globalization wave could be turned back, contained, or redirected, describing the protestors as "a Noah's ark of flat-earth advocates, protectionist trade unions and yuppies looking for their 1960s fix."[8] He then went even further, assuring his readers that globalization should be celebrated and anecdotally noting that working conditions were so good in a Victoria's Secret garment factory in Sri Lanka that he'd let his daughters work there. Fast-forward a decade. Was Friedman surprised by a *Bloomberg News* investigative report revealing that cotton used in that Sri Lankan factory came from forced child labor in Burkina Faso in Africa?[9]

With the Change Is Impossible mind game, defenders of concentrated wealth and power claim that, like it or not, economic globalization is an unstoppable force that makes extreme inequality inevitable. By their account, we're all helpless to alter its course and we must learn to accept that there will always be winners and losers. But what the 1% don't bother to tell us is that for decades they've made themselves the winners—by shaping globalization for their own greed-driven purposes regardless of the devastation it causes.[10]

The bottom line is that, despite their protestations, today's plutocrats are far from helpless when it comes to which priorities they choose to adopt. We see this as well in the trade pacts the United States hammers out with the direct guidance and engagement of our business elites. As economist Josh Bivens has observed, "When trade agreements prohibit a country from copying the technology it buys, that's good business. But if agreements required that each country protect the most basic rights afforded to its workers, that would be protectionism."[11]

Unhealthy Healthcare Costs

The Change Is Impossible mind game is also used by the predatory class to defend escalating healthcare costs. The hospital, pharmaceutical, and insurance industries make record profits, yet many of their wealthiest executives—who collectively take home hundreds of millions of dollars in annual salaries—claim that there's nothing to be done about the situation. Former industry executive Wendell Potter refers to this ploy as the "self-portrait of powerlessness in controlling medical costs."[12] By the account of industry executives, expensive drugs and treatments, the increasing number of elderly Americans, and cutbacks in Medicare reimbursement from the government make rising premiums and other costs for patients inescapable.[13]

But the exorbitant expense of hospitalization, a common source of family bankruptcies, is often about boosting the revenues of for-profit hospitals. Public health scholars Ge Bai and Gerard Anderson found that 49 of the 50 U.S. hospitals with the largest markups for items and services were for-profit hospitals, and almost all of them were owned by larger for-profit health systems.[14] On average these facilities charged more than ten times the Medicare-allowable costs. They do this because they can get away with it—even though almost everyone is adversely affected by skyrocketing healthcare costs, especially the uninsured and the underinsured. According to Potter, very few states restrict such increases, and handsomely paid lobbyists work hard to make sure that doesn't change.[15]

These false claims of seemingly unalterable forces also apply to drug pricing or, perhaps more accurately, price gouging. Pharmaceutical companies make huge profits—in the tens of billions of dollars annually for the largest companies—on their patented medications. Typically, they argue that the high prices reflect underappreciated costs associated with the research behind the drug development and the need to advertise and educate the public. Yet comparable or identical medications are available elsewhere—in some cases, as close as the Canadian border—at much lower prices.

Why the discrepancy? Because drug prices remain unregulated in the United States, and keeping them that way is a top priority for the pharmaceutical industry.[16] According to public policy scholar and former Secretary of Labor Robert Reich, pharmaceutical giants have several strategies to keep this golden goose laying. They lobby for legislation that prohibits the government from negotiating lower wholesale prices through Medicare and Medicaid. They pay off generic drug manufacturers to delay the introduction of equivalent drugs. They aggressively advertise their more expensive brand-name drugs even after generic versions become available, in an effort to mislead the public about their options. And they reformulate medications in minor ways, such as extended-release versions, in order to extend patent protections.[17]

Two specific examples help to drive home these points. Consider first the case of Mylan and its CEO Heather Bresch (the daughter of Joe Manchin, a Democratic U.S. Senator from West Virginia). The company's biggest-selling product, the EpiPen, is a device that delivers a potentially life-saving injection of epinephrine to children and adults experiencing severe allergic reactions. In 2008, before Mylan began instituting substantial annual price hikes, consumers could buy a pair of EpiPens for just over $100. In 2016, the price tag jumped to over $600, precipitating widespread outrage that became front-page news.[18]

Mylan's immediate response to this public relations nightmare was twofold. On the one hand, consumers were promised various belated cost-saving measures.[19] On the other hand, Bresch—who received $19 million in compensation the preceding year—took to CNBC to argue that Mylan was essentially helpless because a "broken system" was the real culprit.[20] Over the course of her TV interview, she made a range of claims, including "No one's more frustrated than me," "We fight every day to get affordable medicine out there," and "This isn't an EpiPen issue. This isn't a Mylan issue. This is a healthcare issue."

The heartless profiteering is even more transparent in a second case: the marketing of Daraprim, a drug that's been around for over a half-century and treats HIV and life-threatening parasitic infections. In 2015, Turing Pharmaceuticals—whose then-CEO Martin Shkreli was also a 32-year-old hedge fund manager—bought Daraprim and immediately jacked up the price from $13.50 to $750 for a single pill. Just before the purchase, internal company emails reveal that Shkreli wrote, "$1 bn [billion] here we come" and "Should be a very handsome investment for all of us." And just after the purchase, another Turing director reacted via email to a single Daraprim order this way: "Another 7.2 million. Pow!"[21]

Facing no regulation or immediate competitors for this generic drug, Turing executives could place hand-over-fist moneymaking above all other considerations, including patient welfare. Like Mylan, in this instance public outrage and political pushback led the company to reconsider the magnitude of its price hike.[22] Separately, Shkreli was subsequently arrested on unrelated securities fraud charges and resigned as Turing's CEO.

As all of these examples illustrate, there's little truth to plutocratic tales of helplessness, in which we're told, with feigned regret, that healthcare costs are beyond everyone's control. Moreover, there's rarely any mention that keeping Americans healthy—and caring for them when they're sick—shouldn't be a profit-driven enterprise in the first place.

Blame It on "Human Nature"

Defenders of extreme wealth and power often claim that something immutable about "human nature" itself makes reducing inequality impossible. In this way, they chalk up the sharp divide between "haves" and "have-nots" to a purportedly unalterable reality: Human beings are driven by self-interest; dog-eat-dog competition is inevitable; and, in the long run, there must always be the victors and the vanquished. To any doubters they say: Sooner or later, you'll regret your naïve optimism.

This point of view isn't only self-serving for the 1%, it also runs contrary to much of what we know to be true about what makes people tick. The idea that people are motivated solely, or even primarily, by self-interest overlooks the intrinsically social nature of human beings. Who isn't familiar with feelings of compassion, empathy, or outrage over the mistreatment of others? Admittedly, we don't experience these sentiments toward everyone; there are some whose struggles arouse little concern in us and others for whom we may even welcome misfortune. Nonetheless, it's clear that most of us care about more than just our individual welfare. And it's equally clear that we're not hard-wired to value rampant consumerism and the blind pursuit of money. At the same time, we're certainly challenged to "expand the circle" of others who we consider part of our moral universe and deserving of our care and respect.[23]

We also know—from psychological research and firsthand experience alike—that the circumstances in which we find ourselves, not inflexible "human nature," usually determine our behavior. Writ large, this means that our societal institutions, laws, and norms influence how we live our lives. The growing field of behavioral economics reveals how small "nudges" can alter the choices we make every day.[24] For instance, organ donations increase when becoming a donor is presented as the default option; school children select healthier foods when these options are displayed more prominently in the cafeteria; people are more likely to enroll in a beneficial retirement plan if participation is automatic unless the employee chooses to opt out; and guests reuse their towels more when they're invited to join the many other patrons supporting the hotel's conservation efforts.[25] Nudges like these remind us that people aren't irredeemably set in their ways. For better or worse, our "natural" tendencies are quite responsive to a range of external interventions.

Nevertheless, today's plutocrats stick to their change-is-impossible arguments through thick and thin. When initiatives they oppose show signs of bearing fruit, they insist that the gains are temporary, matters will soon revert to how they were, and precious resources will have been foolishly wasted. According to their propaganda, you can swim upstream—against human nature—for only so long before the current brings you back to where you started. The purported inevitability of backsliding is attributed to supposedly fundamental inadequacies—in morals, character, or capabilities—of those seeking better lives. Behind this ugly strategy, the 1% hope and expect that public support for the disadvantaged will soon enough evaporate.

WE'LL ALL BE HELPLESS

With this second helplessness appeal, the predatory class claims that the transformations sought by their opponents will leave us all helpless to protect ourselves and the things we value. We're advised that if we don't embrace the status quo— even with its extreme concentrations of wealth and power— we'll soon be much worse off, and without the capacity to undo the damage. Such prospects are often frightening enough that even deeply flawed arguments and policy recommendations can appear persuasive to the general public.

In part, it can be hard to resist the We'll All Be Helpless mind game because we're not very good at judging whether or not our own skepticism is broadly shared by others. Years ago, psychologists Deborah Prentice and Dale Miller examined this problem in an ingenious study aimed at better understanding the worrisome culture of binge drinking at Princeton University.[26] In a private survey, they asked students two questions: how they personally felt about the popularity of alcohol consumption and how they thought other students felt about it.

The researchers discovered that most students actually disliked the pervasive binge drinking norm—but these students mistakenly believed that theirs was the minority view. As a result, they tended to accept the situation without expressing any public concern, and sometimes they even participated in the drinking themselves so as not to be seen as different by their friends. Psychologists call this unrecognized divergence between private attitudes and social norms "pluralistic ignorance." It tends to preserve the status quo, which usually serves the interests of the 1%.

Subsequent research studies focused on issues other than drinking on campus have confirmed these basic findings. The bottom line is that, more often than we realize, we're off base in our estimates of how the majority truly feels about a matter of general interest. Consider this familiar situation. During a classroom lecture, the teacher asks whether anyone doesn't understand what they've just explained. You personally don't understand, but you look around and not a single hand has been raised, so you decide not to raise your own. In this scenario, it's possible that nobody understood the lesson, but by the show of hands, each student might conclude that they are the only one. Meanwhile, the instructor can reasonably assume everyone understood—until the final exam reveals otherwise.

Pluralistic ignorance is driven by our fear of embarrassment or reprisal for views we mistakenly think are likely to be a source of disapproval. The stubborn problem we face is that the preferences people express in public—and the choices they make—can diverge sharply from "private truths" that they're hesitant to communicate to others.[27] If people knew how many others shared their views, it would be more obvious when policies or social norms are out of line with what the public really wants. But instead, collective silence can help plutocrats preserve the status quo indefinitely—especially when political leaders beholden to the 1% disparage the alternatives.

In examining the We'll All Be Helpless mind game, we'll take a careful look at how the 1% use this appeal to block gun reform efforts, lock up undocumented immigrants, and defend poverty wages.

Dire Warnings about Gun Reform

The huge firearms industry relies on this mind game when it promotes the spurious claim that gun reform initiatives will make everyone helpless. We shouldn't be surprised by this campaign, since easy access to deadly weapons—for whoever wants them—means ever-growing profits for today's gun manufacturers and dealers.[28] As a result, percentage-wise, far more Americans die from gun violence—homicides and suicides—than do the citizens of any other wealthy country. The total number in 2018 in the United States is likely to again exceed 30,000—a figure comparable to the number of Americans killed in automobile accidents.[29] Indeed, the far-too-frequent mass killings—including school children in Newtown, Connecticut; churchgoers in Charleston, South Carolina;

co-workers in San Bernadino, California; nightclub attendees in Orlando, Florida; and concert attendees in Las Vegas, Nevada—account for only a small fraction of the bloodshed.

One of the leading purveyors of the We'll All Be Helpless mind game is the National Rifle Association. In an op-ed shortly after President Barack Obama's re-election in 2012, its CEO, Wayne LaPierre, warned, "No wonder Americans are buying guns in record numbers right now, while they still can and before their choice about which firearm is right for their family is taken away forever." In the same piece, he described the NRA as "the indispensable shield against the destruction of our nation's Second Amendment rights" and "the only chance gun owners have to withstand the coming siege."[30] At a press conference a week after the Sandy Hook Elementary School tragedy, LaPierre called for armed security guards in every U.S. school, arguing "the only thing that stops a bad guy with a gun is a good guy with a gun."[31]

There's more. In a 2014 speech at the Conservative Political Action Conference, LaPierre listed "home invaders, drug cartels, carjackers, knockout gamers, and rapers, and haters, and campus killers, airport killers, shopping mall killers" among the threats that assault-style rifles and other guns were needed to stop.[32] It's also worth noting that, although the NRA likes to tout its grassroots membership, it's not without substantial corporate funding. A case in point is the $600,000 check the group received in 2014 from Smith & Wesson. At the time, that gunmaker's CEO remarked, "The existence of the NRA is crucial to the preservation of the shooting sports and to the entire firearms industry."[33]

Riding shotgun with LaPierre are the likes of John Lott, promoter of the now-discredited thesis that more guns mean less crime. In the mainstream press, he's argued that gun reform "will leave individuals more vulnerable and helpless" and that "instead of making places safer, disarming law-abiding citizens leaves them as sitting ducks."[34] The NRA and gun lobby aggressively push this message because it sells guns. Indeed, there's clear evidence that stoking fears about gun restrictions in the aftermath of massacres leads to quick and sharp increases in handgun purchases.[35] But Lott's premise has collapsed under scholarly scrutiny.[36] The National Research Council dismissed his findings and methodology, and researchers at Stanford and Harvard have shown that higher rates of household gun ownership are in fact associated with higher, not lower, homicide rates, both nationally and in state-by-state comparisons.[37]

Unfortunately, gun reform has been thwarted thanks to the influence the gun lobby holds over numerous dutiful members of Congress and local politicians.[38] But the NRA's we'll-all-be-helpless propaganda is winning over the public as well, even though almost everyone supports modest measures such as universal background checks. National polls in recent years show that—for the first time in decades—there's now greater support for "gun rights" than for "gun control." This support is especially strong among those white Americans who, mistakenly, believe crime rates are rising. And whereas people used to report that hunting was their primary reason for owning a gun, now they say it's for personal safety—in other words, as an antidote to helplessness.[39] As NRA-booster Donald Trump argued during the presidential campaign, "You take the guns away from the good people, and the bad ones are going to have target practice."[40]

Putting Undocumented Immigrants behind Bars, Corporate-Style

Members of the 1% rely on this same We'll All Be Helpless mind game when they block immigration reform. In particular, the private prison industry reaps very handsome profits from locking up as many undocumented immigrants as it can. Companies like CoreCivic (the recently rebranded Corrections Corporation of America) and the GEO Group are well served by a climate of fear and panic about porous borders, which is further propelled by nativists' racist rants and their claims of Hispanic conspiracies aimed at reconquering the Southwest.

With taxpayer funding, CoreCivic and GEO now operate roughly half of all U.S. Immigration and Customs Enforcement (ICE) beds in detention facilities for those awaiting immigration court hearings. These companies make billions of dollars, and in their investor reports they caution that immigration reform poses a direct threat to this lucrative business model. How so? Well, profits are likely to decline if immigration enforcement efforts are relaxed; or if fewer people are arrested, convicted, and imprisoned; or if minimum sentences are reduced or early release opportunities for good behavior are increased.[41]

To fend off such possibilities, for-profit prisons spend millions in lobbying and in campaign contributions to sympathetic elected representatives—like Texas congressman John Culberson, a Republican and member of the powerful House Committee on Appropriations. Culberson has done his part to promote the false narrative that undocumented immigrants are dangerous criminals and that if they're not stopped now, they'll soon be beyond our control.[42] During hearings in 2015, he emphasized that "law enforcement lies at the heart of all our liberties" and that "we in Texas feel the brunt of this with the number of illegal criminals coming across the border—the drug runners, the killers and the sex-traffickers. It's appalling and outrageous."[43] Culberson has also insisted that the government take more aggressive steps to meet the requirement that 34,000 detention beds be filled at all times.[44] Lamenting the existence of empty beds, on one occasion he scolded the ICE director, telling her, "I feel very confident you could find an extra 9,000 criminal aliens that needed to be detained to fill those beds in a heartbeat."[45]

Private prison profiteers also benefit from propaganda that condemns the policies of "sanctuary cities," arguing that they make law enforcement officials helpless. These local communities prohibit notification of ICE agents following the arrest of undocumented immigrants for nonviolent offenses such as a broken taillight or driving without a license. Instead, after routine processing, these individuals are released without incarceration and without a review of their immigration status, thereby freeing them from the risk of immediate deportation. Although President Trump has claimed that sanctuary cities "abet criminal behavior,"[46] and his attorney general, Jeff Sessions, has argued that sanctuary policies make "cities and states less safe,"[47] recent research shows that crime rates are actually lower in sanctuary counties than in non-sanctuary counties.[48] At the same time, sanctuary policies reflect more than just a humanitarian awareness of the already fraught circumstances of immigrant families living in the shadows.[49] They also reflect the pragmatic recognition that fostering greater trust of the police in immigrant communities makes solving serious crimes and apprehending wrongdoers easier.

But that logic matters little to high-placed, fearmongering friends of for-profit prisons. They rarely miss an opportunity to raise the specter of future helplessness. For example, former North Carolina Governor Pat McCrory, a Republican, insisted that "public safety officials must have the flexibility and tools to investigate crimes and sanctuary city policies deprive law enforcement of those tools."[50] Similarly, on his presidential campaign website, Senator Marco Rubio of Florida warned, "Illegal immigrants who commit crimes can often be released, free to endanger their communities again, without federal authorities ever having the chance to remove them from the country." And Mark Krikorian, executive director of the anti-immigration Center for Immigration Studies, has argued that failure to remove "illegals" enables them to "embed themselves in our society"; he's called for making their lives so miserable that they'll "self-deport."[51]

The Necessity of Poverty Wages?

As Robert Reich has noted, for decades business leaders have made a habit of predicting that uncontrollable economic disaster will follow any improvements in the lives of low-wage workers. Over a century ago, they warned that laws ending the worst of child labor abuses would force cost-cutting layoffs. They were likewise confident that safety regulations instituted after the deadly Triangle Shirtwaist Factory fire would drive businesses out of New York City.[52] And when President Franklin Delano Roosevelt established the first federal minimum wage with the signing of the Fair Labor Standards Act, the National Publishers Association cautioned that "Rome, 2,000 years ago, fell because the government began fixing the prices of services and commodities," and the National Association of Manufacturers asserted that the act "constitutes a step in the direction of communism, bolshevism, fascism, and Nazism."[53]

That tradition continues today as defenders of extreme inequality turn to the We'll All Be Helpless mind game in opposing increases in the minimum wage. They counter initiatives like the "Fight for $15" movement of fast-food and other low-wage workers—efforts that have already led some states and communities to adopt regulations with the potential to lift many employees out of poverty—by insisting that higher wages will cause us all inescapable and uncontrollable harm. Among the 1%'s most active propaganda shops in this arena is the Employment Policies Institute, run by long-time big business and anti-union lobbyist Rick Berman.

Consider some of the false claims that Michael Saltsman, the research director of Berman's institute, has made. Contrary to the findings of numerous reputable scholars, he's argued that wage hikes inevitably lead to significant job losses and that anyone who thinks otherwise is "fighting the laws of economics."[54] Saltsman has similarly insisted that the automation of functions once held by entry-level workers will be unavoidable if labor costs rise because consumers inflexibly demand low prices. To support this stance, one of Berman's anti-labor websites presents anecdotes of businesses that purportedly couldn't survive mandatory wage hikes. Helplessness-focused descriptions include the "death knell" for a restaurant forced to close its doors, a chiropractor who's moving his business because he "cannot make it anymore," a truckstop with reduced hours because the owner was "forced to cut shifts," and another shuttered restaurant where "skyrocketing costs" were "the nail in its coffin."[55]

Forecasts of doom from defenders of concentrated wealth and power have consistently proved inaccurate, and yet they persist. But Reich has also highlighted a different benchmark that shouldn't be overlooked. As a country, at various points in our history we've recognized that "certain kinds of jobs—jobs that were done by children, or were unsafe, or required people to work too many hours, or below poverty wages—offend our sense of decency."[56] That moral judgment stands even taller than Wall Street's skyscrapers. Today, decency demands that a person working full time should not be trapped in poverty.

DON'T BLAME US

The 1% are quick to boast of their accomplishments, and even faster to cover their tracks when anything with their finger-prints on it blows up—literally or figuratively. In these situations, they turn to the Don't Blame Us mind game, claiming there was nothing they could have done. According to their spin, the blame belongs elsewhere, or the bad outcomes couldn't possibly have been anticipated, or the resulting harm could never have been prevented anyway. The evidence rarely supports such protestations of innocence, but plutocrats still try to frame setbacks or disasters in ways that minimize wide-spread recognition of their own culpability—while continuing to advance their interests.[57]

When representatives of the predatory class make poor decisions—about economic policies, about national priorities, about going to war—they jeopardize the well-being of millions. Few of us will ever make choices with such profoundly bad consequences. But when these same plutocrats then refuse to admit their mistakes, that kind of behavior is probably familiar to most of us. After all, in our personal lives we can perhaps recall a time or two when we denied responsibility for wrongdoing, whether it was running a red light or hurting someone by being unkind.

Psychologists Carol Tavris and Elliot Aronson have offered a detailed analysis of this inclination to justify and excuse our own behavior.[58] They explain that we seek to relieve cognitive dissonance, the psychological discomfort we feel when two of our beliefs, attitudes, or behaviors are in conflict. Given our desire for consistency, we feel pressure to modify one or the other—and usually we make the easier, less demanding change. So, for instance, the smoker who's told their habit could be deadly will ideally quit smoking—but instead they may just convince themselves that the scientific research is flawed. Likewise, doomsday cult members have two options if the Earth isn't destroyed by higher powers on the date they've designated. They can abandon their deeply held convictions or instead conclude that it was their own devotion that miraculously saved the planet.[59] In short, uncomfortable dissonance is reduced through choices that enable us to escape admitting—or perhaps even recognizing—our errors.

Our tendency toward self-justification rather than self-blame doesn't mean that others won't consider us culpable when something goes wrong. Research shows that judgments about blameworthiness depend on a few key variables, including perceptions of controllability, intentionality, and foreseeability.[60] In general, we're more likely to hold people responsible for causing harm when we believe they had control over the outcome, when we think their action or inaction was intentional rather than accidental, and when we judge the situation as one where they should have expected the negative consequences and taken preventive steps. Not surprisingly then, even when the outcomes are disastrous, one way to avoid criticism and disapproval is to persuasively argue that any damage couldn't realistically have been anticipated or avoided—just as plutocrats, regardless of political party, frequently try to do.

In discussing the Don't Blame Us mind game, we'll examine the role played by this appeal in specific contexts, including the 1%'s denial of responsibility for natural disasters, for military and intelligence blunders, and for the Great Recession.

When Disaster Strikes

Don't-blame-us appeals are a familiar refrain from the predatory class whenever environmental disasters strike. They were certainly prominent in President Trump's feeble attempts to defend his administration's slow and inadequate response to Hurricane Maria in late September of 2017. The much-anticipated storm turned Puerto Rico into a humanitarian nightmare as millions of U.S. citizens faced weeks and weeks without electricity, basic medical supplies, or drinking water.

As the islanders' plight worsened, Trump denied that anything was amiss in his administration's relief efforts. On one occasion he insisted, "We have done a great job with the almost impossible situation,"[61] and on another he lamely explained, "This is an island surrounded by water, big water, ocean water."[62] Amid mounting criticism, he then turned to blaming others. When San Juan's mayor, Carmen Yulín Cruz, publicly pleaded for greater urgency from the federal government, Trump responded with a series of tweets from his private golf club in New Jersey, including this one: "Such poor leadership by the Mayor of San Juan, and others in Puerto Rico, who are not able to get their workers to help. They want everything to be done for them when it should be a community effort."[63] The next day he followed up by lambasting his critics as "politically motivated ingrates."[64]

Trump's excuses echoed the don't-blame-us ploys of an earlier White House when Hurricane Katrina breached the levees protecting New Orleans and caused massive losses of life and property in 2005. In the days immediately before Katrina made landfall, the Federal Emergency Management Agency and other independent expert analysts had warned government officials about the prospect of precisely this catastrophic scenario. Yet three days after the hurricane hit, President George W. Bush falsely told a television audience, "I don't think anybody anticipated the breach of the levees. They did anticipate a serious storm."[65] Homeland Security Secretary Michael Chertoff was equally disingenuous in his own claims, calling the disaster "breathtaking in its surprise" and arguing that the "combination of catastrophes exceeded the foresight of the planners, and maybe anybody's foresight."[66]

Hurricanes are far from the only mass tragedies that turn master-of-the-universe one-percenters into helpless innocents. For example, the death and ecological devastation wrought by the 2010 explosion of the Deepwater Horizon in the Gulf of Mexico was the occasion for similar protestations, this time from BP's corporate executives. One company spokesman described the oil rig blowout as "clearly unprecedented."[67] Another explained, "I don't think anybody foresaw the circumstance that we're faced with now."[68] CEO Tony Hayward reportedly bemoaned BP's plight in a meeting with fellow executives in London, asking them, "What the hell did we do to deserve this?"[69] That's a question easily answered. Internal BP documents reveal a long history in which the company failed to follow even its own safety policies, relied on antiquated equipment, performed inadequate inspections, and silenced concerned employees.[70] The BP disaster should have been far from inconceivable regardless, given that dozens of similar blowouts have occurred in the Gulf.[71]

We also shouldn't overlook the many environmental catastrophes that unfold in slow motion—and away from the spotlight—where those with the power to intervene instead focus on denying responsibility and passing the buck. That describes the public health disaster that's befallen the impoverished city of Flint, Michigan. It began several years ago with Governor Rick Snyder, the state's Republican legislature, and the state's so-called emergency managers implementing the predatory class's familiar draconian austerity agenda for the masses.[72] One cost-cutting move involved switching Flint's water supply from Lake Huron to the polluted Flint River.

Visible signs of contamination began to appear almost immediately, but state authorities reassured worried residents that "anyone who is concerned about lead in the drinking water in Flint can relax."[73] Not everyone was fooled, however. General Motors, for example, recognized the corrosive effects of the river water on the auto parts it was manufacturing—and quickly paid to get its water supply from the lake instead.[74] But the families of Flint didn't have that option, and their pleas were dismissed or ignored. As a result, over many months thousands of young children drank tap water poisoned with lead. Today, all of them are at risk of permanent neurological damage, along with learning disabilities and other behavioral problems.[75] And Flint has moved further up the list of majority Black cities where evidence of environmental racism looms large.[76]

Intelligence and Military Blunders

The same Don't Blame Us mind game is also how political leaders often try to justify costly intelligence and military failures. Consider the litany of excuses offered by representatives of the Bush administration following the 9/11 terrorist attacks and the misguided invasion of Iraq.[77] At a press briefing in May 2002, National Security Adviser Condoleezza Rice memorably claimed, "I don't think anybody could have predicted that these people would take an airplane and slam it into the World Trade Center, take another one and slam it into the Pentagon; that they would try to use an airplane as a missile."[78] But her defensive objections were contradicted by evidence that the White House received numerous alerts in the weeks and months leading up to the attacks, including a specific warning that hijacked planes might be used as weapons.[79]

The primary rationale for invading Iraq—the threat posed by Saddam Hussein's purported weapons of mass destruction—was another highly consequential misrepresentation for which the White House later claimed no responsibility. When no WMDs were found, one official after another—President Bush, Vice President Cheney, Rice, and others—insisted that "everyone" had believed the weapons were there, and that they shouldn't be blamed for believing that too. For instance, White House political operative Karl Rove asserted, "Everybody in the West, every major intelligence agency in the world, thought that Saddam Hussein had weapons of mass destruction."[80] But this self-protective claim of unanimity is simply untrue. U.S. intelligence agencies had not even reached their own consensus view before the invasion, and the independent International Atomic Energy Agency had reported, "We have to date found no evidence that Iraq has revived its nuclear weapon program since the elimination of the program in the 1990s."[81]

Similarly, after the initial days of "shock and awe," the invasion of Iraq bogged down and became far more difficult and costly than the assurances the Bush administration had given the American public. At that point, key officials resorted to a variety of helplessness ploys to defend their deeply flawed choices. In a December 2004 town hall meeting with troops stationed in Kuwait, Defense Secretary Donald Rumsfeld offered a no-other-option-available explanation—"You go to war with the Army you have, not the Army you might want or wish to have at a later time"—as if the war had been forced upon us. At that same event, he responded to concerns raised by a soldier about insufficient armor on their vehicles this way: "You can have all the armor in the world on a tank and a tank can be blown up."[82] Two years later, as an Iraqi insurgency raged and the death toll increased, and despite the many warnings that had preceded it, Vice President Cheney told those gathered at a National Press Club luncheon, "I don't think anybody anticipated the level of violence that we've encountered"[83]—which again was far from the truth.

Wall Street and the Great Recession

Hollow cries of helplessness and don't-blame-us appeals also reverberated following the financial collapse that inaugurated the Great Recession of the 2000s. Plutocrats were quick to point fingers at others they insisted were responsible for the suffering of millions of Americans who lost jobs, homes, and life savings. New York City's former mayor, billionaire Michael Bloomberg, for example, singled out Congress for blame when discussing concerns raised by Occupy Wall Street back in 2011:

> I hear your complaints. Some of them are totally unfounded. It was not the banks that created the mortgage crisis. It was, plain and simple, Congress who forced everybody to go and give mortgages to people who were on the cusp...And now we want to go vilify the banks because it's one target, it's easy to blame them and Congress certainly isn't going to blame themselves.[84]

Bloomberg's narrow account ignores much of what we know to be true. It was Wall Street—with Republican and Democratic support—that lobbied for extensive deregulation and then rushed to take advantage of the home-buying frenzy. It was the banks that created exotic and poorly understood mortgage-based products to which credit rating agencies like Moody's and Standard & Poor's gave inflated endorsements. Once these fee-generating instruments were in place, the risk of loan defaults was transferred to third-party investors—including the banks' unsuspecting customers. Mortgage companies meanwhile relaxed lending standards so they could offer many more prospective homebuyers expensive sub-prime loans. When the housing bubble burst, the value of the massive investments tied to real estate prices plummeted. The whole system collapsed. Taxpayer money became the rescue line for the reckless, greed-driven banks that were deemed "too big to fail."[85]

During this period, the 1% also used the Don't Blame Us mind game to denounce the financially strapped and destitute homeowners themselves. Business channel CNBC repeatedly cast those who couldn't make their mortgage payments as "losers" undeserving of sympathy. In one segment, after an interviewee noted that some people had been preyed upon by unscrupulous lenders, one TV host disparagingly responded, "The phrase 'predatory lending' always kills me because how do you trick someone into—how do you force someone to borrow money? Don't borrow it if you can't afford it!" A colleague then chimed in, "It takes two to tango. You can't cheat an honest man."[86] Of course the notion that homebuyers were more blameworthy than huge mortgage companies like Countrywide Financial is absurd. There's overwhelming documentation proving mortgage lenders took unwarranted shortcuts, misled homebuyers about what they'd owe, filed false legal papers with phony signatures, and pushed people into costlier subprime loans even when they qualified for standard mortgages.[87]

And then there are the fabulously wealthy Wall Street executives who've insisted that they too were helpless to anticipate or prevent the devastation that unfolded. Consider Robert Rubin, whose resume includes stints as co-chairman of Goldman Sachs, Treasury Secretary under Bill Clinton, and board member of Citigroup for a decade thereafter—and a personal bank account of over $100 million. Rubin was among the influential figures who aggressively pushed for deregulation of the banks before the financial crisis. When later asked whether he should be faulted for contributing to the damage that ensued, Rubin offered that "everyone" should have done more, but he still resorted to the familiar plea of helplessness: "I've thought about this a lot. ...I don't know what I could have done without operating responsibilities."[88] Meanwhile, former

Goldman Sachs partner Steven Mnuchin, Trump's distressing choice for Treasury Secretary, is among those who made a fortune during the crisis, by buying a distressed bank and then foreclosing on tens of thousands of homeowners.[89]

RESISTANCE IS FUTILE

When they find the status quo favorable to their interests, today's plutocrats erect innumerable obstacles to progressive reforms. They do so with a presumption of impunity that's the mirror image of the helplessness they hope to instill in everyone else. With the Resistance Is Futile mind game, the 1% send a clear warning to the rest of us: They're in charge and that's not going to change. Sometimes they drive this point home through verbal threats; at other times they rely upon intimidating demonstrations of power.

Those who want to hold onto wealth and power have the upper hand whenever the daunting reality of extreme inequality generates widespread hopelessness and passivity. These reactions are understandable, and they've led some psychologists to emphasize the importance of "small wins" when it comes to confronting social problems and organizing for change.[90] Even though it's likely to take many small victories to make a meaningful dent, evidence suggests that this approach is a very effective strategy for chipping away at large obstacles.

Small wins are valuable whenever change is especially tough, because even committed individuals will eventually abandon a cause if there are no signs of progress toward a long-term goal. So small victories offer a unique advantage: They're easier to achieve and harder for adversaries to obstruct. Moreover, celebrating these modest successes helps to remind everyone that progress is indeed possible. In turn, these favorable experiences serve not only to keep people motivated, but they also encourage others who have witnessed the victories to join the effort, thereby increasing the human and material resources available to expand the fight.

The powerful positive feelings that flow from a sense of progress—even progress on a small scale—have been documented in a variety of areas, including research into job satisfaction. In one study, employees assigned to complex and creative projects were asked to keep daily diaries in which they tracked their best and worst workdays over a period of several months. When the researchers examined the data, they found noteworthy fluctuations in the workers' mood and motivation at the end of each day. The days that the employees deemed best were those during which meaningful progress had been made, and those rated as worst involved project setbacks.[91] Such results highlight the fact that neither huge breakthroughs nor massive failures are necessary to significantly affect how we feel about our efforts.

In exploring the Resistance Is Futile mind game, let's now take a detailed look at how the 1% use this appeal to perpetuate racial inequities, exploit low-wage workers, and exert financial control over our electoral politics.

Trapped by Racial Injustice

None of the predatory class's efforts to render the disadvantaged helpless is more troubling than the entrenched, racially biased system that controls, oppresses, and blocks communities of color from equal justice and equal opportunity. It's been more than a half-century since Democratic Governor George Wallace of Alabama—"segregation now, segregation tomorrow, segregation forever"[92]—defiantly blocked the doors at the University of Alabama to prevent Vivian Malone and James Hood from entering. Such overt racist acts of intimidation by high-profile politicians are perhaps less common today, but the Resistance Is Futile mind game is alive and well. Moreover, institutional norms and policies continue to trap victims in a web of adversity from which they are often powerless to escape.[93]

Civil rights attorney and scholar Michelle Alexander has described how young Black men are shoehorned into dilapidated schools, unable to find jobs that pay a living wage, arrested in disproportionate numbers for nonviolent crimes in impoverished neighborhoods, and then incarcerated at astounding and again disproportionate rates. As she writes, "Mass incarceration depends for its legitimacy on the widespread belief that all those who appear trapped at the bottom actually chose their fate."[94] Borrowing the birdcage metaphor of political theorist Iris Marion Young, Alexander also notes that the realities of this externally imposed helplessness are obscured from the public, who fail to see the full picture:

> If one thinks about racism by examining only one wire of the cage, or one form of disadvantage, it is difficult to understand how and why the bird is trapped. Only a large number of wires arranged in a specific way, and connected to one another, serve to enclose the bird and to ensure that it cannot escape.

After release from prison, future prospects and participation in mainstream society are even more severely constrained. For instance, more than 10% of Black men of voting age were ineligible to vote in the 2014 election because they were classified as felons, many for nonviolent offenses.[95] Drug convictions can make social supports like food stamps, welfare, and federal housing assistance off limits as well.[96] These restrictions compound the difficulties of re-entry to society after a prison term, already a daunting undertaking given the obstacles to finding a decent-paying job.

Beyond the disturbing realities of mass incarceration and its aftermath alone, the Black community is targeted in other ways that can promote helplessness and despair. For example, racial profiling—and its associated negative stereotypes about criminality—subject African Americans to seemingly inescapable surveillance, harassment, and other intrusions in their daily lives.[97] Earlier, we looked at reprehensible voter suppression efforts. Related strategies further minimize the political voice of communities of color. The gerrymandering of voting districts often diminishes or eliminates the influence of non-white voters. It also affects which candidates win local and national elections by creating easier paths to office for non-minority politicians who are friendly to the plutocratic agenda.[98]

Workers Pushed to the Brink

Most workers in the United States are "at-will" employees. Working without a contract or union representation, they can be fired at any time for almost any reason. In terms of job security, this represents a profound level of helplessness imposed upon tens of millions of Americans. Even the handful of legal restrictions that limit employers from having total control—for instance, you can't be fired due to discrimination or for reporting health or safety violations—place the burden of proving wrongful termination on employees.[99] Most people who lose a job have little time to pursue such complaints anyway; they're too busy trying to find new work to support themselves and their families. Meanwhile, the mere threat of dismissal is often enough to dissuade workers from exercising their rights.

For large U.S. employers, this imposition of powerlessness extends far beyond the cavalier firing of individual employees. Companies routinely prioritize profit-boosting cost-cutting above all else. Low-wage workers are limited to part-time hours to make sure they don't qualify for healthcare benefits.[100] Universities hire large numbers of adjunct faculty because they're cheaper than salaried professors.[101] Management demands significant concessions whenever union contracts come up for renewal.[102] And domestic factories are shuttered with production moved overseas to wherever workers can be exploited even more effectively.[103]

Corporate behemoths also exert their coercive power over small-business owners who simply can't compete with their merciless price-cutting. In this context, Amazon quickly comes to mind. Having moved beyond books alone to selling everything to everyone, the online retailer's dominance has steadily grown. How does the company lure cost-conscious customers away from local retail outlets of all kinds through unbeatable prices? By taking advantage of low-wage workers, by avoiding the added expense of sales taxes wherever it can, and by encouraging a growing trend whereby shoppers first explore their options on Main Street and then go home and buy the products they've selected through Amazon instead.[104]

At the same time, the retailing giant garners tax breaks and other accommodations from local governments in exchange for building its huge warehouses—"fulfillment centers"—in particular places. Yet despite the hype, evidence suggests that these operations ultimately provide worse jobs and for fewer workers, while adversely affecting the town's local suppliers and infrastructure.[105] As for the ruthlessness underlying Amazon's success, billionaire CEO Jeff Bezos reportedly once described his approach to negotiating discounts from publishers as similar to "the way a cheetah would pursue a sickly gazelle."[106]

Money in Politics

Today's plutocrats have also enfeebled the public in another way: by taking ever-firmer control over the funding of our elections. Recent polling shows that a remarkable 85% of Americans believe fundamental changes or a complete overhaul are needed in how our political campaigns are funded.[107] But that kind of mandate is likely to fall on deaf ears in Congress because so many of those who hold elected office secure their positions with hefty campaign backing from the 1%. For these politicians, citizen helplessness can protect rather than undermine their selfish interests.

The corrupting role of money in politics—and its disempowerment of average Americans—is certainly nothing new.[108] But this dangerous trend accelerated with the Supreme Court's 2010 verdict in *Citizens United v. Federal Election Commission.*

In that case, the 5-4 majority ruled that corporations—and unions—can spend unrestricted amounts on political activities that aren't directly tied to a specific candidate or party. This opened the floodgates for political spending sprees by the super-rich.[109] Today, an individual can give only up to $2,700 to a candidate running for federal office. But wealthy donors can give millions of dollars to "Super PACs" and other so-called independent groups. That's exactly what they're doing, sometimes without their identities ever being disclosed.[110]

The most glaring problem with this system is that the legal requirement of independence from candidates isn't taken seriously. The rules that are supposed to prevent coordination between these groups and campaign staff have proven ineffective because they're essentially disregarded.[111] Many Super PACs promote a single candidate—and at times are even run by that politician's former advisers—without any repercussions. This makes a mockery of the Court's assurance that independent expenditures "do not give rise to corruption or the appearance of corruption."[112]

Access to wealthy donors and their networks of influence affects more than who wins our elections. Perhaps even more problematically, it determines who can even afford to run for office. We already have far too many candidates whose views and priorities reflect the desires of their 1% donors. Worthy opponents with different commitments—including third-party candidates—find themselves virtually powerless when it comes to funding a credible campaign under the current rules. People of color are now well over a third of all Americans, but they're only 10% of those elected to national office.[113] The entire process works to further mute the voice of regular Americans, adding to the helplessness so many feel about politics today. This suits the predatory class just fine.

SUMMING UP: THE PLUTOCRATS' HELPLESSNESS MIND GAMES

In this chapter, we've examined four helplessness mind games exploited by today's plutocrats to protect their tremendous wealth and power. Let's review each of them.

With the Change Is Impossible mind game, the 1% insist that the world is shaped by complex forces far too powerful to be altered by human intervention. Closer analysis, however, reveals that defenders of extreme inequality don't lack the capacity to exert influence over these forces. Rather, they simply lack the motivation to do so. Indeed, even when they're not the direct cause of others' misery, too often they're comfortable as bystanders, unwilling to use their enormous resources to benefit the common good.

In other contexts, plutocrats turn to we'll-all-be-helpless appeals. They warn us that change will lead to harmful repercussions that we'll all be powerless to combat. Here they aim to frighten us into accepting a status quo that serves their own interests but causes widespread damage to the public good. The 1% know that if they get us to focus on some trumped-up downside of change, we're likely to turn our backs on those who suffer the most under the current regime.

Today's plutocrats are also quick to use the Don't Blame Us mind game in claiming there was nothing they could do when circumstances take a turn for the worse. Given their inordinate wealth and power, these cries of helplessness and blamelessness should be subjected to careful scrutiny. Although they strut the stage boasting about their purported talents and accomplishments, members of the 1% head for the shadows when it's time to accept responsibility for their policy failures. Instead of admitting culpability and making efforts at redress, the predatory class serenades us with disingenuous denials that anything different could have been done.

Finally, representatives of the predatory class use resistance-is-futile appeals to convince the rest of us that we're helpless to wrest our lives and our country from their control. They work to demoralize, sideline, and ostracize those who seek greater equality and opportunity. This ploy frequently works. If we're convinced that we can't succeed, our change efforts soon grind to a halt or never get off the ground. But we should remember that the 1% are susceptible to the disempowering effects of perceived helplessness too—if we can convincingly demonstrate that they can't defend the status quo any longer.

With these four mind games, we've now covered the five core concerns upon which today's plutocrats so readily prey: vulnerability, injustice, distrust, superiority, and helplessness. It's time to put together what we've learned and, in the final chapter, examine how to best tackle the challenges these ploys pose for our collective well-being.

7

COUNTERING THE MIND GAMES
BUILDING A BETTER SOCIETY

*"Ordinary people exercise power in American politics
mainly at those extraordinary moments when they rise up
in anger and hope, defy the rules that ordinarily govern
their daily lives, and, by doing so, disrupt the workings
of the institutions in which they are enmeshed."*

— FRANCES FOX PIVEN[1]

As the preceding chapters have shown, today's plutocrats use an extensive repertoire of psychological mind games to target our core concerns about vulnerability, injustice, distrust, superiority, and helplessness. In so doing, they aim to suppress popular outrage over inequality and stifle calls for progressive change. Despite all the evidence that extreme inequality is hurting ordinary Americans, these ploys have produced a sad yet impressive track record. The 1%'s greed-driven agenda seems to march forward with frustrating consistency, time and time again defeating the common good.

These mind games have proven so effective precisely because they tap into real issues that are important in our daily lives. Each of the five psychological domains we've explored is a key lens through which we make sense of the world around us. That's why appeals that manipulate these concerns find such fertile ground in our psyches. It's also why it can be hard to recognize that, contrary to their expressions of commitment to the public interest, the true goals of the predatory class are to secure their fortunes and outsized influence—at the expense of everyone else.

But a more equal and more decent society isn't out of reach. Getting there, however, requires us to confront and defeat the 1%'s relentless campaign of lies and distortions. This book is intended as a contribution to that urgent struggle. If we're successful in countering their propaganda, the plutocrats' hollow tales will lose their allure, their selfish motives will be laid bare, and the public will realize how the privileged few have fleeced and betrayed the country—and the people—that made their enormous wealth and power possible. In this final chapter, we'll turn our attention to how we can accomplish these goals.

THE PROGRESSIVE VISION—WHAT MOST AMERICANS WANT

First, let's briefly consider what the United States could look like if the rule of the 1% crumbles. It isn't hard to identify the kinds of policies that might be implemented if we can break the stranglehold of the predatory class. Indeed, among progressive leaders and organizations there's considerable agreement on what the path ahead should include.

The priorities include tackling climate change and protecting the environment by curtailing fracking, offshore drilling, and mountaintop removal; ending institutional racism, mass incarceration, and police brutality; ensuring a living wage for everyone, and building the workforce through investments in "green" jobs and infrastructure repair; offering a Medicare-type, single-payer health insurance option to all Americans, and using Medicare's bargaining leverage to bring down healthcare costs; establishing humane immigration policies that include a path to citizenship; reducing our bloated defense budget and the hundreds of military bases we maintain overseas; raising taxes on the wealthiest Americans and the hugely profitable businesses many of them run; limiting the size of the largest banks and preventing them from gambling with depositors' money; helping homeowners with underwater mortgages; making public college affordable for all, and reducing student debt; removing barriers that make both registering and voting more difficult; requiring that corporations be accountable to their employees, communities, and the environment rather than to their shareholders alone; and getting "big money" out of our politics and elections.

That's not a complete list, but it obviously covers a lot of ground. Despite the predictable objections from representatives of the plutocracy, these are not ideas from the political fringe. Many of these policy recommendations are widely supported by the American people, as national polls over the past few years show:[2]

- 61% feel that only those at the top have a chance to get ahead in today's economy.

- 66% think that money and wealth should be distributed more evenly.

- 76% favor raising the minimum wage to $10.10 per hour, and 59% favor raising it to $15 per hour.

- 66% prefer candidates who recognize global warming and support increased reliance on renewable forms of energy.

- 78% believe the government should limit the greenhouse gas emissions of businesses.

- 59% would support a government healthcare plan similar to Medicare to compete with the private market.

- 85% support requiring paid sick leave for employees.

- 79% think that post-high school education is too expensive to be affordable for everyone in the United States.

- 70% support the use of federal funds to provide high-quality preschool education for every child.

- 74% think big corporations have too much political influence.

- 84% believe money has too much influence in our elections.

- 69% believe corporations don't pay their fair share of taxes.

- 68% favor raising taxes on people who earn over $1 million annually.

- 61% approve of labor unions.

Polling numbers like these are encouraging. Still, it takes much more to produce transformative social change because plutocrats are "all in" when it comes to defending their fortress. That means they're ever-ready and eager to use the psychologically potent mind games in their quivers in order to sow doubt, weaken resolve, fracture opposition, and ensure that the public's avowed policy preferences never materialize.

INOCULATING OURSELVES AGAINST THE 1%'S MIND GAMES

That's why a key step in thwarting the 1% is to personally resist the sway of their manipulative ploys. As Noam Chomsky wrote back in 1989, "Citizens of the democratic societies should undertake a course of intellectual self-defense to protect themselves from manipulation and control, and to lay the basis for more meaningful democracy."[3] Such preventative strategies have never been more crucial than they are today. Of course, implementing them isn't easy because, as we've seen, tapping into our core concerns can give plutocratic appeals the solid ring of truth even though they're as flimsy as a con artist's promises.

But here's some good news. Years of research on the psychology of persuasion shows us how we can hold firm against the propaganda of the predatory class. Of particular relevance is what's called "attitude inoculation."[4] The basic idea comes from the familiar public health approach used to prevent contracting and spreading a dangerous virus. Consider the flu vaccine. When you get a flu shot, you're receiving a modest dose of the actual influenza virus. Your body responds by building up antibodies, which will prove essential in fighting off the full-blown virus if it later attacks as you go about your daily life. A flu shot doesn't always work, but it improves your odds. That's why we're encouraged to get one each year before the flu season begins.

The 1%'s mind games are like a virus, one that can "infect" us with false and destructive beliefs. Here too, inoculation is the best defense. Having been warned that this "plutocratic virus" is prevalent and heading our way, we can become more vigilant and prepare in advance for the onslaught. How can we do that? By confronting and evaluating their appeals in a less threatening and less stressful environment. In doing so, we learn both to recognize them and to build and practice the counterarguments—the "antibodies"—that we'll need when we're later faced with an all-out plutocratic mind game assault. As psychologists Anthony Pratkanis and Elliot Aronson have explained, "We cannot resist propaganda by burying our heads in the sand. The person who is easiest to persuade is the person whose beliefs are based on slogans that have never been seriously challenged and examined."[5]

Political Mind Games was written as just this kind of critical inoculation. In earlier chapters, we've seen exactly what the 1%'s mind games look like, how they're used, why they work, and the ways in which they're flawed and misleading. At the same time, we've also fortified ourselves with evidence, arguments, and rebuttals that limit the influence their appeals can have over us. In short, we're "immunized"—and that means we're now much better positioned to help others fend off these manipulative ploys too.[6]

COUNTERING THE MIND GAMES WITH APPEALS OF OUR OWN

Still, convincing the public that the reign of the 1% is unhealthy and illegitimate—and that it can be overturned—is a difficult undertaking. After all, the plutocrats' mind games are carefully designed to obstruct just this kind of broad awakening. But what's hard isn't impossible, and we've already seen that their ploys can be exposed and debunked as little more than self-serving tales.

At the same time, while it's morally wrong to manipulatively target the public's core concerns to advance narrow interests, our lives do indeed revolve around issues of vulnerability, injustice, distrust, superiority, and helplessness. This means that progressives can and should appeal to these same concerns—but in ways that encourage people to work together for the common good.

In recent years that's exactly what's been happening on a wide range of fronts. "Fight for $15" began as a campaign to raise the minimum wage for fast-food workers, but it's turned into a much broader movement across the country.[7] Spurred on by efforts of the Water Protectors who gathered for months near the Standing Rock Sioux Reservation in North Dakota, activist groups have slowed the fossil fuel industry's assault on the environment,[8] with successes in pushing local bans on fracking and restrictions on offshore drilling.[9] On the education front, the spin of the 1% promoting charter schools and high-stakes testing has encountered stiff resistance, as teachers and parents in Seattle, Chicago, and other communities are objecting to the fraud, waste, and harm associated with many of the corporate reformers' ventures.[10] Trade deals that prioritize the interests and profits of multinational corporations are facing fierce grassroots opposition.[11] And activist efforts that illuminate the moral blight of mass incarceration and discriminatory policing have gained public and political support as well.[12]

It's true that many of these promising developments are facing bitter headwinds from the Trump White House. But the unexpected success of Vermont Senator Bernie Sanders' campaign for the Democratic Party's 2016 presidential nomination and his continuing national popularity are among the encouraging measures of the current political climate. Sanders came up short in his contest against the eventual primary winner, former Secretary of State Hillary Clinton. But his forceful message highlighting the corrupting influences of big money on our elections and our way of life generated tremendous enthusiasm among millions of voters—especially youthful ones—and dread among members of the predatory class who abhor close scrutiny of their actions.[13]

Just as noteworthy are the huge waves of protests and demonstrations that emerged in the weeks and months since Donald Trump's inauguration. The hundreds of thousands of diverse participants in the January 2017 Women's March on Washington—not to mention the many offshoot marches around the country—far outnumbered those who came to the nation's capital to witness the president's swearing-in ceremony a day earlier.[14] Likewise, broad grassroots opposition to Trump's early executive orders—including a travel ban on Muslims seeking entry into the United States[15]—has been intense and, at least for now, seemingly irrepressible.

Many of the contested areas we've explored in the preceding chapters are likely to become increasingly fierce battlegrounds in the 2018 midterm elections and well beyond. With progressive values offering a direct challenge to the plutocrats' psychological appeals, let's take a closer look at how several of these struggles are unfolding.

Minimum Wage Campaigns

Campaigns aimed at increasing the minimum wage present a clear threat to the wishes and selfish interests of the predatory class. In their defense of poverty wages, representatives of the 1% rely on a variety of mind games. They use the Change Is Dangerous and Change Is Unjust mind games to warn that higher pay will imperil opportunities for low-wage workers and unfairly toss many into unemployment lines. (Not true.) They turn to the It's a False Alarm mind game to argue that minimum wage workers are just teenagers doing temporary part-time work. (Also false.) They use we'll-make-you-sorry ploys, threatening to take their factories and warehouses elsewhere if municipalities want to require a living wage. They trot out the They're Misguided and Misinformed mind game, insisting that advocates for low-wage workers don't really understand the economic principles involved. (Again, untrue.) And the most reprehensible among the elitist mouthpieces enlist the No Injustice Here and They're Losers mind games, assuring the public that minimum wage earners are pathetic human beings undeserving of our concern.

Today's plutocrats, with their beholden "think tanks," chambers of commerce, and allied business groups, are accustomed to carrying the day with these messages. But they've encountered strong opposition, and the push for minimum wage hikes has gained strength in many areas across the country. New York and California, home to the two largest cities in the United States, have already enacted laws that will gradually lift their minimum wages to $15 per hour. Smaller municipalities, such as Seattle and Washington, D.C., have moved in the same direction. These developments demonstrate the success that campaigns like the fast-food "Fight for $15" can achieve when they counter the 1%'s appeals.[16] Despite the personal risks involved, low-wage workers organized, engaged in rallies and strikes, drew media attention and then, once in the spotlight, shared hopes and life stories that were very different from how they were portrayed by the plutocrats' manipulative mind games.

There's a compelling progressive narrative to be told here. It too recognizes our core concerns, but in a manner antithetical to the 1%'s self-serving appeals. It reminds us that vulnerability is indeed a pressing issue, because poverty wages subject workers and their families to daily lives fraught with insecurity and uncertainty over whether basic needs can be met and unexpected emergencies can be overcome. It also illuminates where injustice really lies: working long and hard and yet still being unable to make ends meet is profoundly unfair, all the more so when the fruits of one's labors merely add to the enormous wealth of a privileged few. It identifies the rightful targets of our distrust as the CEOs of giant corporations and their political allies who refuse to place the common good over their self-aggrandizing pursuits, and who thereby betray our fundamental social contract. Likewise, this account warns that the greatness or superiority of our country is best measured by the circumstances of those who are struggling to achieve the American Dream—not by the number of greed-driven billionaires who call it home. And finally, it emphasizes that, despite a rigged system designed to mire us in helplessness, a living wage for all Americans isn't out of reach if we organize effectively and refuse to settle for less.

Challenging the Fossil Fuel Industry

Climate change and environmental conservation are another arena in which corporate honchos are facing increasingly stiff resistance from the American public. Mind games from representatives of the fossil fuel industry form a constant drumbeat. They offer it's-a-false-alarm appeals, insisting that concerns about global warming, or fracking, or pipeline leaks are overblown. They use they're-devious-and-dishonest ploys in an effort to discredit the overwhelming scientific consensus that human activity lies at the root of the greenhouse gas problem. They turn to the Change Is Unjust mind game, arguing that many good jobs will be lost if we shift to clean and renewable sources. And they rely on the Resistance Is Futile mind game to persuade activists that opposition to ExxonMobil and other energy behemoths is a fool's errand that's destined to fail. None of these claims withstands careful scrutiny.

Yet, even though oil and gas executives find comfort in the Trump administration's promotion of their denialism, opponents are gaining strength and chalking up victories over rich and powerful profiteers. Defying the industry's aura of invincibility, activists working locally across the country have slowed and sometimes blocked the assault on the environment. They've formed diverse coalitions—like the Standing Rock Sioux and military veterans in opposing the Dakota Access Pipeline—to delay the construction of massive pipelines with protests and legal judgments; they've garnered bans on fracking in numerous municipalities; and they've pushed the scientific community to devote more attention to environmental issues. At the same time, advocates have more broadly succeeded in awakening the public. National polls show that more Americans than ever before are expressing great concern about climate change, and skepticism toward the corporate deniers is growing as well.[17]

Here too there's a progressive narrative to communicate, loudly and directly. Refusing to curtail the destructive consequences of climate change heightens our vulnerability, endangers our national security, and imperils future generations. The fossil fuel industry's persistence in degrading the environment for profit is an injustice with countless innocent victims, especially the economically disadvantaged who are the ones most immediately impacted by the adverse repercussions of pollution, pipeline leaks, and global warming. Through their decades of lies and lack of transparency, these same companies and their political allies have demonstrated that distrust is the appropriate stance for the public as we search for solutions to the crisis. Any claim to superiority as a nation will be repudiated if we ignore science and fail to commit ourselves to respecting and protecting the natural world and its bountiful wonders. Finally, we can—and must—overcome our feelings of personal helplessness, by uniting together to upend the stubborn resolve of greed-driven interests.

Accountability for "War on Terror" Torture

As a third example, I offer a more personal account. Since 2007, I've joined with a small group of colleagues in working to oppose the use of torture in the U.S. "war on terror" and, more specifically, to reset the moral compass of my own profession of psychology.[18]

After the 9/11 attacks, whether drawn by the call of patriotism or lucrative paydays, psychologists became key players in a brutal war machine that methodically broke the bodies and minds of prisoners at Abu Ghraib, Guantánamo Bay, and CIA "black sites."[19] Over time we came to learn—with a mixture of horror and dismay—that their roles were indispensable. Government policies required that a psychologist be on hand whenever a detainee was subjected to torturous techniques like waterboarding. The Bush administration gave a perverse rationale: The presence of health professionals supposedly constituted clear evidence—in the form of expert guidance— that there was no intent to cause severe pain or suffering.

Throughout this period, the leadership of the American Psychological Association—the largest membership organization of psychologists in the world, with a $100 million annual budget—failed to adequately defend psychology's bedrock do-no-harm principles.[20] Instead, key APA leaders—eager to expand the profession's reach, curry favor with Department of Defense bigwigs, and share in the government's war-on-terror largesse—endorsed the participation of psychologists in national security detention and interrogation operations. They did so despite growing allegations that prisoners were being abused and tortured, insisting that psychologists helped to ensure that these operations were "safe, legal, ethical, and effective."[21]

When we called upon the APA to right its ship, our advocacy efforts were met with denials, stonewalling, and personal attacks. Some status quo defenders turned to the It's a Dangerous World mind game, arguing that coercive actions, even extreme ones, were necessary to protect the country from dire threats. Others turned to we're-the-victims ploys, claiming that the APA was being unfairly maligned with unsupported allegations. For example, the association's ethics director dismissed reports of detainee abuse as "long on hearsay and innuendo, short on facts."[22] APA leaders also relied on the They're Misguided and Misinformed mind game; one APA president condemned us as "opportunistic commentators masquerading as scholars."[23] We saw our share of we'll-make-you-sorry appeals as well, with one high-profile military psychologist boasting, "I confronted one of my critics and threatened to shut his mouth for him if he didn't do it himself."[24] All of these arguments disguised the facts and hid the truth from the public.

Our years-long anti-torture campaign, which required that we debunk the APA's mind games, had many steps and relied on aid from a range of allies. First, we educated ourselves about what was happening at the detention sites, how psychologists were involved, and the APA's stance amid growing reports of abuses. Second, we confronted the APA's leadership with disturbing reports and evidence, and we called for greater transparency and justifications regarding the organization's responses to allegations of torture. Third, we worked to debunk the misrepresentations that followed from various APA leaders. Fourth, as evidence of wrongdoing grew stronger, we demanded that the APA acknowledge its misdeeds, pursue accountability, and enact policy reforms to prevent similar failures in the future. Throughout, we built support among professional colleagues and the public, providing them with detailed analyses of the ongoing controversy, with petitions to sign and circulate, and with an understanding of how critical these issues were to the ethical foundations and future of the profession.

Finally, in 2014, the APA leadership grudgingly authorized a comprehensive independent review of its past actions. We weren't surprised when the "Hoffman Report" confirmed our worst suspicions. The lengthy report concluded that the APA—despite growing evidence of detainee mistreatment and the profound ethical conflicts this raised for health professionals—had secretly collaborated with Department of Defense officials in a coordinated plan to promote policies that supported the government's desire for psychologist participation in its detention and interrogation operations. Soon after the report's damning findings were released, and almost 14 years after September 11, 2001, the APA took important steps to formally prohibit its members from participating in national security interrogations. That enlightened policy remains in place today. But opposition to it exists in certain quarters, so vigilance remains a necessity.

For our coalition, the case against torture has always been clear and compelling—and it too can be understood in terms of the same five core concerns. Rather than making us safer, these grotesque methods instead increase our country's vulnerability by contributing to the radicalization of a new generation of impassioned adversaries. Equally important, torture is a profound injustice, an assault on our basic commitment to human decency and dignity. When, as a nation, we engage in such abhorrent practices, we also engender distrust among our own allies, who become uncertain of our guiding principles. In a similar fashion, the resort to cruelty undercuts our aspirations to be a moral authority around the globe. Finally, if we accept the view that torture is the only way to escape helplessness when it comes to keeping us safe, then we fall prey to abandoning the laws and values necessary to preserve a vibrant democracy.

ENGAGING AND UNITING

Many of the 1%'s mind games are direct attempts to discourage the building of a broad-based progressive movement. These appeals warn that change efforts will imperil us, that reforms will be unfair to many Americans, that the opposition are extremists who can't be trusted and don't value our country's traditions, and that climbing aboard isn't worth our time and energy because these efforts are destined to fail anyway. Such claims are self-serving, and it's no surprise that the predatory class is eager to make opposition organizing as difficult as possible. But their ploys do usefully highlight some of the key psychological considerations facing organizers and movements alike.

One basic challenge is that it often takes time and reflection for a person to shift from the role of uncertain bystander to engaged activist. In part, that's because the transition may require some reconsideration of one's identity, as well as adjustments to daily routines. Participation is also easier when a course of action with a reasonable likelihood of success has been identified. But sometimes that path toward political progress can be very hard to find—especially since defenders of extreme inequality do whatever they can to obscure it. Yet another stumbling block is the risk of personal harm—frequently highlighted by the 1%—that's associated with any undertaking where powerful interests are aligned against you. These dangers are diminished when large numbers unite together, but they never entirely disappear.

On the other side of the ledger, however, history shows that a relatively small base of organized and committed individuals can win over and mobilize a disengaged public—if they resist the plutocrats' efforts to make them feel helpless. Mark and Paul Engler, scholars of nonviolent civil resistance, explain that a core group of activists is able to broaden a movement's influence by doing a few key things.[25] First, they reliably show up as visible and energized participants in whatever actions a group undertakes.[26] Second, when election season arrives, they vote for the candidates that demonstrate the greatest support for their particular cause. Third, they embrace opportunities to share their views—with people they know and people they don't—in an effort to persuade them to reconsider their opinions. And fourth, even when such efforts are greeted with disdain within their social or professional networks, these active supporters persist in working to change minds.

At the same time, a fledgling social movement can't succeed if its most dedicated participants marginalize themselves by failing to encourage or find rewarding ways for thousands or millions of less committed individuals to also contribute. Grassroots organizer and author Jonathan Smucker warns that organizers become increasingly isolated if they fail to nurture a broad continuum with multiple levels of involvement. When that happens, they lose the necessary connections with the broader society they hope to change. In the worst case, even those who share the activists' vision may opt not to join "because they are not interested in assimilating into—or being identified with—a self-marginalizing fringe subculture, or because they see a lack of strategy."[27]

As a further obstacle to movement building, today's plutocrats welcome—and encourage with their mind games—divisions within the country over cultural, racial, religious, gender, and class differences. These are barriers to collective action that can be hard to overcome because they lead to counterproductive conflicts, misdirected blame, and scapegoating for tenuous circumstances. When that happens, the 1%, despite being vastly outnumbered, are able to preserve their wealth and power without having to face organized and far-ranging opposition.

This manipulative divide-and-conquer strategy recalls an episode of *The Twilight Zone*, the classic 1960s television series from anti-war and anti-racism activist Rod Serling.[28] When a mysterious roar and flash of light disturb a quiet summer evening, a young boy warns that creatures from outer space have arrived in human form. His notion seems farfetched until lights, phones, and automobiles stop working up and down Maple Street. At first neighbors unite in a search for answers. But soon they're accusing each other of plotting an extraterrestrial invasion. As mob violence erupts, one alien watching from above explains to another, "All we need do is sit back and watch...Their world is full of Maple Streets. And we'll go from one to the other and let them destroy themselves." Narrator Serling offers this warning to viewers at the end:

> The tools of conquest do not necessarily come with bombs and explosions and fallout. There are weapons that are simply thoughts, attitudes, prejudices—to be found only in

the minds of men. For the record, prejudices can kill and suspicion can destroy and a thoughtless frightened search for a scapegoat has a fallout all its own for the children and the children yet unborn.

What's clear is that to overturn and reverse the conquests of the predatory class, we need to build resilient coalitions that transcend our differences. A truly transformative social movement requires us to nurture a common group identity, one that links all people who recognize that our country has arrived at a very dark and disturbing place, and that we must now find our way out together.[29] In this context, one of the most effective unifying forces is shared outrage over extreme inequality. It can join the disadvantaged and oppressed with those who are fortunate enough to have greater security and resources.

When such outrage unites individuals and groups that differ from each other, it creates a superordinate group and breaks down familiar ingroup-outgroup boundaries.[30] In this way, outrage over inequality can merge the direct victims of discrimination with those who find discrimination morally repugnant even though they themselves haven't experienced it. Similarly, this outrage can bring together in common cause people struggling to make ends meet and those who, while better off, are convinced that it's simply wrong for anyone to go without adequate food, shelter, or healthcare.

What also makes shared outrage especially potent is its collective action orientation. It pushes for sustained engagement against the individuals, groups, and institutions that benefit from extreme inequality and seek to perpetuate it. As a political force, shared outrage goes beyond the mere acknowledgement of regrettable circumstances in the world. It insists on explanations for what's wrong, seeks accountability for the wrongdoing, and combats illegitimate attempts to blame victims for their plight. A chorus of voices rising up as one also prevents any single group from becoming an isolated target for condemnation or retribution from powerful entrenched interests.

Ideally, a superordinate group includes people from all stations in life, including some who've obtained tremendous wealth and power. With social networks and material resources that can amplify the message and carry it to other audiences, these individuals can be valuable allies and participants. Even some proud, card-carrying members of the plutocracy may be susceptible to changing their views. Chuck Collins of the Institute for Policy Studies refers to the choice they face as "coming home." As he describes it, "We need the wealthy to opt back in to our communities, not from a charitable arm's-length distance but up close and personal. This is the pathway toward a truly more egalitarian society."[31]

The nonpartisan Moral Monday movement is among the encouraging examples of encompassing coalitions driven by outrage over injustice and inequality. Founded by North Carolina NAACP president Reverend William Barber II, the group has held regular demonstrations—including acts of civil disobedience—to protest assaults on voter rights, workers' rights, and civil rights.[32] Barber has explained the organizing approach as one of building "fusion coalitions" aimed at countering the 1%'s divide-and-conquer strategy: "If you have a moral narrative, say economics are moral, budgets are moral, education is moral...and then you talk about the impact on real people...people see their common identity."[33]

"THE FIERCE URGENCY OF NOW"

Replacing the greed-driven agenda of the 1% with a moral agenda that benefits everyone is a daunting project, particularly in the current political climate. Beyond their extraordinary wealth, today's plutocrats have a champion in the White House, indebted politicians and high-paid lobbyists throughout Washington, and high-profile media outlets and spokespersons. As we've seen, all of these forces work to inundate us with elaborate and expensive propaganda campaigns that frame issues to the plutocrats' liking, shape the public's perceptions of right and wrong, and undermine prospects for solidarity among those working for change. But despite it all, the vision of a more humane, more caring, and more equal society still animates most Americans.

Yet this particular political moment isn't unique after all. Back when Trump was just promoting himself as a real estate mogul and entertainer, other plutocracy-enabling leaders—in both major parties—were already establishing their snake-oil bona fides, using psychological mind games to hustle an insufficiently skeptical public. In some ways, then, Trump's move to the nation's capital simply reinvigorated and reinforced the well-entrenched predatory playbook that was already enriching the few at the expense of the public interest. Senator Elizabeth Warren summarized the situation well at a post-election Democratic Party retreat in early 2017:

> Our moment of crisis didn't begin with the election of Donald Trump...We were already in crisis because for years and years and years, Washington has worked just great for the rich and the powerful, but far too often, it hasn't worked for anyone else. We were already in a moment of crisis because for years and years and years, the economy has worked just great for those who have already made it, but far too often, it hasn't worked for anyone else. We were already in a moment of crisis because for years and years and years, we've been living in a nation where opportunity is quietly disappearing. A country that is giving fewer and fewer kids a real chance to succeed.[34]

At the same time, there's no denying that Trump has brought to the White House something worse than the typical one-per-center: a toxic brew of bigotry, belligerence, and brutality. The significance of this is far-reaching. Those who are now disadvantaged—especially people of color and other marginalized groups—face even tougher times as scapegoating has intensified and misdirected hostility has become increasingly commonplace. That's why collective resistance efforts must combine unwavering support for those most immediately at risk with a clear recognition of what we all share: voices that have grown weaker, opportunities that have grown scarcer, and children whose futures have grown dimmer.

Ultimately it isn't hard to understand that extreme concentrations of wealth and power are incompatible with democracy and the good society. But as I've argued here, what's less well understood is exactly *how* today's plutocrats have leveraged specific psychological appeals to achieve their aims. By ruthlessly exploiting our concerns about vulnerability, injustice, distrust, superiority, and helplessness—concerns that should serve as guideposts for improving the general welfare—they've succeeded in advancing their own narrow interests while blocking effective opposition to their rule. Exposing and countering these destructive mind games therefore becomes more urgent every day.

In this crucial work, progressives must bring these same concerns to the forefront—but in ways that illuminate and advance the common good. This means showing how the real vulnerabilities that Americans experience every day include the perils of economic insecurity, inadequate healthcare, and destruction of the environment. It means calling attention to daily injustices, whether that's working hard for less than a living wage or facing discrimination in housing, education, or law enforcement. It means making the case that a distrustful posture can help protect us from outside threats, but not if it leads to unprincipled militarism and the abandonment of international alliances—and that distrust of concentrated and unfettered power at home is equally indispensable.

So too, it means taking pride in this country's accomplishments and democratic aspirations, not as a pedestal for self-righteousness but as the inspiration to put our national strength to good purpose, whether the goal is eradicating hunger or protecting human rights. Finally, it means empowering the American people—including the many suffering from helplessness, hopelessness, or apathy—by enlisting their efforts in creating a reinvigorated progressive movement, one that gives all of us a meaningful voice in the political process. The challenge awaits us.

ACKNOWLEDGMENTS

For many years, I've been the fortunate beneficiary of insights and inspiration from diverse communities of scholars and social justice advocates. My experiences at the University of Pennsylvania's Solomon Asch Center for Study of Ethnopolitical Conflict were essential in developing the psychological framework I present in *Political Mind Games*. My engagement with fellow members of Psychologists for Social Responsibility and the Coalition for an Ethical Psychology have helped me to better understand and appreciate the challenges and rewards of collective efforts aimed at progressive change.

Numerous friends and colleagues have been very generous as I've worked on this project. For their time, feedback, and encouragement, I am particularly grateful to Jean Maria Arrigo, Trudy Bond, Yosef Brody, Lina Cherfas, Michael Feuer, Arancha Garcia del Soto, Malik Isasis, Deborah Levenson, Ian Lustick, Kathie Malley-Morrison, Barry Mann, Anthony Marsella, Julianne McKinney, Diane Perlman, Ken Pope, Gene Richardson, Stephen Soldz, and Jeffrey Winkler.

I am also deeply indebted to my family—especially my wife, Judy; my children, Josh, Ben, and Sarah; and their partners, Aaron, Amy, and Max—for a rare combination of steadfast support and uncommon insight.

The views expressed in *Political Mind Games*, along with any errors, are solely my own.

NOTES

CHAPTER 1
America's Plutocrats: Who They Are and How They Succeed

1   Jesse Bricker, Lisa J. Dettling, Alice Henriques, Joanne W. Hsu, Lindsay Jacobs, Kevin B. Moore, Sarah Pack, John Sabelhaus, Jeffrey Thompson, and Richard A. Windle, "Changes in U.S. Family Finances from 2013 to 2016: Evidence from the Survey of Consumer Finances," *Federal Reserve Bulletin*, September 2017, https://www.federalreserve.gov/publications/files/scf17.pdf; Emmanuel Saez and Gabriel Zucman, "Wealth Inequality in the United States since 1913: Evidence from Capitalized Income Tax Data," National Bureau of Economic Research, October 2014, http://eml.berkeley.edu/~saez/saez-zucmanNBER14wealth.pdf; Emmanuel Saez, "U.S. Top One Percent of Income Earners Hit New High in 2015 Amid Strong Economic Growth," Washington Center for Equitable Growth, July 1, 2016, http://equitablegrowth .org/research-analysis/u-s-top-one-percent-of-income-earners -hit-new-high-in-2015-amid-strong-economic-growth/; Thomas Piketty, *Capital in the Twenty-First Century* (Cambridge, MA: Harvard University Press, 2014); Thomas Piketty, Emmanuel Saez, and Gabriel Zucman, "Distributional National Accounts: Methods and Estimates for the United States," Washington Center for Equitable Growth, December 2016, http://cdn.equitablegrowth.org /wp-content/uploads/2017/02/24163023/120716-WP-distributional -national-accounts.pdf; Chuck Collins and Josh Hoxie, "Billionaire Bonanza: The Forbes 400 and the Rest of Us," Institute for Policy Studies, December 2015, http://www.ips-dc.org/wp-content /uploads/2015/12/Billionaire-Bonanza-The-Forbes-400-and-the -Rest-of-Us-Dec1.pdf; Dylan Matthews, "You're Not Imagining It: The Rich Really Are Hoarding Economic Growth," *Vox*, August 8, 2017, https://www.vox.com/policy-and-politics/2017/8/8/16112368 /piketty-saez-zucman-income-growth-inequality-stagnation-chart.

2   Josh Bivens, "Inequality, Exhibit A: Walmart and the Wealth
    of American Families," Economic Policy Institute, July 17, 2012,
    http://www.epi.org/blog/inequality-exhibit-wal-mart-wealth-american/.

3   Lawrence Mishel and Alyssa Davis, "CEO Pay Continues to Rise as
    Typical Workers Are Paid Less," Economic Policy Institute, June 12,
    2014, http://s1.epi.org/files/2014/ceo-pay-continues-to-rise.pdf.

4   Richard Wilkinson and Kate Pickett, *The Spirit Level: Why Greater
    Equality Makes Societies Stronger* (New York: Bloomsbury Press,
    2009); Joseph E. Stiglitz, *The Price of Inequality: How Today's Divided
    Society Endangers Our Future* (New York: W.W. Norton, 2012); Robert
    Frank, *Falling behind: How Rising Inequality Harms the Middle Class*
    (Oakland, CA: University of California Press, 2007); David Cay Johnston,
    ed., *Divided: The Perils of Our Growing Inequality* (New York: New
    Press, 2014); Christopher Hayes, *Twilight of the Elites: America after
    Meritocracy* (New York: Crown Publishers, 2012); Jeff Faux, *The Servant
    Economy: Where America's Elite Is Sending the Middle Class* (Hoboken,
    NJ: John Wiley & Sons, 2012); Goran Therborn, *The Killing Fields of
    Inequality* (Cambridge, UK: Polity Press, 2013); Hedrick Smith, *Who
    Stole the American Dream?* (New York: Random House, 2012); Anthony
    B. Atkinson, *Inequality: What Can Be Done?* (Cambridge, MA: Harvard
    University Press, 2015); Dean Baker, *Rigged: How Globalization and the
    Rules of the Modern Economy Were Structured to Make the Rich Richer*
    (Washington, DC: Center for Economic and Policy Research, 2016).

5   Pew Research Center, "Most See Inequality Growing, but Partisans
    Differ over Solutions," January 23, 2014, http://www.people-press
    .org/2014/01/23/most-see-inequality-growing-but-partisans-differ
    -over-solutions/; New York Times/CBS News Poll, "Americans' Views
    on Income Inequality and Workers' Rights," June 3, 2015, http://www
    .nytimes.com/interactive/2015/06/03/business/income-inequality
    -workers-rights-international-trade-poll.html; Pew Research Center,
    "Most Say Government Policies Since Recession Have Done Little to
    Help Middle Class, Poor," March 2015, http://www.people-press.org
    /files/2015/03/03-04-15-Economy-release.pdf.

6   Michael I. Norton and Dan Ariely, "Building a Better America—One
    Wealth Quintile at a Time," *Perspectives on Psychological Science* 6
    (2011): 9-12.

7   David Callahan and Mijin Cha, "Stacked Deck: How the Dominance
    of Politics by the Affluent & Business Undermines Economic Mobility
    in America," Demos, 2013, http://www.demos.org/sites/default/files
    /publications/Demos-Stacked-Deck.pdf; Benjamin I. Page, Larry M.
    Bartels, and Jason Seawright, "Democracy and the Policy Preferences
    of Wealthy Americans," *Perspectives on Politics* 11 (2013): 51-73.

8   John Kenneth Galbraith, *The Good Society: The Humane Agenda*
    (New York: Houghton Mifflin, 1996); Robert N. Bellah, Richard Madsen,
    William M. Sullivan, Ann Swidler, and Steven M. Tipton: *The Good
    Society* (New York: Knopf, 1991).

9   Martin Gilens and Benjamin I. Page, "Testing Theories of American
    Politics: Elites, Interest Groups, and Average Citizens," *Perspectives
    on Politics* 12 (2014): 564-581.

10 Edward S. Herman and Noam Chomsky, *Manufacturing Consent: The
    Political Economy of the Mass Media* (New York: Pantheon Books, 1988).

11 Adam Smith, *Wealth of Nations* (New York: Modern Library Edition,
    1994).

12 James K. Galbraith, "The Predator State: Enron, Tyco, WorldCom...
    and the U.S. Government?" *Mother Jones*, May/June 2006,
    http://www.motherjones.com/politics/2006/05/predator-state.

13 Nathan Schneider, "From Occupy Wall Street to Occupy Everywhere,"
    The Nation, October 12, 2011, http://www.thenation.com/article/occupy
    -wall-street-occupy-everywhere/; Jonathan Matthew Smucker, *Hegemony
    How-To: A Roadmap for Radicals* (Oakland, CA: AK Press, 2017).

14 Jane Mayer, *Dark Money: The Hidden History of the Billionaires behind
    the Rise of the Radical Right* (New York: Knopf, 2016); G. William
    Domhoff, *Who Rules America: The Triumph of the Corporate Rich* (New
    York: McGraw-Hill Education, 2013); Nomi Prins, *All the Presidents'
    Bankers: The Hidden Alliances That Drive American Power* (New York:
    Nation Books, 2014); Charles H. Ferguson, *Predator Nation: Corporate
    Criminals, Political Corruption, and the Hijacking of America* (New
    York: Crown Business, 2012); David Sirota, *Hostile Takeover: How Big
    Money & Corruption Conquered Our Government—and How We Take
    It Back* (New York: Crown Publishers, 2006); Kenneth P. Vogel, *Big
    Money: 2.5 Billion Dollars, One Suspicious Vehicle, and a Pimp—on
    the Trail of the Ultra-Rich Hijacking American Politics* (New York:
    Public Affairs, 2014); Bill Moyers, "How Wall Street Occupied America,"
    The Nation, November 2, 2011, http://www.thenation.com/article/how
    -wall-street-occupied-america/.

15 Matt Rocheleau, "Trump's Cabinet Picks So Far Worth a Combined
    $13B," *Boston Globe*, December 20, 2016, https://www.bostonglobe.com
    /metro/2016/12/20/trump-cabinet-picks-far-are-worth-combined
    /XvAJmHCgkHhO3lSxgIKvRM/story.html.

16 Derek Wallbank, "Millionaires' Club in Congress Exceeds Half of
    Members," *Bloomberg*, January 10, 2014, https://www.bloomberg.com
    /news/articles/2014-01-10/millionaires-club-in-u-s-congress-is-the
    -new-50-percent.

17 Christopher Hayes, *Twilight of the Elites: America after Meritocracy*
    (New York: Crown Publishers, 2012).

18 Chrystia Freeland, *Plutocrats: The Rise of the New Global Super-Rich and
    the Fall of Everyone Else* (New York: Penguin, 2012); James K. Galbraith,
    *The Predator State: How Conservatives Abandoned the Free Market and
    Why Liberals Should Too* (New York: The Free Press, 2008); Paul Street,
    They Rule: The 1% vs. Democracy (New York: Routledge, 2016); Barbara
    Ehrenreich, *This Land Is Their Land: Reports from a Divided Nation*
    (New York: Metropolitan Books, 2008).

19   Chuck Collins, *Born on Third Base: A One Percenter Makes the Case for Tackling Inequality, Bringing Wealth Home, and Committing to the Common Good* (White River Junction, VT: Chelsea Green, 2016).

20   Erica Payne and the Patriotic Millionaires, "Renegotiating Power and Money in America," 2015, http://patrioticmillionaires.org/book /powerandmoney.pdf.

21   Sam Pizzigati, *The Rich Don't Always Win* (New York: Seven Stories, 2012).

22   Roy J. Eidelson and Judy I. Eidelson, "Dangerous Ideas: Five Beliefs That Propel Groups toward Conflict," *American Psychologist* 58 (2003): 182-192.

23   Sean Ransom, "Donald Trump's Brilliant Manipulation of the Science of Group Conflict," *Sociological Images*, October 12, 2016, https://thesocietypages.org/socimages/2016/10/12/trumps-brilliant -manipulation-of-the-science-of-group-conflict/.

24   Associated Press, "Read Donald Trump's Speech to the Republican Convention," *Fortune*, July 22, 2016, http://www.politico.com/story /2016/07/full-transcript-donald-trump-nomination-acceptance -speech-at-rnc-225974.

25   Washington Post, "Full Text: Donald Trump Announces a Presidential Bid," June 16, 2015, https://www.washingtonpost.com/news/post-politics /wp/2015/06/16/full-text-donald-trump-announces-a-presidential-bid/.

26   Donald J. Trump, *Great Again: How to Fix Our Crippled America* (New York: Threshold Editions, 2016).

27   Michael E. Miller, "Donald Trump on a Protester: 'I'd Like to Punch Him in the Face,'" *Washington Post*, February 23, 2016, https://www .washingtonpost.com/news/morning-mix/wp/2016/02/23 /donald-trump-on-protester-id-like-to-punch-him-in-the-face/.

28   Hadas Gold, "Donald Trump: We're Going to 'Open Up' Libel Laws," *Politico*, February 26, 2016, http://www.politico.com/blogs /on-media/2016/02/donald-trump-libel-laws-219866.

29   Washington Post, "Full Text: Donald Trump Announces a Presidential Bid," June 16, 2015, https://www.washingtonpost.com/news/post-politics /wp/2015/06/16/full-text-donald-trump-announces-a-presidential-bid/.

30   Associated Press, "Read Donald Trump's Speech to the Republican Convention," *Fortune*, July 22, 2016, http://www.politico.com/story /2016/07/full-transcript-donald-trump-nomination-acceptance -speech-at-rnc-225974.

31   Robert Farley, "Trump's Bogus Voter Fraud Claims," FactCheck.org, October 19, 2016, http://www.factcheck.org/2016/10/trumps-bogus -voter-fraud-claims/.

32 MSNBC, "MSNBC's Chris Jansing Interviews Donald Trump One-on-One in Wisconsin," April 5, 2016, http://info.msnbc.com/_news/2016/04/05/35354489-msnbcs-chris-jansing-interviews-donald-trump-one-on-one-in-wisconsin.

33 Donald J. Trump, *Great Again: How to Fix Our Crippled America* (New York: Threshold Editions, 2016).

34 Fox News, "Donald Trump Lays Out Foreign and Domestic Strategies," *O'Reilly Factor*, September 9, 2015, http://www.foxnews.com/transcript/2015/09/09/donald-trump-lays-out-foreign-and-domestic-strategies/.

35 Maggie Haberman and Richard Perez-Penanov, "Donald Trump Sets Off a Furor with Call to Register Muslims in the U.S.," *New York Times*, November 20, 2015, http://www.nytimes.com/2015/11/21/us/politics/donald-trump-sets-off-a-furor-with-call-to-register-muslims-in-the-us.html.

36 Associated Press, "Read Donald Trump's Speech to the Republican Convention," *Fortune*, July 22, 2016, http://fortune.com/2016/07/22/read-donald-trumps-speech-to-the-republican-convention/.

37 Donald J. Trump, *Great Again: How to Fix Our Crippled America* (New York: Threshold Editions, 2016).

38 Associated Press, "Read Donald Trump's Speech to the Republican Convention," *Fortune*, July 22, 2016, http://fortune.com/2016/07/22/read-donald-trumps-speech-to-the-republican-convention/.

39 Donald J. Trump, *Great Again: How to Fix Our Crippled America* (New York: Threshold Editions, 2016).

40 Emily Greenhouse, "Donald Trump: 'I'm the Most Successful Person Ever to Run for the Presidency,'" *Bloomberg Politics*, June 1, 2015, http://www.bloomberg.com/politics/articles/2015-06-01/donald-trump-i-m-the-most-successful-person-ever-to-run-for-the-presidency-.

41 Donald J. Trump, *Great Again: How to Fix Our Crippled America* (New York: Threshold Editions, 2016).

42 Time, "Donald Trump Explains All," August 20, 2015, http://time.com/4003734/donald-trump-interview-transcript/.

43 Associated Press, "Read Donald Trump's Speech to the Republican Convention," *Fortune*, July 22, 2016, http://fortune.com/2016/07/22/read-donald-trumps-speech-to-the-republican-convention/.

44 Ian Schwartz, "Trump: 'We Will Have So Much Winning If I Get Elected That You May Get Bored with Winning,'" *Real Clear Politics*, September 9, 2015, http://www.realclearpolitics.com/video/2015/09/09/trump_we_will_have_so_much_winning_if_i_get_elected_that_you_may_get_bored_with_winning.html.

45 Associated Press, "Read Donald Trump's Speech to the Republican Convention," *Fortune*, July 22, 2016, http://fortune.com/2016/07/22/read-donald-trumps-speech-to-the-republican-convention/.

46 Los Angeles Times, "Donald Trump's Complete Convention Speech, Annotated," July 21, 2016, http://www.latimes.com/politics/la-na -pol-donald-trump-convention-speech-transcript-20160721-snap -htmlstory.html.

47 Donald J. Trump (@realDonaldTrump), "Crime is out of control, and rapidly getting worse. Look what is going on in Chicago and our inner cities. Not good!" Twitter, July 12, 2016, 7:58 a.m., https://twitter.com/realdonaldtrump/status/752834632907943936.

48 CNN Press Room, "Donald Trump Calls into SOTU, Says What Hillary Clinton Has Done 'Is Criminal,'" July 26, 2015, http://cnnpressroom.blogs.cnn.com/2015/07/26/donald-trump -calls-into-sotu-says-what-hillary-clinton-has-done-is-criminal/.

49 Robert B. Cialdini, *Influence: The Psychology of Persuasion* (New York: William Morrow, 1984); Anthony Pratkanis and Elliot Aronson, *Age of Propaganda: The Everyday Use and Abuse of Persuasion* (New York: W. H. Freeman & Company, 1992); Garth S. Jowett and Victoria O'Donnell, *Propaganda & Persuasion* (Thousand Oaks, CA: Sage Publications, 2012); Richard M. Perloff, *The Dynamics of Persuasion: Communication and Attitudes in the 21st Century* (New York: Lawrence Erlbaum Associates, 2008); Jason Stanley, *How Propaganda Works* (Princeton, NJ: Princeton University Press, 2015); Bryant Welch, *State of Confusion: Political Manipulation and the Assault on the American Mind* (New York: St. Martin's Press, 2008).

50 Richard E. Petty and John T. Cacioppo, "The Elaboration Likelihood Model of Persuasion," *Advances in Experimental Social Psychology* 19 (1986): 123-205; Shelly Chaiken, Akiva Liberman, and Alice H. Eagly, "Heuristic and Systematic Information Processing within and beyond the Persuasion Context," in *Unintended Thought*, eds. James S. Uleman and John Bargh (New York: Guilford Press, 1989), 212-252.

51 Joseph Heller, *Catch-22: A Novel* (New York: Simon & Schuster, 1994).

52 Melanie C. Green, Jennifer Garst, Timothy C. Brock, and Sungeun Chung, "Fact Versus Fiction Labeling: Persuasion Parity despite Heightened Scrutiny of Fact," *Media Psychology* 8 (2006): 267-285; Melanie C. Green and Timothy C. Brock, "The Role of Transportation in the Persuasiveness of Public Narratives," *Journal of Personality and Social Psychology* 79 (2000): 701-721.

53 Garth S. Jowett and Victoria O'Donnell, *Propaganda & Persuasion* (Thousand Oaks, CA: Sage Publications, 2012).

CHAPTER 2
Vulnerability Mind Games: Exploiting Our Fears and Insecurities

1   Henry A. Wallace, "Tell the People Who We Are," September 10, 1948, http://wgf.org/henry-wallace/.

2   Gustave M. Gilbert, *Nuremberg Diary* (New York: Farrar, Straus & Company, 1947).

3   Norman Solomon, *War Made Easy: How Presidents and Pundits Keep Spinning Us to Death* (Hoboken, NJ: John Wiley & Sons, 2005); Roy J. Eidelson, "How Leaders Promote War by Exploiting Our Core Concerns," *Peace Review* 25 (2013): 219-226.

4   White House Archives, "Vice President Speaks at VFW 103rd National Convention," August 26, 2002, http://georgewbush -whitehouse.archives.gov/news/releases/2002/08/20020826.html.

5   White House Archives, "President Bush Outlines Iraq Threat," October 7, 2002, http://georgewbush-whitehouse.archives.gov/news /releases/2002/10/20021007-8.html.

6   Karen DeYoung, "A Rhetorical Weave on Iraq," *Washington Post*, December 5, 2002, https://www.washingtonpost.com/archive/politics /2002/12/05/a-rhetorical-weave-on-iraq/b71bba50-c79f-43e2-ae7e -ff630143d345/.

7   Sheldon Rampton and John Stauber, *Weapons of Mass Deception: The Uses of Propaganda in Bush's War on Iraq* (New York: Tarcher/ Penguin, 2003).

8   Dick Cheney, "Sixth Annual Barbara K. Olson Memorial Lecture," National Lawyers Convention, November 17, 2006, http://www.fed -soc.org/library/doclib/20080314_OlsonLectCheney.pdf.

9   White House Archives, "President Bush Discusses the Iraq War Supplemental," April 16, 2007, http://georgewbush-whitehouse .archives.gov/news/releases/2007/04/20070416.html.

10 John Schwarz, "It Didn't Just Start Now: John Kelly Has Always Been a Hard-Right Bully," *The Intercept*, October 21, 2017, https://theintercept .com/2017/10/21/it-didnt-just-start-now-john-kelly-has-always-been -a-hard-right-bully/.

11 Associated Press, "CIA's Final Report: No WMD Found in Iraq," April 25, 2005, http://www.nbcnews.com/id/7634313/ns/world_news -mideast_n_africa/t/cias-final-report-no-wmd-found-iraq/.

12 Fairleigh Dickinson University, "Ignorance, Partisanship Drive False Beliefs about Obama, Iraq," PublicMind Poll, January 2015, http://publicmind.fdu.edu/2015/false/final.pdf.

13   Program on International Policy Attitudes, "The American Public on the 9/11 Decade: A Study of American Public Opinion," September 8, 2011, https://www.brookings.edu/wp-content/uploads/2016/06/0908 _opinion_poll_telhami.pdf.

14   Douglas L. Kriner and Francis X. Shen, *The Casualty Gap: The Causes and Consequences of American Wartime Inequalities* (New York: Oxford University Press, 2010).

15   John Tirman, "Bush's War Totals," *The Nation*, January 28, 2009, https://www.thenation.com/article/bushs-war-totals/.

16   Matthias Gebauer and Holger Stark, "Ex-US Intelligence Chief on Islamic State's Rise: 'We Were Too Dumb,'" *Spiegel Online International*, November 29, 2015, http://www.spiegel.de/international/world/former -us-intelligence-chief-discusses-development-of-is-a-1065131.html; Ishaan Tharoor, "Iraq's Crisis: Don't Forget the 2003 U.S. Invasion," *Washington Post*, June 16, 2014, https://www.washingtonpost.com /news/worldviews/wp/2014/06/16/iraqs-crisis-dont-forget-the-2003 -u-s-invasion/.

17   Daniel Trotta, "Iraq War Costs U.S. More Than $2 Trillion: Study," *Reuters*, March 14, 2013, http://www.reuters.com/article/2013/03/14 /us-iraq-war-anniversary-idUSBRE92D0PG20130314; Amy Belasco, "The Cost of Iraq, Afghanistan, and Other Global War on Terror Operations since 9/11," Congressional Research Service, December 8, 2014, http://www.fas.org/sgp/crs/natsec/RL33110.pdf.

18   William D. Hartung, "The Military-Industrial Complex Revisited: Shifting Patterns of Military Contracting in the Post-9/11 Period," Watson Institute for International and Public Affairs at Brown University, 2011, http://watson.brown.edu/costsofwar/files/cow/imce /papers/2011/The%20Military-Industrial%20Complex%20Revisited .pdf; William D. Hartung, *Prophets of War: Lockheed Martin and the Making of the Military-Industrial Complex* (New York: Nation Books, 2011); Andrew J. Bacevich, *America's War for the Greater Middle East: A Military History* (New York: Random House, 2016).

19   Mike Lofgren, *The Deep State: The Fall of the Constitution and the Rise of a Shadow Government* (New York: Viking, 2016).

20   Lee Fang, "Jeb Bush, Hosted by Defense Contractor-Backed Group, Calls Iraq War 'a Pretty Good Deal,'" *The Intercept*, August 13, 2015, https://firstlook.org/theintercept/2015/08/13/jeb-bush-hosted -defense-contractor-backed-group-calls-iraq-war-pretty-good-deal/.

21   White House, "Remarks by President Trump at Swearing-In of Attorney General Sessions," February 9, 2017, https://www.whitehouse.gov/the -press-office/2017/02/09/remarks-president-trump-swearing-attorney -general-sessions.

22   Jeff Nesbit, "We Have Lost the War on Drugs," *U.S. News & World Report*, December 21, 2015, http://www.usnews.com/news/blogs/at-the-edge/articles/2015-12-21/the-war-on-drugs-is-over-and-we-lost; Graham Boyd, "The Drug War Is the New Jim Crow," NACLA Report on the Americas, July/August 2001, https://www.aclu.org/other/drug-war-new-jim-crow; Christopher J. Coyne and Abigail R. Hall, "Four Decades and Counting: The Continued Failure of the War on Drugs," Cato Institute, April 12, 2017, https://www.cato.org/publications/policy-analysis/four-decades-counting-continued-failure-war-drugs; Altaf Rahamatulla, "The War on Drugs Has Failed. What's Next?" Ford Foundation, March 23, 2017, https://www.fordfoundation.org/ideas/equals-change-blog/posts/the-war-on-drugs-has-failed-what-s-next/.

23   Ronald Reagan, "Radio Address to the Nation on Economic Growth and the War on Drugs," October 8, 1988, https://www.reaganlibrary.archives.gov/archives/speeches/1988/100888a.htm.

24   CBS News, "War on Drugs Aids War on Terror," December 14, 2001, http://www.cbsnews.com/news/bush-war-on-drugs-aids-war-on-terror/.

25   Department of Justice, "Attorney General Jeff Sessions Delivers Remarks on Efforts to Combat Violent Crime and Restore Public Safety before Federal, State and Local Law Enforcement," March 15, 2017, https://www.justice.gov/opa/speech/attorney-general-jeff-sessions-delivers-remarks-efforts-combat-violent-crime-and-restore.

26   Alison Durkee, "Jeff Sessions and Marijuana: What Has Trump's Attorney General Said about Legal Pot?" Mic.com, December 21, 2016, https://mic.com/articles/162999/jeff-sessions-and-marijuana-what-has-trump-s-attorney-general-said-about-legal-pot.

27   Jonathan Stray, "FAQ: What You Need to Know about the NSA's Surveillance Programs," *ProPublica*, June 27, 2013, https://www.propublica.org/article/nsa-data-collection-faq; Spencer Ackerman; "Ron Wyden: NSA Review Panel Offers 'Substantial, Meaningful Reforms,'" *Guardian*, December 18, 2013, https://www.theguardian.com/world/2013/dec/18/nsa-review-panel-reform-ron-wyden.

28   Transcript, "Hearing on the Nomination of Gen. Michael Hayden to Be Director of the CIA," *Washington Post*, May 18, 2006, http://www.washingtonpost.com/wp-dyn/content/article/2006/05/18/AR2006051800823.html.

29   Peter Baker and David E. Sanger, "Obama Calls Surveillance Programs Legal and Limited," *New York Times*, June 7, 2013, http://www.nytimes.com/2013/06/08/us/national-security-agency-surveillance.html.

30   Eric Bradner, "Trump: 'Err on the Side of Security,'" *CNN*, December 1, 2015, http://www.cnn.com/2015/12/01/politics/donald-trump-nsa-surveillance/index.html.

31 Joseph Cox, "How Private Contractors Are Profiting from Government Surveillance," *Vice News*, February 11, 2014, http://www.vice.com/en_uk /read/nsa-private-companies-profit-from-surveillance; Matthew Rosenberg, "At Booz Allen, a Vast U.S. Spy Operation, Run for Private Profit," *New York Times*, October 6, 2016, http://www.nytimes.com /2016/10/07/us/booz-allen-hamilton-nsa.html; Kenneth Lipp, "AT&T Is Spying on Americans for Profit," *Daily Beast*, October 25, 2016, http://www.thedailybeast.com/atandt-is-spying-on-americans-for-profit.

32 Andrea Peterson, "Obama Can't Point to a Single Time the NSA Call Records Program Prevented a Terrorist Attack," *Washington Post*, December 23, 2013, https://www.washingtonpost.com/news/the-switch /wp/2013/12/23/obama-cant-point-to-a-single-time-the-nsa-call -records-program-prevented-a-terrorist-attack/; Justin Elliott and Theodoric Meyer, "No Evidence behind Broad Claims of NSA's Effectiveness," *Progressive*, October 23, 2013, http://progressive.org /dispatches/evidence-behind-broad-claims-nsa-s-effectiveness/.

33 Carol Rose and Kade Crockford, "'Keep Fear Alive': A Misguided Call to Double Down On Localized Secret Policing," WBUR Cognoscenti, February 3, 2015, http://www.wbur.org/cognoscenti/2015/02/03 /domestic-spying-homeland-security-carol-rose-kade-crockford.

34 U.S. House of Representatives Committee on the Budget, "Paul Ryan Video Release on Surpassing $15 Trillion in National Debt," November 16, 2011, http://budget.house.gov/news/documentsingle.aspx ?DocumentID=269248.

35 U.S. Department of Defense News, "Debt Is Biggest Threat to National Security, Chairman Says," September 22, 2011, http://archive.defense .gov/news/newsarticle.aspx?id=65432.

36 Jamie Weinstein, "Exclusive: Bowles on Ryan: 'I'm Not Going to Act Like I Don't Like Him,'" *Daily Caller*, August 14, 2012, http://dailycaller .com/2012/08/14/exclusive-bowles-on-ryan-im-not-going-to-act-like- i-dont-like-him/.

37 Mary Bottari, "Pete Peterson's Puppet Populists," *The Nation*, February 20, 2013, http://www.thenation.com/article/173018/pete-petersons -puppet-populists.

38 Dean Baker, "Patently Absurd Logic on Budget Deficits and Debt," *Huffington Post*, April 18, 2016, http://www.huffingtonpost.com/dean -baker/patently-absurd-logic-on_b_9724338.html; Paul Krugman, "Debt Is Good," *New York Times*, August 21, 2015, https://www.nytimes .com/2015/08/21/opinion/paul-krugman-debt-is-good-for-the -economy.html; Jeff Spross, "Don't Worry about the Rising National Debt. Seriously, Just Don't." *The Week*, January 29, 2015, http:// theweek.com/articles/536307/dont-worry-aboutthe-rising-national- debt-seriously-just-don't.

39 Jeff Faux, *The Servant Economy: Where America's Elite Is Sending the Middle Class* (Hoboken, NJ: John Wiley & Sons, 2012); Dean Baker, *Plunder and Blunder: The Rise and Fall of the Bubble Economy* (Sausalito, CA: PoliPoint Press, 2009).

40 Josh Eidelson, "Starbucks Tycoon Bullies the Baristas," *The Nation*, January 30, 2013, https://www.thenation.com/article/starbucks-tycoon-bullies-baristas/.

41 Dean Baker and David Rosnick, "The Impact of Social Security Cuts on Retiree Income," Center for Economic and Policy Research, July 2010, http://www.cepr.net/documents/publications/ss-2010-07.pdf.

42 Frank Newport, "Many Americans Doubt They Will Get Social Security Benefits," Gallup, August 13, 2015, http://www.gallup.com/poll/184580/americans-doubt-social-security-benefits.aspx.

43 Robert Reich, "Budget Baloney: Why Social Security Isn't a Problem for 26 Years, and the Best Way to Fix It Permanently," *Huffington Post*, February 16, 2011, http://www.huffingtonpost.com/robert-reich/budget-baloney-why-social_b_824331.html; Dean Baker, "Social Security Trustees Report without the Hysteria," *Huffington Post*, July 27, 2015, http://www.huffingtonpost.com/dean-baker/social-security-trustees_b_7883640.html; Dean Baker and Mark Weisbrot, *Social Security: The Phony Crisis* (Chicago, IL: University of Chicago Press, 1999); James K. Galbraith, *The Predator State: How Conservatives Abandoned the Free Market and Why Liberals Should Too* (New York: The Free Press, 2008).

44 Sarah Anderson and Scott Klinger, "Platinum-Plated Pensions: The Retirement Fortunes of CEOs Who Want to Cut Your Social Security," Institute for Policy Studies, November 19, 2013, http://www.ips-dc.org/wp-content/uploads/2013/11/Platinum-Plated_Pensions.pdf; Sarah Anderson and Scott Klinger, "A Tale of Two Retirements," Institute for Policy Studies, October 28, 2015, http://foreffectivegov.org/files/two-retirements.pdf.

45 Daniel Kahneman and Amos Tversky, "Prospect Theory: An Analysis of Decision under Risk," *Econometrica* 47 (1979): 263-291.

46 Scott Eidelman and Christian S. Crandall, "A Psychological Advantage for the Status Quo," in *Social and Psychological Bases of Ideology and System Justification*, eds. John T. Jost, Aaron C. Kay, and Hulda Thorisdottir (New York: Oxford University Press, 2009), 85-106; Nadia Y. Bashir, Penelope Lockwood, Alison L. Chasteen, Daniel Nadolny, and Indra Noyes, "The Ironic Impact of Activists: Negative Stereotypes Reduce Social Change Influence," *European Journal of Social Psychology* 43 (2013): 614-626; Laurie T. O'Brien and Christian S. Crandall, "Perceiving Self-Interest: Power, Ideology, and Maintenance of the Status Quo," *Social Justice Research* 18 (2005): 1-24.

47 Jared Bernstein, *Crunch: Why Do I Feel So Squeezed?* (Oakland, CA: Berrett-Koehler, 2008).

48 Ronald Reagan, "Radio Address on Socialized Medicine," American Rhetoric's Online Speech Bank, http://www.americanrhetoric.com /speeches/ronaldreagansocializedmedicine.htm.

49 U.S. Senate Committee on Health, Education, Labor and Pensions, "Diverting Non-Urgent Emergency Room Use: Can It Provide Better Care and Lower Costs?" May 11, 2011, https://www.gpo.gov/fdsys/pkg /CHRG-112shrg81788/html/CHRG-112shrg81788.htm.

50 U.S. Representative Tom Price (R-GA), Press Release, February 8, 2012, http://tomprice.house.gov/press-release/price-mandate-ought-be -reversed-right-religious-freedom-protected-and-entire-health.

51 John Geyman, "Affordable Care Act: Imploding and beyond Repair," *The Hill*, October 21, 2016, http://thehill.com/blogs/congress-blog /healthcare/301988-affordable-care-act-imploding-and-beyond-repair.

52 Steven Brill, *America's Bitter Pill: Money, Politics, Backroom Deals, and the Fight to Fix Our Broken Healthcare System* (New York: Random House, 2015); Tom Hamburger and Kim Geiger, "Healthcare Insurers Get Upper Hand," *Los Angeles Times*, August 24, 2009, http://www .latimes.com/nation/la-na-healthcare-insurers24-2009aug24-story.html.

53 Associated Press-Yahoo Poll, Knowledge Works, December 2007, http://surveys.ap.org/data/KnowledgeNetworks/AP-Yahoo_2007-08 _panel02.pdf.

54 OECD, "Health at a Glance 2013: OECD Indicators," Organisation for Economic Co-operation and Development, 2013, http://www .oecd.org/els/health-systems/Health-at-a-Glance-2013.pdf; Alice Chen, Emily Oster, and Heidi Williams, "Why Is Infant Mortality Higher in the US Than in Europe?" NBER Working Paper No. 20525, September 2014 (revised August 2015), http://www.nber.org/papers /w20525.pdf; Christopher Ingraham, "Our Infant Mortality Rate Is a National Embarrassment," *Washington Post*, September 29, 2014, http://www.washingtonpost.com/blogs/wonkblog/wp/2014/09/29 /our-infant-mortality-rate-is-a-national-embarrassment/.

55 Angie Drobnic Holan, "Sarah Palin Falsely Claims Barack Obama Runs a 'Death Panel,'" *Politifact*, August 10, 2009, http://www .politifact.com/truth-o-meter/statements/2009/aug/10/sarah-palin /sarah-palin-barack-obama-death-panel/.

56 Josiah Ryan, "Bachmann: Obamacare the 'Crown Jewel' of Socialism," *The Hill*, January 19, 2011, http://thehill.com/blogs/floor-action/house/ 138933-bachmann-obamacare-the-crown-jewel-of-socialism-.

57 Brian Beutler, "Inside the Tea Partiers Anti-Health Care Organizing Campaign," *Talking Points Memo*, August 3, 2009, http:// talkingpointsmemo.com/dc/inside-the-tea-partiers-anti-health-care -organizing-campaign.

58 Lee Fang, "Right-Wing Harassment Strategy against Dems Detailed in Memo: 'Yell,' 'Stand Up and Shout Out,' 'Rattle Him,'" *Think Progress*, July 31, 2009, http://thinkprogress.org/politics/2009/07/31/53761 /recess-harassment-memo/.

59 T. R. Reid, *The Healing of America: A Global Quest for Better, Cheaper, and Fairer Health Care* (New York: Penguin Books, 2009); Max Fisher, "Here's a Map of the Countries That Provide Universal Health Care (America's Still Not on It)," *The Atlantic*, June 28, 2012, http://www .theatlantic.com/international/archive/2012/06/heres-a-map-of-the -countries-that-provide-universal-health-care-americas-still-not-on-it /259153/; Adam Gaffney, Steffie Woolhandler, David U. Himmelstein, and Marcia Angell, "Moving Forward from the Affordable Care Act to a Single-Payer System," *American Journal of Public Health* 106 (2016): 987-988, http://ajph.aphapublications.org/doi/pdf/10.2105/ AJPH.2015.303157.

60 Wendell Potter, *Deadly Spin: An Insurance Company Insider Speaks Out on How Corporate PR Is Killing Health Care and Deceiving Americans* (New York: Bloomsbury Press, 2010); Jeffrey Young, "How Your Health Insurance Company Can Still Screw You, Despite Obamacare," *Huffington Post*, July 21, 2014, http://www.huffingtonpost .com/2014/07/21/health-insurance-obamacare_n_5599544.html.

61 James K. Galbraith, *The Predator State: How Conservatives Abandoned the Free Market and Why Liberals Should Too* (New York: The Free Press, 2008).

62 Mallory Shelbourne, "Poll: Majority Disapprove of GOP Healthcare Plan," *The Hill*, May 11, 2017, http://thehill.com/policy/healthcare /332957-poll-majority-disapprove-of-gop-healthcare-plan.

63 Congressional Budget Office Cost Estimate, "American Health Care Act," March 13, 2017, https://www.cbo.gov/sites/default/files/115th -congress-2017-2018/costestimate/americanhealthcareact.pdf; Matthew Yglesias, "The Hidden Reason Republicans Are So Eager to Repeal Obamacare," *Vox*, January 17, 2017, http://www.vox.com /policy-and-politics/2017/1/17/14263918/affordable-care-act-tax-cut; Brian Beutler, "The Media's Failure to Correct Republicans' Obscene Trumpcare Lies," *New Republic*, March 20, 2017, https://newrepublic .com/article/141439/medias-failure-correct-republicans-obscene -trumpcare-lies; Robert Pear, "G.O.P. Health Bill Would Leave 23 Million More Uninsured in a Decade, C.B.O. Says," *New York Times*, May 24, 2017, https://www.nytimes.com/2017/05/24/us/politics /cbo-congressional-budget-office-health-care.html; Margot Sanger-Katz, "Shifting Dollars from Poor to Rich Is a Key Part of the Senate Health Bill," *New York Times*, June 22, 2017, https://www.nytimes .com/2017/06/22/upshot/shifting-dollars-from-poor-to-rich-is-a -key-part-of-the-senate-health-bill.html.

64 Lara Seligman, "Polls," *The Hill*, February 25, 2013, http://thehill.com /polls/284579-the-hill-poll-voters-pentagon-should-bear-the-brunt-of -deficit-cuts.

65 Ian Lustick, *Trapped in the War on Terror* (Philadelphia, PA: University of Pennsylvania Press, 2006).

66 Howard P. "Buck" McKeon, "McKeon: Obama Cuts Would Gut U.S. Defense," *USA Today*, April 28, 2011, http://usatoday30.usatoday.com /news/opinion/forum/2011-04-28-McKeon-blasts-Obama-defense -cuts_n.htm.

67 The Foreign Policy Initiative, "FPI Fact Sheet: The Dangers of Deep Defense Cuts: What America's Civilian and Military Leaders Are Saying," May 23, 2012, http://www.foreignpolicyi.org/content /dangers-deep-defense-cuts-what-america's-civilian-and-military -leaders-are-saying.

68 Marion C. Blakey, "Opposing View: Defense Cuts Threaten Security, Economy," *USA Today*, August 5, 2012, http://usatoday30.usatoday .com/news/opinion/story/2012-08-02/Marion-Blakey-Aerospace -Industries-Association/56720838/1.

69 Mike Lofgren, *The Deep State: The Fall of the Constitution and the Rise of a Shadow Government* (New York: Viking, 2016).

70 K.K. Rebecca Lai, Troy Griggs, Max Fisher, and Audrey Carlsen, "Is America's Military Big Enough?" *New York Times*, March 22, 2017, https://www.nytimes.com/interactive/2017/03/22/us/is-americas -military-big-enough.html.

71 Brad Plumer, "America's Staggering Defense Budget, in Charts," *Washington Post*, January 7, 2013, http://www.washingtonpost.com /blogs/wonkblog/wp/2013/01/07/everything-chuck-hagel-needs -to-know-about-the-defense-budget-in-charts/.

72 Lee Fang and Zaid Jilani, "Defense Contractors Cite 'Benefits' of Escalating Conflicts in the Middle East," *The Intercept*, December 14, 2015, https://theintercept.com/2015/12/04/defense-contractors-cite -benefits-of-escalating-conflicts-in-the-middle-east/; Marc Pilisuk and Jennifer Rountree, *The Hidden Structure of Violence: Who Benefits from Global Violence and War* (Santa Barbara, CA: Praeger, 2007).

73 Citizens for Responsibility and Ethics in Washington, "Strategic Maneuvers: The Revolving Door from the Pentagon to the Private Sector," November 2012, http://crew.3cdn.net/3363b253a6744add9a _7sm6i6qfx.pdf.

74 Aerospace Industries Association, "Analysis Projects One Million Jobs at Risk from Defense Cuts," October 25, 2011, http://www.aia-aerospace .org/newsroom/aia_news/analysis_projects_one_million_jobs_at _risk_from_defense_cuts/.

75 Robert Pollin and Heidi Garrett-Peltier, "The U.S. Employment Effects of Military and Domestic Spending Priorities: 2011 Update," Political Economy Research Institute at University of Massachusetts, Amherst, December 2011, http://www.peri.umass.edu/fileadmin/pdf/published _study/PERI_military_spending_2011.pdf.

76 Lara Seligman, "Polls," *The Hill*, February 25, 2013, http://thehill.com /polls/284579-the-hill-poll-voters-pentagon-should-bear-the-brunt -of-deficit-cuts; Richard Kogan and Isaac Shapiro, "Congressional Budget Plans Get Two-Thirds of Cuts from Programs for People with Low or Moderate Incomes," Center on Budget and Policy Priorities, July 2, 2015, http://www.cbpp.org/sites/default/files/atoms/files /3-23-15bud.pdf.

77 Dwight D. Eisenhower, "The Chance for Peace," April 16, 1953, http://www.presidency.ucsb.edu/ws/?pid=9819.

78 Naomi Klein, *This Changes Everything: Capitalism vs. the Climate* (New York: Simon & Schuster, 2014); Naomi Klein, "Climate Change Is a People's Shock," *The Nation*, September 16, 2014, https://www .thenation.com/article/climate-change-peoples-shock/; Bill McKibben, "A World at War," *New Republic*, August 15, 2016, https://newrepublic .com/article/135684/declare-war-climate-change-mobilize-wwii; Bill McKibben, "Global Warming's Terrifying New Math," *Rolling Stone*, July 19, 2012, http://www.rollingstone.com/politics/news /global-warmings-terrifying-new-math-20120719.

79 Naomi Klein, *This Changes Everything: Capitalism vs. the Climate* (New York: Simon & Schuster, 2014); Dana Nuccitelli, "Climate Change Could Impact the Poor Much More Than Previously Thought," *Guardian*, January 26, 2015, http://www.theguardian.com /environment/climate-consensus-97-per-cent/2015/jan/26/climate -change-could-impact-poor-much-more-than-previously-thought; Alicia Mundy and Colleen McCain Nelson, "Climate Change Is Harming Economy, Report Says," *Wall Street Journal*, May 6, 2014, http://www .wsj.com/articles/SB10001424052702303417104579545510182551226.

80 John Cook, Dana Nuccitelli, Sarah A. Green, Mark Richardson, Barbel Winkler, Rob Painting, Robert Way, Peter Jacobs, and Andrew Skuce, "Quantifying the Consensus on Anthropogenic Global Warming in the Scientific Literature," *Environmental Research Letters* 8 (2013): 1-7, http://dx.doi.org/10.1088/1748-9326/8/2/024024.

81 Sheldon Rampton and John Stauber, *Trust Us, We're Experts: How Industry Manipulates Science and Gambles with Your Future* (New York: Tarcher/Putnam, 2002).

82 Heather Haddon, "Donald Trump: 'I Don't Believe in Climate Change,'" *Wall Street Journal*, September 24, 2015, http://blogs.wsj.com/washwire/ 2015/09/24/donald-trump-i-dont-believe-in-climate-change/.

83 Michael Shear, "Trump Will Withdraw U.S. from Paris Climate Agreement," *New York Times*, June 1, 2017, https://www.nytimes.com /2017/06/01/climate/trump-paris-climate-agreement.html.

84 Brady Dennis and Steven Mufson, "Thousands of Emails Detail EPA Head's Close Ties to Fossil Fuel Industry," *Washington Post*, February 22, 2017, https://www.washingtonpost.com/news/energy-environment /wp/2017/02/22/oklahoma-attorney-generals-office-releases-7500 -pages-of-emails-between-scott-pruitt-and-fossil-fuel-industry/.

85 Scott Pruitt and Luther Strange, "The Climate-Change Gang," *National Review*, May 17, 2016, http://www.nationalreview.com/article/435470 /climate-change-attorneys-general; Coral Davenport, "E.P.A. Chief Doubts Consensus View of Climate Change," *New York Times*, March 9, 2017, https://www.nytimes.com/2017/03/09/us/politics/epa-scott- pruitt-global-warming.html.

86 James Inhofe, "The Science of Climate Change Senate Floor Statement," July 28, 2003, http://www.epw.senate.gov/speechitem.cfm?party=rep &id=230594.

87 Denver Nicks, "The Craziest Senator," *Daily Beast*, July 29, 2009, http://www.thedailybeast.com/articles/2009/07/29/the-craziest -senator.html.

88 Jeff Tollefson, "Documents Spur Investigation of Climate Sceptic," *Nature*, February 2015, http://www.nature.com/news/documents -spur-investigation-of-climate-sceptic-1.16972; Eric Lipton and Brooke Williams, "Researchers or Corporate Allies? Think Tanks Blur the Line," *New York Times*, August 7, 2016, http://www.nytimes.com/2016/08 /08/us/politics/think-tanks-research-and-corporate-lobbying.html; Riley E. Dunlap and Peter J. Jacques, "Climate Change Denial Books and Conservative Think Tanks: Exploring the Connection," *American Behavioral Scientist* 57 (2013): 699–731, https://www.ncbi.nlm.nih.gov /pmc/articles/PMC3787818/pdf/10.1177_0002764213477096.pdf.

89 Jim Lakely, "'Do You Still Believe in Global Warming?' Billboards Hit Chicago," Heartland Institute, May 3, 2012, https://www.heartland .org/press-releases/2012/05/03/do-you-still-believe-global-warming -billboards-hit-chicago.

90 Brian Vastag, "Group Pulls Plug on Billboard Linking Global Warming Believers to Terrorists," *Washington Post*, May 4, 2012, http://www .washingtonpost.com/national/health-science/group-pulls-plug-on -billboard-linking-global-warming-believers-to-terrorists/2012/05 /04/gIQAU2q51T_story.html.

91 Neela Banerjee, "Climate Change Skepticism Seeps into Science Classrooms," *Los Angeles Times*, January 16, 2012, http://articles.latimes .com/2012/jan/16/nation/la-na-climate-change-school-20120116.

92 Heartland Institute, "2012 Fundraising Plan," http://www.desmogblog .com/sites/beta.desmogblog.com/files/(1-15-2012)%202012 %20Fundraising%20Plan.pdf.

93 Katie Worth, "Climate Change Skeptic Group Seeks to Influence 200,000 Teachers," *Frontline*, March 28, 2017, http://www.pbs.org/wgbh/frontline/article/climate-change-skeptic-group-seeks-to-influence-200000-teachers/.

94 Kate Sheppard, "Chamber: Global Warming Is Good for You," *Mother Jones*, October 2, 2009, http://www.motherjones.com/mojo/2009/10/more-chamber-commerces-climate-denial.

95 CBS This Morning, "ExxonMobil CEO: 'My Philosophy Is to Make Money,'" March 7, 2013, http://www.cbsnews.com/videos/exxonmobil-ceo-my-philosophy-is-to-make-money/.

96 Council on Foreign Relations: "CEO Speaker Series: A Conversation with Rex W. Tillerson," June 27, 2012, http://www.cfr.org/world/ceo-speaker-series-conversation-rex-w-tillerson/p35286; Sara Jerving, Katie Jennings, Masako Melissa Hirsch, and Susanne Rust, "What Exxon Knew about the Earth's Melting Arctic," *Los Angeles Times*, October 9, 2015, http://graphics.latimes.com/exxon-arctic/.

97 Chris Mooney and Brady Dennis, "Tillerson Doesn't Deny Climate Change—but Dodges Questions about Exxon's Role in Sowing Doubt," *Washington Post*, January 11, 2017, https://www.washingtonpost.com/news/energy-environment/wp/2017/01/11/tillerson-says-u-s-should-maintain-its-seat-at-table-on-fighting-global-climate-change/.

98 Center for Economic and Policy Research, "Getting It Wrong on Trade: TPP Is Not Good for Workers," March 14, 2015, http://www.cepr.net/blogs/beat-the-press/getting-it-wrong-on-trade-tpp-is-not-good-for-workers; David Rosnick, "Gains from Trade? The Net Effect of the Trans-Pacific Partnership Agreement on U.S. Wages," Center for Economic and Policy Research, September 2013, http://www.cepr.net/documents/publications/TPP-2013-09.pdf.

99 Elizabeth Warren, "The Trans-Pacific Partnership Clause Everyone Should Oppose," *Washington Post*, February 25, 2015, http://www.washingtonpost.com/opinions/kill-the-dispute-settlement-language-in-the-trans-pacific-partnership/2015/02/25/ec7705a2-bd1e-11e4-b274-e5209a3bc9a9_story.html.

100 Matt Bai, "Why Obama Is Happy to Fight Elizabeth Warren on the Trade Deal," Yahoo! *Politics*, May 9, 2015, https://www.yahoo.com/politics/why-obama-is-happy-to-fight-elizabeth-warren-on-118537612596.html.

101 White House, "Joint Press Conference with President Obama and Prime Minister Najib of Malaysia," April 27, 2014, https://www.whitehouse.gov/the-press-office/2014/04/27/joint-press-conference-president-obama-and-prime-minister-najib-malaysia.

102 United States Environmental Protection Agency, "Hydraulic Fracturing for Oil and Gas: Impacts from the Hydraulic Fracturing Water Cycle on Drinking Water Resources in the United States," December 2016, https://cfpub.epa.gov/ncea/hfstudy/recordisplay.cfm?deid=332990; Chris Mooney, Steven Mufson, and Brady Dennis, "EPA's Science Advisers Challenge Agency Report on the Safety of Fracking," *Washington Post*, August 12, 2016, https://www.washingtonpost.com/news/energy-environment/wp/2016/08/11/epas-science-advisers-challenge-agency-report-on-the-safety-of-fracking/; Jennifer S. Harkness, Gary S. Dwyer, Nathaniel R. Warner, Kimberly M. Parker, William A. Mitch, and Avner Vengosh, "Iodide, Bromide, and Ammonium in Hydraulic Fracturing and Oil and Gas Wastewaters: Environmental Implications," *Environmental Science & Technology* 49 (2015): 1955–1963, http://pubs.acs.org/doi/abs/10.1021/es504654n; Gayathri Vaidyanathan, "Fracking Can Contaminate Drinking Water," *Scientific American*, April 4, 2016, https://www.scientificamerican.com/article/fracking-can-contaminate-drinking-water/.

103 Danielle Paquette, "Live Near Fracking? You're More Likely to Report Health Problems, New Study Says," *Washington Post*, September 10, 2014, https://www.washingtonpost.com/news/storyline/wp/2014/09/10/live-near-fracking-youre-more-likely-to-report-health-problems-new-study-says/.

104 Abrahm Lustgarten, "Opponents to Fracking Disclosure Take Big Money from Industry," *ProPublica*, January 14, 2011, http://www.propublica.org/article/opponents-to-fracking-disclosure-take-big-money-from-industry#naturalgascaucus.

105 Erik Milito, "Innovation, Science, and Fracking," Energy Tomorrow, June 9, 2016, http://energytomorrow.org/blog/2016/06/09/innovation-science-and-fracking.

106 Elizabeth Grossman, "What Do We Really Know about Roundup Weed Killer?" *National Geographic*, April 23, 2015, http://news.nationalgeographic.com/2015/04/150422-glyphosate-roundup-herbicide-weeds/; Rene Ebersole, "Did Monsanto Ignore Evidence Linking Its Weed Killer to Cancer?" *The Nation*, October 12, 2017, https://www.thenation.com/article/did-monsanto-ignore-evidence-linking-its-weed-killer-to-cancer/.

107 Sharon Lerner, "New Evidence about the Dangers of Monsanto's Roundup," *The Intercept*, May 17, 2016, https://theintercept.com/2016/05/17/new-evidence-about-the-dangers-of-monsantos-roundup/.

108 Monsanto Newsroom, "Monsanto Reinforces Decades of Data and Regulatory Review Clearly Document Safety of Glyphosate," March 23, 2015, http://news.monsanto.com/press-release/research-and-development/monsanto-reinforces-decades-data-and-regulatory-review-clearl; Genna Reed, "Monsanto's Four Tactics for Undermining Glyphosate Science Review," Union of Concerned Scientists, March 23, 2017, http://blog.ucsusa.org/genna-reed/monsantos-four-tactics-for-undermining-glyphosate-science-review.

109 Bill Sells, "What Asbestos Taught Me about Managing Risk," *Harvard Business Review*, March-April 1994, https://hbr.org /1994/03/what-asbestos-taught-me-about-managing-risk.

110 Ryan Jaslow, "Big Tobacco Kept Cancer Risk in Cigarettes Secret: Study," CBS News, September 30, 2011, http://www.cbsnews.com /news/big-tobacco-kept-cancer-risk-in-cigarettes-secret-study/.

111 Doron Levin, "Here Are Some of Worst Car Scandals in History," *Fortune*, September 26, 2015, http://fortune.com/2015/09/26/auto -industry-scandals/; Tim Higgins and Nick Summers, "GM Recalls: How General Motors Silenced a Whistle-Blower," *Bloomberg Businessweek*, June 19, 2014, http://www.businessweek.com/articles /2014-06-18/gm-recalls-whistle-blower-was-ignored-mary-barra -faces-congress.

112 Tara Golshan, "Harassment Victims Experienced Retaliation When They Spoke Up," *Vox*, October 15, 2017, https://www.vox.com/identities /2017/10/15/16438750/weinstein-sexual-harassment-facts.

113 Solomon E. Asch, *Social Psychology* (Englewood Cliffs: Prentice-Hall, 1955).

114 Stanley Milgram, "Behavioral Study of Obedience," *Journal of Abnormal and Social Psychology* 67 (1963): 371-378.

115 Aram Roston, "Walmart 'Unable to Substantiate' Forced Labor Claims at Seafood Supplier," *Daily Beast*, June 14, 2012, http://www.thedailybeast.com/articles/2012/06/14/walmart-unable -to-substantiate-forced-labor-claims-at-seafood-supplier.html.

116 Josh Eidelson, "Guest Workers Who Sparked June Walmart Supplier Walk-out Hail Strike Wave's Spread," *The Nation*, December 1, 2012, http://www.thenation.com/article/guest-workers-who-sparked-june -walmart-supplier-walk-out-hail-strike-waves-spread/.

117 Ann Zimmerman, "Pro-Union Butchers at Wal-Mart Win a Battle, but Lose the War," *Wall Street Journal*, April 11, 2000, http://www.wsj.com /articles/SB955407680495911513.

118 Joel Robert, "Wal-Mart Shuts Unionizing Store," CBS News, February 9, 2005, http://www.cbsnews.com/news/wal-mart-shuts-unionizing-store/.

119 Reuters, "Walmart Illegally Closed Union Store, Court Says," *New York Times*, June 27, 2014, http://www.nytimes.com/2014/06/28/business /international/walmart-illegally-closed-union-store-court-says.html.

120 Josh Eidelson, "Walmart Fires Eleven Strikers in Alleged Retaliation," *The Nation*, June 22, 2013, http://www.thenation.com/article/walmart -fires-eleven-strikers-alleged-retaliation/.

121 Robert Evatt, "Plumbing Trucks Arrive at Closed Wal-Mart, No Permits Filed Yet," *Tulsa World*, April 22, 2015, http://www.tulsaworld.com /business/retail/plumbing-trucks-arrive-at-closed-wal-mart-no -permits-filed/article_eb6513d8-48d8-590d-a9e4-5d3a3eb17ae7.html.

122 Paul Fletcher, "Ricketts Shuts Down Local News Sites DNAInfo and Gothamist in Wake of Union Vote," *Forbes*, November 3, 2017, https://www.forbes.com/sites/paulfletcher/2017/11/03/ricketts-shuts-down-local-newsites-dnainfo-and-gothamist/.

123 Kate Bronfenbrenner, "No Holds Barred: The Intensification of Employer Opposition to Organizing," Economic Policy Institute, May 20, 2009, http://epi.3cdn.net/edc3b3dc172dd1094f_0ym6ii96d.pdf; Kate Bronfenbrenner, "A War against Workers Who Organize," *Washington Post*, June 3, 2009, http://www.washingtonpost.com/wp-dyn/content/article/2009/06/02/AR2009060202967.html.

124 Human Rights Watch, "Unfair Advantage: Workers' Freedom of Association in the United States under International Human Rights Standards," August 2000, https://www.hrw.org/reports/pdfs/u/us/uslbr008.pdf.

125 Annie Linskey, "Warren Fires Back at Banks Halting Donations to Democrats," *Boston Globe*, March 27, 2015, https://www.bostonglobe.com/news/politics/2015/03/27/senator-elizabeth-warren-shoots-back-wall-street-after-banks-reportedly-withhold-contributions-democrats/UsePAiAo9hb1mRYGQc4FpL/story.html.

126 Alicia Mundy, "Adelson to Keep Betting on the GOP," *Wall Street Journal*, December 4, 2012, http://www.wsj.com/articles/SB10001424127887323717004578159570568104706.

127 CBS News, "Democratic Debate Transcript: Clinton, Sanders, O'Malley in Iowa," November 14, 2015, http://www.cbsnews.com/news/democratic-debate-transcript-clinton-sanders-omalley-in-iowa/.

128 Ashley Lopez, "Koch Brothers Set Sights on Florida Supreme Court Justices," Florida Center for Investigative Reporting, October 1, 2012, http://fcir.org/2012/10/01/koch-brothers-set-sights-on-florida-supreme-court-justices/.

129 Moyers & Company, "Justice, Not Politics," October 12, 2012, http://billmoyers.com/episode/justice-not-politics/.

130 Norm Ornstein, "Courting Corruption: The Auctioning of the Judicial System," *The Atlantic*, October 15, 2014, http://www.theatlantic.com/politics/archive/2014/10/courting-corruption-the-auctioning-of-the-judicial-system/381524/.

131 Josh Eidelson, "Big Political Money Now Floods Judges' Races, Too," *Bloomberg Businessweek*, July 31, 2014, http://www.bloomberg.com/bw/articles/2014-07-31/big-political-money-now-floods-judges-races-too.

132 John Nichols and Robert W. McChesney, *Dollarocracy: How the Money and Media Election Complex Is Destroying America* (New York: Nation Books, 2013).

133 Paul Bond, "Leslie Moonves on Donald Trump: 'It May Not Be Good for America, but It's Damn Good for CBS,'" *Hollywood Reporter*, February 29, 2016, http://www.hollywoodreporter.com/news/leslie-moonves-donald-trump-may-871464.

134 Michael Hudson, "Whistleblowers Ignored, Punished by Lenders, Dozens of Former Employees Say," Center for Public Integrity, November 22, 2011, http://www.publicintegrity.org/2011/11/22/7461/whistleblowers-ignored-punished-lenders-dozens-former-employees-say.

135 Tim Higgins and Nick Summers, "GM Recalls: How General Motors Silenced a Whistle-Blower," *Bloomberg Businessweek*, June 19, 2014, http://www.businessweek.com/articles/2014-06-18/gm-recalls-whistleblower-was-ignored-mary-barra-faces-congress.

136 Matthew Daly, "VA Settles Complaints of Three Phoenix Whistleblowers," *Associated Press*, September 29, 2014, http://www.pbs.org/newshour/rundown/va-settles-complaints-three-phoenix-whistleblowers/.

137 Naomi Wolf, "Revealed: How the FBI Coordinated the Crackdown on Occupy," *Guardian*, December 29, 2012, http://www.theguardian.com/commentisfree/2012/dec/29/fbi-coordinated-crackdown-occupy.

138 Colin Moynihan, "Officials Cast Wide Net in Monitoring Occupy Protests," *New York Times*, May 22, 2014, http://www.nytimes.com/2014/05/23/us/officials-cast-wide-net-in-monitoring-occupy-protests.html.

139 Sarah Knuckey, Katherine Glenn, and Emi MacLean, "Suppressing Protest: Human Rights Violations in the U.S. Response to Occupy Wall Street," The Global Justice Clinic, NYU School of Law and the Walter Leitner International Human Rights Clinic at the Leitner Center for International Law and Justice, Fordham Law School, July 2012, http://chrgj.org/wp-content/uploads/2012/10/suppressingprotest.pdf.

140 Jim Dwyer, "A Spray Like a Punch in the Face," *New York Times*, September 27, 2011, http://www.nytimes.com/2011/09/28/nyregion/a-burst-of-pepper-spray-like-a-punch-in-the-face.html.

141 Robinson Meyer, "The Legal Case for Blocking the Dakota Access Pipeline," *The Atlantic*, September 9, 2016, https://www.theatlantic.com/technology/archive/2016/09/dapl-dakota-sitting-rock-sioux/499178/; Sam Levin, "Revealed: FBI Terrorism Taskforce Investigating Standing Rock Activists," *Guardian*, February 10, 2017, https://www.theguardian.com/us-news/2017/feb/10/standing-rock-fbi-investigation-dakota-access; Sam Levin, "Veterans at Standing Rock See Police Retribution after Arrest and Charges," *Guardian*, February 13, 2017, https://www.theguardian.com/us-news/2017/feb/13/standing-rock-veterans-police-arrest-north-dakota; Susie Nielson, "The Media's Standing Rock Problem Looks a Lot Like Its Black Lives Matter Problem," *Quartz*, November 22, 2016, https://qz.com/843368/false-balance-in-the-coverage-of-the-police-violence-at-standing-rock-is-undermining-the-nodapl-movement/; Roy Eidelson, "The Sustaining Fires of Standing Rock: A Movement Grows," *Psychology Today*, March 17, 2017, https://www.psychologytoday.com/blog/dangerous-ideas/201703/the-sustaining-fires-standing-rock-movement-grows.

142 Julia Carrie Wong, "Standing Rock Protest: Hundreds Clash with Police over Dakota Access Pipeline," *Guardian*, November 21, 2016, https://www.theguardian.com/us-news/2016/nov/21/standing-rock -protest-hundreds-clash-with-police-over-dakota-access-pipeline.

CHAPTER 3

Injustice Mind Games: Hijacking Our Beliefs about Right and Wrong

1   Howard Zinn, *A People's History of the United States* (London: Longman, 1980).

2   Dale T. Miller, "Disrespect and the Experience of Injustice," *Annual Review of Psychology* 52 (2001): 527-553.

3   Morton Deutsch, "Justice and Conflict," in *The Handbook of Conflict Resolution: Theory and Practice*, eds. Morton Deutsch, Peter T. Coleman, and Eric C. Marcus (San Francisco, CA: Jossey-Bass, 2006), 43-68.

4   Tom R. Tyler, "Psychological Perspectives on Legitimacy and Legitimation," *Annual Review of Psychology* 57 (2006): 375-400.

5   Abby Jackson, "The Walmart Family Is Teaching Hedge Funds How to Profit from Publicly Funded Schools," *Business Insider*, March 17, 2015, http://www.businessinsider.com/walmart-is-helping-hedge-funds -make-money-off-of-charter-schools-2015-3.

6   Gordon Lafer, "Do Poor Kids Deserve Lower-Quality Education Than Rich Kids? Evaluating School Privatization Proposals in Milwaukee, Wisconsin," Economic Policy Institute, April 24, 2014, http://s1.epi.org /files/2014/school-privatization-milwaukee.pdf; Center for Research on Education Outcomes, "National Charter School Study Executive Summary 2013," Stanford University, 2013, http://credo.stanford.edu /documents/NCSS%202013%20Executive%20Summary.pdf; Kevin Carey, "Dismal Voucher Results Surprise Researchers as DeVos Era Begins," *New York Times*, February 23, 2017, https://www.nytimes.com /2017/02/23/upshot/dismal-results-from-vouchers-surprise-researchers -as-devos-era-begins.html; Martin Carnoy, "School Vouchers Are Not a Proven Strategy for Improving Student Achievement," Economic Policy Institute, February 28, 2017, http://www.epi.org/files/pdf/121635.pdf.

7   Jane Mayer, "Betsy DeVos: Trump's Big-Donor Education Secretary," *New Yorker*, November 23, 2016, http://www.newyorker.com/news /news-desk/betsy-devos-trumps-big-donor-education-secretary; Douglas N. Harris, "Betsy DeVos and the Wrong Way to Fix Schools," *New York Times*, November 25, 2016, http://www.nytimes.com/2016 /11/25/opinion/betsy-devos-and-the-wrong-way-to-fix-schools.html; Patrick J. Kearney, "An Open Letter to Betsy DeVos from America's Public School Teachers," *Huffington Post*, December 5, 2016, http:// www.huffingtonpost.com/entry/an-introduction-from-public-school- teachers-to-betsy_us_5845e2fbe4b0707e4c8171a3; Valerie Strauss, "To Trump's Education Pick, the U.S. Public School System Is a 'Dead End,'" *Washington Post*, December 21, 2016, https://www.washingtonpost.com /news/answer-sheet/wp/2016/12/21/to-trumps-education-pick-the-u-s -public-school-system-is-a-dead-end/.

8   Jay A. Fernandez, "How Did 'Superman' Fly with the D.C. Elite?" *Hollywood Reporter*, September 16, 2010, http://www.hollywoodreporter .com/news/how-did-superman-fly-dc-27963.

9   David Welna, "Romney Tries to Mend Fences with Latinos," NPR, May 23, 2012, http://www.npr.org/2012/05/23/153519648/romney-tries-to -mend-fences-with-latinos.

10 Ted Cruz, "Sen. Cruz: We Shouldn't Put Our Future on a Waiting List," January 28, 2015, http://www.cruz.senate.gov/?p=press_release&id=2127.

11 Michael B. Katz and Mike Rose, eds., *Public Education under Siege* (Philadelphia, PA: University of Pennsylvania Press, 2013); Dana Goldstein, *The Teacher Wars: A History of America's Most Embattled Profession* (New York: Doubleday, 2014); Joanne Barkan, "Charitable Plutocracy: Bill Gates, Washington State, and the Nuisance of Democracy," *Nonprofit Quarterly*, April 11, 2016, https://nonprofitquarterly.org/2016/04/11/charitable-plutocracy -bill-gates-washington-state-and-the-nuisance-of-democracy/.

12 Helen F. Ladd, *Education and Poverty: Confronting the Evidence*, Duke Sanford School of Public Policy Working Papers Series, SAN11- 01, November 4, 2011, http://files.eric.ed.gov/fulltext/ED536952.pdf; National Center for Education Statistics, "The Condition of Education 2016," U.S. Department of Education, May 2016, http://nces.ed.gov /pubs2016/condition_of_ed_2016144.pdf.

13 Christopher Hayes, *Twilight of the Elites: America after Meritocracy* (New York: Crown Publishers, 2012).

14 Diane Ravitch, *Reign of Error: The Hoax of the Privatization Movement and the Danger to America's Public Schools* (New York: Alfred A. Knopf, 2013); Peter Edelman, *So Rich, So Poor: Why It's So Hard to End Poverty in America* (New York: The New Press, 2012).

15 Emma Brown, Valerie Strauss, and Danielle Douglas-Gabriel, "Trump's First Full Education Budget: Deep Cuts to Public School Programs in Pursuit of School Choice," *Washington Post*, May 17, 2017, https://www .washingtonpost.com/local/education/trumps-first-full-education -budget-deep-cuts-to-public-school-programs-in-pursuit-of-school -choice/2017/05/17/2a25a2cc-3a41-11e7-8854-21f359183e8c_story .html; Moriah Balingit, "DeVos Rescinds 72 Guidance Documents Outlining Rights for Disabled Students," *Washington Post*, October 21, 2017, https://www.washingtonpost.com/news/education/wp/2017/10 /21/devos-rescinds-72-guidance-documents-outlining-rights-for -disabled-students/; Ryan Kilpatrick, "Education Secretary Betsy DeVos Withdraws Obama-Era Student Loan Protections," *Fortune*, April 12, 2017, http://fortune.com/2017/04/12/betsy-devos-student-loans-obama/; Todd Spangler, "Betsy DeVos Scraps Obama-era College Sexual Misconduct Rules," *USA Today*, September 22, 2017, https://www .usatoday.com/story/news/politics/2017/09/22/betsy-devos-college -sexual-misconduct-guidelines/693690001/.

16 Diane Ravitch, *Reign of Error: The Hoax of the Privatization Movement and the Danger to America's Public Schools* (New York: Alfred A. Knopf, 2013).

17 Ballotpedia, "Voter Identification Laws by States," http://ballotpedia.org/Voter_identification_laws_by_state.

18 News21, "Comprehensive Database of U.S. Voter Fraud Uncovers No Evidence That Photo ID Is Needed," August 12, 2012, http://votingrights.news21.com/article/election-fraud/; Sami Edge, "A Review of Key States with Voter ID Laws Found No Voter Impersonation Fraud," Center for Public Integrity, August 21, 2016, https://www.publicintegrity.org/2016/08/21/20078/review-key-states-voter-id-laws-found-no-voter-impersonation-fraud.

19 Justin Levitt, "The Truth about Voter Fraud," Brennan Center for Justice at New York University School of Law, 2007, http://www.brennancenter.org/sites/default/files/legacy/The %20Truth%20About%20Voter%20Fraud.pdf.

20 Emily Guskin and Scott Clement, "Poll: Nearly Half of Americans Say Voter Fraud Occurs Often," *Washington Post*, September 15, 2016, https://www.washingtonpost.com/news/the-fix/wp/2016/09/15 /poll-nearly-half-of-americans-say-voter-fraud-occurs-often/.

21 Brennan Center for Justice, "Citizens without Proof: A Survey of Americans' Possession of Documentary Proof of Citizenship and Photo Identification," Voting Rights & Elections Series, New York University School of Law, November 2006, http://www.brennancenter.org/sites /default/files/legacy/d/download_file_39242.pdf; Zoltan Hajnal, Nazita Lajevardi, and Lindsay Nielson, "Voter Identification Laws and the Suppression of Minority Votes," *Journal of Politics*, 79 (2017): 363-379; Alice Speri, "Voter Suppression Is the Real Election Scandal," *The Intercept*, October 27, 2016, https://theintercept.com/2016/10/27 /voter-suppression-is-the-real-election-scandal/; Greg Palast, "The GOP's Stealth War against Voters," *Rolling Stone*, August 24, 2016, http://www.rollingstone.com/politics/features/the-gops-stealth-war -against-voters-w435890; Ari Berman, "A New Study Shows Just How Many Americans Were Blocked from Voting in Wisconsin Last Year," *Mother Jones*, September 25, 2017, http://www.motherjones.com /politics/2017/09/a-new-study-shows-just-how-many-americans -were-blocked-from-voting-in-wisconsin-last-year/.

22 Greg Abbott, "Helping Stamp Out Voter Fraud in Texas," *Hill Country News*, March 10, 2006, http://www.hillcountrynews.com/opinion /columnists/article_5ba237e2-e6da-5e2c-b87d-1f1bb79e87ad.html.

23 James J. Woodruff II, "America's Vote Fraud Epidemic," *The Hill*, September 20, 2010, http://thehill.com/blogs/congress-blog /campaign/119699-americas-vote-fraud-epidemic.

24 Jane Mayer, "The Voter-Fraud Myth," *New Yorker*, October 29, 2012, http://www.newyorker.com/magazine/2012/10/29/the-voter-fraud-myth.

25 John Fund, "Winning the Fight for Voter-ID," *National Review*, January 19, 2014, http://www.nationalreview.com/article/368864/winning-fight-voter-id-john-fund.

26 Reince Priebus, "Anti Voter Fraud Reforms Are Practical, Not Partisan," *US News & World Report*, June 6, 2011, http://www.usnews.com/opinion/articles/2011/06/06/anti-voter-fraud-reforms-are-practical-not-partisan.

27 Republican Party Platform, 2012, http://www.ontheissues.org/Archive/2012_RNC_Platform_Republican_Party.htm.

28 Republican Party Platform, 2016, https://prod-static-ngop-pbl.s3.amazonaws.com/static/home/data/platform.pdf.

29 Jenna Johnson, "Trump Urges Supporters to Monitor Polling Places in 'Certain Areas,'" *Washington Post*, October 1, 2016, https://www.washingtonpost.com/news/post-politics/wp/2016/10/01/trump-urges-supporters-to-monitor-polling-places-in-certain-areas/; Maggie Haberman and Matt Flegenheimer, "Donald Trump, a 'Rigged' Election and the Politics of Race," *New York Times*, August 21, 2016, http://www.nytimes.com/2016/08/22/us/politics/donald-trump-a-rigged-election-and-the-politics-of-race.html.

30 Editorial Board, "Voter Harassment, Circa 2012," *New York Times*, September 21, 2012, http://www.nytimes.com/2012/09/22/opinion/voter-harassment-circa-2012.html.

31 Stephanie Saul, "Looking, Very Closely, for Voter Fraud," *New York Times*, September 16, 2012, http://www.nytimes.com/2012/09/17/us/politics/groups-like-true-the-vote-are-looking-very-closely-for-voter-fraud.html.

32 Kevin Diaz, "Houston Group at Center of Trump Voter Fraud Allegations," *Houston Chronicle*, November 28, 2016, http://www.houstonchronicle.com/news/houston-texas/houston/article/Houston-group-at-center-of-Trump-voter-fraud-10641221.php.

33 White House, "President Announces Formation of Bipartisan Presidential Commission on Election Integrity," May 11, 2017, https://www.whitehouse.gov/the-press-office/2017/05/11/president-announces-formation-bipartisan-presidential-commission.

34 Josh Siegel, "Votes of Thousands Who Haven't Proven Citizenship Could 'Swing' Kansas Elections," *Daily Signal*, September 8, 2016, http://dailysignal.com/2016/09/08/votes-of-thousands-who-havent-proven-citizenship-could-swing-kansas-elections/.

35 John Nichols, "ALEC Exposed: Rigging Elections," *The Nation*, July 12, 2011, http://www.thenation.com/article/alec-exposed-rigging-elections/.

36 Wendy R. Weiser, "Voter Suppression: How Bad? (Pretty Bad)," *American Prospect*, Fall 2014, http://prospect.org/article/22-states -wave-new-voting-restrictions-threatens-shift-outcomes-tight-races.

37 Editorial Board, "Jeff Sessions as Attorney General: An Insult to Justice," *New York Times*, November 18, 2016, http://www.nytimes.com /2016/11/19/opinion/jeff-sessions-as-attorney-general-an-insult-to -justice.html; Alice Speri, "Career Racist Jeff Sessions Is Donald Trump's Pick for Attorney General," *The Intercept*, November 18, 2016, https:// theintercept.com/2016/11/18/career-racist-jeff-sessions-is-donald -trumps-pick-for-attorney-general/.

38 Melvin J. Lerner and Carolyn H. Simmons, "Observer's Reaction to the 'Innocent Victim': Compassion or Rejection?" *Journal of Personality and Social Psychology* 4 (1966): 203-210; Melvin J. Lerner, *The Belief in a Just World: A Fundamental Delusion* (New York: Plenum, 1980); Carolyn L. Hafer and Becky L. Choma, "Belief in a Just World, Perceived Fairness, and Justification of the Status Quo," in *Social and Psychological Bases of Ideology and System Justification*, eds. John T. Jost, Aaron C. Kay, and Hulda Thorisdottir (New York: Oxford University Press, 2009), 107-125.

39 Zick Rubin and Letita Anne Peplau, "Who Believes in a Just World?" *Journal of Social Issues* 31 (1975): 65-89.

40 Carolyn L. Hafer and Laurent Begue, "Experimental Research on Just-World Theory: Problems, Developments, and Future Challenges," *Psychological Bulletin* 131 (2005): 128-167; William Ryan, *Blaming the Victim* (New York: Vintage Books, 1976).

41 Action 4 News, Pittsburgh, "Sen. Santorum Wants to Penalize Hurricane Victims," *Huffington Post*, March 28, 2008, http://www.huffingtonpost .com/2005/09/06/sen-santorum-wants-to-pen_n_6942.html.

42 Bill O'Reilly, "Keeping the Record Straight on the Katrina Story," *Fox News*, September 6, 2005, http://www.foxnews.com/story/2005/09 /06/keeping-record-straight-on-katrina-story.html.

43 Jaime Omar Yassin, "Demonizing the Victims of Katrina," *Fairness & Accuracy in Reporting*, November 1, 2005, http://fair.org/extra-online -articles/demonizing-the-victims-of-katrina/.

44 George Zornick, "The Eleven Craziest Things Newt Gingrich Has Ever Said," *The Nation*, May 11, 2011, http://www.thenation.com/blog /160588/eleven-craziest-things-newt-gingrich-has-ever-said.

45 Jeffrey H. Birnbaum, "Lenders Fighting Mortgage Rewrite," *Washington Post*, February 22, 2008, http://www.washingtonpost.com/wp-dyn /content/article/2008/02/21/AR2008022102687.html.

46 John Tamny, "The Ongoing, and Hideous Lie about 'Victimized' Mortgage Holders," *Forbes*, March 5, 2013, http://www.forbes.com /sites/johntamny/2013/03/05/the-ongoing-and-hideous-lie-about -victimized-mortgage-walkers.

47   Erik Wasson, "Rand Paul Slams Jobless Benefits Extension Plan,"
The Hill, December 8, 2013, http://thehill.com/policy/finance/192405
-rand-paul-opposes-extending-jobless-benefits.

48   Richard Vedder, "The Wages of Unemployment," *Wall Street Journal*,
January 15, 2013, http://www.wsj.com/articles/SB10001424127887324
46160457819314169099174.

49   Augustine Faucher, "How We Know the Stimulus Is Working," *Moody's
Analytics*, December 4, 2009, https://www.economy.com/dismal
/analysis/free/119925; Douglas W. Elmendorf, "Policies for Increasing
Economic Growth and Employment in the Short Term," Congressional
Budget Office, February 23, 2010, http://www.cbo.gov/sites/default
/files/02-23-employment_testimony.pdf.

50   Peter A. Galuszka, *Thunder on the Mountain: Death at Massey and the
Dirty Secrets behind Big Coal* (New York: St. Martin's Press, 2012).

51   Giovanni Russonello, "Massey Had Worst Mine Fatality Record Even
before April Disaster," Investigative Reporting Workshop, American
University, November 23, 2010, http://investigativereportingworkshop
.org/investigations/coal-truth/story/massey-had-worst-mine-fatality
-record-even-april-d/.

52   Amanda Frost, "One Dollar for Every West Virginian," *Slate*, October 10,
2008, http://www.slate.com/articles/news_and_politics/jurisprudence
/2008/10/one_dollar_for_every_west_virginian.single.html; Supreme
Court of the United States, Hugh M. Caperton, Et Al., Petitioners V.
A. T. Massey Coal Company, Inc., Et Al. on Writ of Certiorari to the
Supreme Court of Appeals of West Virginia, No. 08-22, June 8, 2009,
https://www.law.cornell.edu/supct/pdf/08-22P.ZO.

53   Kim Geiger and Bob Drogin, "West Virginia Coal Mine Rescue Crews
Race against Time," *Los Angeles Times*, April 8, 2010, http://articles
.latimes.com/2010/apr/08/nation/la-na-coal-mine-main8-2010apr08.

54   Ken Ward Jr., "Investigators Dismiss Massey's View That Disaster
'Unavoidable,'" *Charleston Gazette-Mail*, July 22, 2010, http://www
.wvgazette.com/News/201007220815.

55   J. Davitt McAteer and Associates: "Upper Big Branch: The April 5,
2010, Explosion: A Failure of Basic Coal Mine Safety Practices," Report
to the Governor, Governor's Independent Investigation Panel, May 2011,
http://www.npr.org/documents/2011/may/giip-massey-report.pdf.

56   Mine Safety and Health Administration Press Release, "US Labor
Department's MSHA Cites Corporate Culture as Root Cause of Upper
Big Branch Mine Disaster," December 6, 2011, http://www.dol.gov/opa
/media/press/msha/msha20111734.htm.

57   Sabrina Tavernise and Clifford Krauss, "Mine Owner Will Pay $209
Million in Blast That Killed 29 Workers," *New York Times*, December
6, 2011, http://www.nytimes.com/2011/12/07/us/mine-owner-to-pay
-200-million-in-west-virginia-explosion.html.

58 Ken Ward Jr., "Longtime Massey Energy CEO Don Blankenship Indicted," *Charleston Gazette-Mail*, November 13, 2014, http://www.wvgazette.com/article/20141113/GZ01/141119629; Alan Blinder, "Mixed Verdict for Donald Blankenship, Ex-Chief of Massey Energy, after Coal Mine Blast," *New York Times*, December 3, 2015, http://www.nytimes.com/2015/12/04/us/donald-blankenship-massey-energy-upper-big-branch-mine.html; Associated Press, "The Latest: Ex-coal CEO Says He's Not Guilty of Any Crime," April 6, 2016, http://bigstory.ap.org/1a5a91e3e4024062b806272d85008768.

59 Kim Geiger, Tom Hamburger, and Doug Smith, "Families of Dead Miners Feel Let Down by Washington," *Los Angeles Times*, May 8, 2011, http://articles.latimes.com/2011/may/08/nation/la-na-coal-mine-safety-20110508; Ben Adler, "To the Donors Go the Spoils," *Vice News*, March 29, 2017, https://news.vice.com/story/trump-gave-the-coal-industry-a-gift-this-week-heres-what-it-cost.

60 Peter A. Galuszka, *Thunder on the Mountain: Death at Massey and the Dirty Secrets behind Big Coal* (New York: St. Martin's Press, 2012).

61 Douglas Starr, "The Interview: Do Police Interrogation Techniques Produce False Confessions?" *New Yorker*, December 9, 2013, http://www.newyorker.com/magazine/2013/12/09/the-interview-7.

62 John T. Jost, Mahzarin R. Banaji, and Brian A. Nosek, "A Decade of System Justification Theory: Accumulated Evidence of Conscious and Unconscious Bolstering of the Status Quo," *Political Psychology* 25 (2004): 881-919; Gary Blasi and John T. Jost, "System Justification Theory and Research: Implications for Law, Legal Advocacy, and Social Justice," *California Law Review* 94 (2006), 1119-1168; Aaron C. Kay and Justin Friesen, "On Social Stability and Social Change: Understanding When System Justification Does and Does Not Occur," *Psychological Science* 20 (2011): 360-364.

63 James R. Kluegel and Eliot R. Smith, *Beliefs about Inequality: Americans' Views of What Is and What Ought to Be* (Hawthorne, NY: Aldine de Gruyter, 1986).

64 Brenda Major, Dean B. McFarlin, and Diana Gagnon, "Overworked and Underpaid: On the Nature of Gender Differences in Personal Entitlement," *Journal of Personality and Social Psychology* 47 (1984): 1399-1412; Jessica Schieder and Elise Gould, "'Women's Work' and the Gender Pay Gap," Economic Policy Institute, July 20, 2016, http://www.epi.org/files/pdf/110304.pdf.

65 Aaron C. Kay and John T. Jost, "Complementary Justice: Effects of 'Poor but Happy' and 'Poor but Honest' Stereotype Exemplars on System Justification and Implicit Activation of the Justice Motive," *Journal of Personality and Social Psychology* 85 (2003): 823–837.

66 Bruce Drake, "Polls Show Strong Support for Minimum Wage Hike," Pew Research Center, March 4, 2014, http://www.pewresearch.org/fact-tank/2014/03/04/polls-show-strong-support-for-minimum-wage-hike/.

67 Greg Sargent, "Bring It On: Battle over Minimum Wage Is Underway," *Washington Post*, February 13, 2013, https://www.washingtonpost.com /blogs/plum-line/wp/2013/02/13/bring-it-on-battle-over-minimum -wage-is-underway/.

68 Journal Editorial Report, "How to Become American?" *Wall Street Journal*, February 3, 2013, http://www.wsj.com/articles /SB10001424127887324445904578282074152947286.

69 James Sherk and John Ligon, "Unprecedented Minimum-Wage Hike Would Hurt Jobs and the Economy," Heritage Foundation, Issue Brief #4102 on Labor, December 5, 2013, http://www.heritage.org/research /reports/2013/12/unprecedented-minimum-wage-hike-would-hurt -jobs-and-the-economy.

70 Kate Taylor, "Fast-food CEO Says He's Investing in Machines Because the Government Is Making It Difficult to Afford Employees," *Business Insider*, March 16, 2016, http://www.businessinsider.com/carls-jr-wants -open-automated-location-2016-3.

71 Andrew Kaczynski, "Trump Labor Pick in 2011 on His Fast-Food Workers: We Hire 'the Best of the Worst,'" *CNN Money*, January 23, 2017, http://money.cnn.com/2017/01/23/news/kfile-puzder-best-of -the-worst/index.html.

72 John Schmitt, "Why Does the Minimum Wage Have No Discernible Effect on Employment?" Center for Economic and Policy Research, February 2013, http://www.cepr.net/documents/publications/min -wage-2013-02.pdf.

73 Ben Wolcott, "2014 Job Creation Faster in States That Raised the Minimum Wage," Center for Economic and Policy Research Blog, June 30, 2014, http://www.cepr.net/blogs/cepr-blog/2014-job -creation-in-states-that-raised-the-minimum-wage.

74 John Schmitt, "Why Does the Minimum Wage Have No Discernible Effect on Employment?" Center for Economic and Policy Research, February 2013, http://www.cepr.net/documents/publications/min -wage-2013-02.pdf; Catherine Ruetschlin and Amy Traub, "A Higher Wage Is Possible: How Walmart Can Invest in Its Workforce without Costing Customers a Dime," Demos, November 2013, http://www .demos.org/sites/default/files/publications/A%20Higher%20Wage %20Is%20Possible.pdf.

75 Jared Bernstein, "Minimum Wage: Who Makes It?" *New York Times*, June 9, 2014, http://www.nytimes.com/2014/06/10/upshot/minimum -wage.html.

76 Drew DeSilver and Steve Schwarzer: "Making More Than Minimum Wage, but Less Than $10.10 an Hour," Pew Research Center, November 5, 2014, http://www.pewresearch.org/fact-tank/2014/11/05/making -more-than-minimum-wage-but-less-than-10-10-an-hour/; Linda Tirado, *Hand to Mouth: Living in Bootstrap America* (New York: G. P. Putnam's Sons, 2014).

77   Rush Limbaugh Show, "Are You Willing to Pay Double for a Big Mac?"
August 30, 2013, http://www.rushlimbaugh.com/daily/2013/08/30
/are_you_willing_to_pay_double_for_a_big_mac.

78   Travis Holum, "What Will a Minimum Wage Increase Cost You
at McDonald's?" *Motley Fool*, June 8, 2014, http://www.fool.com
/investing/general/2014/06/08/what-will-a-higher-minimum
-wage-cost-you-at-mcdona.aspx.

79   Barbara Ehrenreich, *Nickled and Dimed: On (Not) Getting By in
America* (New York: Henry Holt, 2001).

80   Steven Greenhouse, *The Big Squeeze: Tough Times for the American
Worker* (New York: Alfred A. Knopf, 2008); Josh Bivens, *Failure by
Design: The Story behind America's Broken Economy* (Ithaca, NY:
Cornell University Press, 2011).

81   Lydia DePillis, "The $15 Minimum Wage Sweeping the Nation Might
Kill Jobs—and That's Okay," *Washington Post*, April 1, 2016, https://
www.washingtonpost.com/news/wonk/wp/2016/04/01/the-15
-minimum-wage-sweeping-the-nation-might-kill-jobs-and-thats-okay/.

82   Sarah Anderson, "Off the Deep End: The Wall Street Bonus Pool and
Low-Wage Workers," Institute for Policy Studies, March 2017, http://
www.ips-dc.org/wp-content/uploads/2017/03/Wall-Street-bonuses
-v-minimum-wage-2017-final.pdf.

83   Heather Mac Donald, "To See Its Value, See How Crime Rose
Elsewhere," *New York Times*, July 22, 2013, http://www.nytimes.com
/roomfordebate/2012/07/17/does-stop-and-frisk-reduce-crime/to-see
-its-value-see-how-crime-rose-elsewhere.

84   See Dylan Matthews, "Ray Kelly Says Stop & Frisk Saves Lives.
There's No Good Evidence for That," *Washington Post*, August 20, 2013,
http://www.washingtonpost.com/blogs/wonkblog/wp/2013/08/20
/ray-kelly-says-stop-frisk-saves-lives-theres-no-good-evidence-for-that/;
New York City Department of Investigation, Office of the Inspector
General for the NYPD, "An Analysis of Quality-of-Life Summonses,
Quality-of-Life Misdemeanor Arrests, and Felony Crime in New York
City, 2010-2015," June 22, 2016, http://www1.nyc.gov/assets/oignypd
/downloads/pdf/Quality-of-Life-Report-2010-2015.pdf; Nick Pinto,
"NYPD Watchdog Shatters Bratton's 'Broken Windows'—Now What?"
Village Voice, June 28, 2016, http://www.villagevoice.com/news/nypd
-watchdog-shatters-brattons-broken-windows-now-what-8796746.

85   Margot Alder, "At 'Stop-And-Frisk' Trial, Cops Describe Quota-Driven
NYPD," NPR, March 21, 2013, http://www.npr.org/2013/03/21
/174941454/at-stop-and-frisk-trial-cops-describe-quota-driven-nypd.

86   New York Civil Liberties Union, "New NYCLU Report Finds NYPD
Stop-and-Frisk Practices Ineffective, Reveals Depth of Racial
Disparities," May 9, 2012, http://www.nyclu.org/news/new-nyclu
-report-finds-nypd-stop-and-frisk-practices-ineffective-reveals-depth
-of-racial-dispar.

87 Andrea Peyser, "The Court of Lawlessness," *New York Post*, July 9, 2012, http://nypost.com/2012/07/09/the-court-of-lawlessness/.

88 Ross Tuttle and Eric Schneider, "Stopped-and-Frisked: 'For Being a F**king Mutt' [VIDEO]," *The Nation*, October 8, 2012, http://www.thenation.com/article/170413/stopped-and-frisked-being-fking-mutt-video.

89 Joseph Goldstein, "Judge Rejects New York's Stop-and-Frisk Policy," *New York Times*, August 12, 2013, http://www.nytimes.com/2013/08/13/nyregion/stop-and-frisk-practice-violated-rights-judge-rules.html.

90 Associated Press: "NYC Mayor Lambastes Stop-and-Frisk Ruling," *Politico*, August 13, 2013, http://www.politico.com/story/2013/08/stop-and-frisk-michael-bloomberg-new-york-95474.html.

91 Michael Bloomberg, "'Stop and Frisk' Keeps New York Safe," *Washington Post*, August 18, 2013, http://www.washingtonpost.com/opinions/michael-bloomberg-stop-and-frisk-keeps-new-york-safe/2013/08/18/8d4cd8c4-06cf-11e3-9259-e2aafe5a5f84_story.html.

92 S. A. Miller, "Violent Crime Will Go Up If Stop-and-Frisk Ends: Ray Kelly," *New York Post*, August 18, 2013, http://nypost.com/2013/08/18/violent-crime-will-go-up-if-stop-and-frisk-ends-ray-kelly/.

93 Rebecca Leber, "NYC Police Said Stop-and-Frisks Reduce Violent Crime. This Chart Says Otherwise." *New Republic*, December 2, 2014, http://www.newrepublic.com/article/120461/nypd-stop-and-frisk-drops-79-percent-and-crime-drops-too.

94 Aaron Blake, "The First Trump-Clinton Presidential Debate Transcript, Annotated," *Washington Post*, September 26, 2016, https://www.washingtonpost.com/news/the-fix/wp/2016/09/26/the-first-trump-clinton-presidential-debate-transcript-annotated/.

95 Eileen Sullivan, "White House Helps Pay for NYPD Muslim Surveillance" *Associated Press*, February 27, 2012, http://www.ap.org/content/ap-in-the-news/2012/white-house-helps-pay-for-nypd-muslim-surveillance.

96 John Avlon, "The Case for Ray Kelly as Obama's New Homeland Security Director," *Daily Beast*, July 12, 2013, http://www.thedailybeast.com/articles/2013/07/12/the-case-for-ray-kelly-as-obama-s-new-homeland-security-director.html.

97 Andrew Siff, "Ray Kelly Floated as Possible Replacement for Departing Homeland Security Chief Janet Napolitano," NBC 4 New York, http://www.nbcnewyork.com/news/local/NYPD-Commissioner-Ray-Kelly-Homeland-Security-Chief-Janet-Napolitano-215335781.html.

98 Jennifer Epstein, "Obama Would Consider Ray Kelly to Replace Janet Napolitano," *Politico*, July 16, 2013, http://www.politico.com/politico44/2013/07/obama-would-consider-ray-kelly-to-replace-janet-napolitano-168507.html.

99 Fritz Strack and Thomas Mussweiler, "Explaining the Enigmatic Anchoring Effect: Mechanisms of Selective Accessibility," *Journal of Personality and Social Psychology* 73 (1997): 437-446.

100 Dietram A. Scheufele and David Tewksbury, "Framing, Agenda Setting, and Priming: The Evolution of Three Media Effects Models," *Journal of Communication* 57 (2007): 9-20; Noam Chomsky, *Necessary Illusions: Thought Control in Democratic Societies* (Cambridge, MA: South End Press, 1989).

101 Sasha Abramsky, *The American Way of Poverty: How the Other Half Still Lives* (New York: Nation Books, 2013); Linda Tirado, *Hand to Mouth: Living in Bootstrap America* (New York: G. P. Putnam's Sons, 2014).

102 Thom Hartmann, *Cracking the Code: How to Win Hearts, Change Minds, and Restore America's Original Vision* (San Francisco, CA: Berrett-Koehler Publishers, 2007).

103 Pew Research Center, "Federal Tax System Seen in Need of Overhaul," March 19, 2015, http://www.people-press.org/files/2015/03/3-19-15 -Taxes-release.pdf.

104 Eric Peterson, "Tax Inversions Deals Show Upside Down Corporate Tax Code," Americans for Prosperity, July 17, 2014, http:// americansforprosperity.org/article/tax-inversions-deals-show-upside -down-corporate-tax-code.

105 Review & Outlook, "The Non-Taxpaying Class," *Wall Street Journal*, November 20, 2002, http://www.wsj.com/articles /SB1037748678534174748.

106 David Corn, "SECRET VIDEO: Romney Tells Millionaire Donors What He REALLY Thinks of Obama Voters," *Mother Jones*, September 17, 2012, http://www.motherjones.com/politics/2012/09/secret-video -romney-private-fundraiser; Joel F. Handler and Yeheskel Hasenfeld, *Blame Welfare: Ignore Poverty and Inequality* (New York: Cambridge University Press, 2007).

107 Rush Limbaugh Show, "Here We Go Again: 'Let Democrats Win!'" November 22, 2011, http://www.rushlimbaugh.com/daily/2011/11/22 /here_we_go_again_let_democrats_win.

108 Timothy Noah, "Eric Cantor: Tax The Poor!" *New Republic*, April 25, 2012, http://www.newrepublic.com/blog/timothy-noah/102966 /eric-cantor-tax-the-poor.

109 Floyd Norris, "Corporate Profits Grow and Wages Slide," *New York Times*, April 4, 2014, http://www.nytimes.com/2014/04/05/business /economy/corporate-profits-grow-ever-larger-as-slice-of-economy-as -wages-slide.html.

110 Noam Scheiber and Patricia Cohen, "For the Wealthiest, a Private Tax System That Saves Them Billions," *New York Times*, December 29, 2015, http://www.nytimes.com/2015/12/30/business/economy/for-the-wealthiest-private-tax-system-saves-them-billions.html; Sarah Anderson and Scott Klinger, "Burning Our Bridges," Center for Effective Government and Institute for Policy Studies, April 1, 2015, http://www.ips-dc.org/wp-content/uploads/2015/03/IPS_Burning-Bridges-Report.pdf; Sarah Anderson, Chuck Collins, Scott Klinger, and Sam Pizzigati, "Executive Excess 2011: The Massive CEO Rewards for Tax Dodging," Institute for Policy Studies, August 31, 2011, http://www.ips-dc.org/wp-content/uploads/2011/08/Executive-Excess-CEO-Rewards-for-Tax-Dodging.pdf; Sarah Anderson and Sam Pizzigati, "The Wall Street CEO Bonus Loophole," Institute for Policy Studies, August 31, 2016, http://www.ips-dc.org/wp-content/uploads/2016/08/IPS-report-on-CEO-bonus-loophole-embargoed-until-Aug-31-2016.pdf.

111 Citizens for Tax Justice, "Fifteen (of Many) Reasons Why We Need Corporate Tax Reform: Companies from Various Sectors Use Legal Tax Dodges to Avoid Taxes," April 11, 2016, http://ctj.org/ctjreports/10corporations0416final.pdf.

112 Jeff Immelt, "Bernie Sanders Says We're 'Destroying the Moral Fabric' of America. He's Wrong." LinkedIn, April 6, 2016, https://www.linkedin.com/pulse/facts-matter-jeff-immelt.

113 Lowell McAdam, "Feeling the Bern of Reality—The Facts about Verizon and the 'Moral Economy,'" LinkedIn, April 13, 2016, https://www.linkedin.com/pulse/feeling-bern-reality-facts-verizon-moral-economy-lowell-mcadam.

114 NBC News: Meet the Press, May 8, 2016, http://www.nbcnews.com/meet-the-press/meet-press-may-8-2016-n570111; Louis Jacobson and Linda Qiu, "For the Third Time, Donald Trump, U.S. Is Not 'Highest Taxed Nation in the World,'" *PolitiFact*, May 8, 2016, http://www.politifact.com/truth-o-meter/statements/2016/may/08/donald-trump/donald-trump-us-not-highest-taxed-nation-in-world/.

115 Kevin Drawbaugh, "Burger King to Save Millions in U.S. Taxes in 'Inversion': Study," *Reuters*, December 11, 2014, http://www.reuters.com/article/2014/12/11/us-usa-tax-burgerking-idUSKBN0JP0CI20141211.

116 Congressional Record, V. 149, PT. 1, January 7, 2003 to January 17, 2003, 1086.

117 John Thune, "Working toward Repealing Destructive and Unnecessary Death Tax," April 10, 2015, http://www.thune.senate.gov/public/index.cfm/2015/4/working-toward-repealing-destructive-and-unnecessary-death-tax.

118 House Committee on Ways and Means, "The Death Tax: The 'Wrong Tax at the Wrong Time,'" April 16, 2015, http://waysandmeans.house.gov/the-death-tax-the-wrong-tax-at-the-wrong-time/.

119 White House Office of the Press Secretary, "Briefing by Secretary of the Treasury Steven Mnuchin and Director of the National Economic Council Gary Cohn," April 26, 2017, https://www.whitehouse.gov/the -press-office/2017/04/26/briefing-secretary-treasury-steven-mnuchin -and-director-national.

120 Chye-Ching Huang and Brandon Debot, "Ten Facts You Should Know about the Federal Estate Tax," Center on Budget and Policy Priorities, March 23, 2015, http://www.cbpp.org/research/ten-facts-you-should-know-about-the-federal-estate-tax.

121 Karlyn Bowman, "A Killer Tax," *Forbes*, December 7, 2009, http://www .forbes.com/2009/12/04/polls-estate-death-tax-opinions-columnists -karlyn-bowman.html.

122 William W. Beach, "Seven Reasons Why Congress Should Repeal, Not Fix, the Death Tax," Heritage Foundation, WebMemo #2688, November 9, 2009, http://www.heritage.org/research/reports/2009/11/seven -reasons-why-congress-should-repeal-not-fix-the-death-tax.

123 Ilyana Kuziemko, Michael Norton, Emmanuel Saez, and Stefanie Stantcheva, "What Do Americans Think Should Be Done about Inequality?" Washington Center for Equitable Growth, March 26, 2015, http://d3b0lhre2rgreb.cloudfront.net/ms-content/uploads /sites/10/2015/03/25142544/032615-inequality-survey-ib.pdf.

124 Tax Policy Center, "A Preliminary Analysis of the Unified Framework," Urban Institute and Brookings Institution, October 27, 2017, http:// www.taxpolicycenter.org/sites/default/files/publication/144971/a -preliminary-analysis-of-the-unified-framework_2.pdf; John Nichols, "Senate Republicans Are Trying to Give the 1 Percent a $1.9 Trillion Tax Break," *The Nation*, October 20, 2017, https://www.thenation .com/article/senate-republicans-are-trying-to-give-the-1-percent-a -1-9-trillion-tax-break/.

125 Mark Denbeaux, Joshua Denbeaux, David Gratz, John Gregorek, Matthew Darby, Shana Edwards, Shane Hartman, Daniel Mann, and Helen Skinner, "Report on Guantanamo Detainees: A Profile of 517 Detainees through Analysis of Department of Defense Data," Center for Policy and Research, Seton Hall School of Law, February 8, 2006, http://law.shu.edu/publications/guantanamoReports/guantanamo _report_final_2_08_06.pdf.

126 Center for Constitutional Rights, "Report on Torture and Cruel, Inhuman, and Degrading Treatment of Prisoners at Guantánamo Bay, Cuba," July 2006, https://ccrjustice.org/sites/default/files/assets /Report_ReportOnTorture.pdf.

127 Guardian, "Torture Scandal: The Images That Shamed America," http://www.theguardian.com/gall/0,8542,1211872,00.html.

128 DoD News Briefing, Secretary of Defense Donald H. Rumsfeld, January 22, 2002, http://avalon.law.yale.edu/sept11/dod_brief139.asp.

129 Excerpts of Rumsfeld Testimony, *Washington Post*, May 7, 2004, http://www.washingtonpost.com/wp-dyn/articles/A9173-2004May7_3.html.

130 Sara Wood, "Rumsfeld: America Is 'Not What's Wrong with the World,'" *American Forces Press Service*, September 22, 2006, http://archive.defense.gov/news/newsarticle.aspx?id=1146.

131 Charles Babington, "Senator Critical of Focus on Prisoner Abuse," *Washington Post*, May 12, 2004, http://www.washingtonpost.com/wp-dyn/articles/A18915-2004May11.html.

132 Dick Durbin, "Treatment of Detainees at Guantanamo Bay," June 14, 2005, http://www.durbin.senate.gov/newsroom/press-releases/treatment-of-detainees-at-guantanamo-bay.

133 Joel Roberts, "Furor over Senator's Gitmo Remarks," CBS News, June 21, 2005, http://www.cbsnews.com/news/furor-over-senators-gitmo-remarks/.

134 Fox News, "Durbin Revises and Extends Gitmo Remarks," June 17, 2005, http://www.foxnews.com/story/2005/06/17/durbin-revises-and-extends-gitmo-remarks.html.

135 Michelle Malkin, "The Treacherous Dick Durbin," June 16, 2005, http://michellemalkin.com/2005/06/16/the-treacherous-dick-durbin/.

136 Greg Miller and Julian E. Barnes, "Rumsfeld Blamed in Detainee Abuse Scandals," Real Independent News & Film, December 12, 2008, http://rinf.com/alt-news/human-rights/rumsfeld-blamed-in-detainee-abuse-scandals/.

137 Plato, Republic, trans. Benjamin Jowett, http://classics.mit.edu/Plato/republic.html.

CHAPTER 4
Distrust Mind Games: Misdirecting Our Doubts and Suspicions

1   Tennessee Williams, *Camino Real* (New York: New Directions Publishing, 2008).

2   Susan T. Fiske, Amy J. C. Cuddy, and Peter Glick, "Universal Dimensions of Social Cognition: Warmth and Competence," *TRENDS in Cognitive Sciences* 11 (2007): 77-83.

3   Paul Rozin and Edward B. Royzman, "Negativity Bias, Negativity Dominance, and Contagion," *Personality and Social Psychology Review* 5 (2001): 296–320; Roy F. Baumeister, Ellen Bratslavsky, Catrin Finkenauer, and Kathleen D. Vohs, "Bad Is Stronger Than Good," *Review of General Psychology* 5 (2001): 323-370; Russell Hardin, *Trust & Trustworthiness* (New York: Russell Sage Foundation, 2002).

4   New York Times, "Full Transcript and Video: Trump News Conference," February 16, 2017, https://www.nytimes.com/2017/02/16/us/politics/donald-trump-press-conference-transcript.html.

5   Donald J. Trump (@realDonaldTrump), "Just leaving Florida. Big crowds of enthusiastic supporters lining the road that the FAKE NEWS media refuses to mention. Very dishonest!" Twitter, February 12, 2017, 5:19 a.m., https://twitter.com/realDonaldTrump/status/830904083519242241

6   Donald J. Trump (@realDonaldTrump), "The FAKE NEWS media (failing @nytimes, @NBCNews, @ABC, @CBS, @CNN) is not my enemy, it is the enemy of the American People!" Twitter, February 17, 2017, 1:48 p.m., https://twitter.com/realdonaldtrump/status/832708293516632065.

7   Donald J. Trump (@realDonaldTrump), "FAKE NEWS media knowingly doesn't tell the truth. A great danger to our country. The failing @nytimes has become a joke. Likewise @CNN. Sad!" Twitter, February 24, 2017, 10:09 p.m., https://twitter.com/realdonaldtrump/status/835325771858251776.

8   Donald J. Trump (@realDonaldTrump), "The Fake News Media works hard at disparaging & demeaning my use of social media because they don't want America to hear the real story!" Twitter, May 28, 2017, 8:20 p.m., https://twitter.com/realdonaldtrump/status/868985285207629825.

9   Donald J. Trump (@realDonaldTrump), "The Fake News Media has never been so wrong or so dirty. Purposely incorrect stories and phony sources to meet their agenda of hate. Sad!" Twitter, June 13, 2017, 6:35 a.m., https://twitter.com/realdonaldtrump/status/874576057579565056.

10   Donald J. Trump (@realDonaldTrump), "With all of its phony
     unnamed sources & highly slanted & even fraudulent reporting,
     #Fake News is DISTORTING DEMOCRACY in our country!"
     Twitter, July 16, 2017, 7:15 a.m., https://twitter.com/realdonaldtrump
     /status/886544734788997125.

11   David Leonhardt and Stuart A. Thompson, "Trump's Lies," *New York
     Times*, June 23, 2017, https://www.nytimes.com/interactive/2017/06
     /23/opinion/trumps-lies.html; Glenn Kessler, Michelle Ye Hee Lee,
     and Meg Kelly, "President Trump's First Six Months: The Fact-check
     Tally," *Washington Post*, July 20, 2017, https://www.washingtonpost
     .com/news/fact-checker/wp/2017/07/20/president-trumps-first-six
     -months-the-fact-check-tally.

12   Washington Post, "Washington Post-ABC News Poll April 17-20, 2017,"
     April 27, 2017, https://www.washingtonpost.com/politics/polling
     /washington-postabc-news-poll-april-1720/2017/04/27/186260fe
     -27d9-11e7-928e-3624539060e8_page.html.

13   Andrea Flynn, Susan Holberg, Dorian Warren, and Felicia Wong,
     "Rewrite the Racial Rules: Building an Inclusive American Economy,"
     Roosevelt Institute, June 2016, http://rooseveltinstitute.org/wp
     -content/uploads/2016/06/Structural-Discrimination-Final.pdf;
     Dedrick Asante-Muhammad, Chuck Collins, Josh Hoxie, and Emanuel
     Nieves, "The Ever-Growing Gap," CFED and Institute for Policy Studies,
     August 2016, http://www.ips-dc.org/wp-content/uploads/2016/08/The
     -Ever-Growing-Gap-CFED_IPS-Final-1.pdf.

14   National Center for Law and Economic Justice, "Poverty in the United
     States," November 4, 2015, http://nclej.org/wp-content/uploads/2015
     /11/2014PovertyStats.pdf.

15   Rakesh Kochhar, Richard Fry, and Paul Taylor, "Wealth Gaps Rise
     to Record Highs between Whites, Blacks, Hispanics," Pew Research
     Center, July 26, 2011, http://www.pewsocialtrends.org/2011/07/26
     /wealth-gaps-rise-to-record-highs-between-whites-blacks-hispanics/.

16   New York Civil Liberties Union, "Stop-and-Frisk Data," 2015,
     http://www.nyclu.org/content/stop-and-frisk-data.

17   Human Rights Watch, "Decades of Disparity: Drug Arrests and Race in
     the United States," March 2009, http://www.hrw.org/sites/default/files
     /reports/us0309web_1.pdf.

18   The Sentencing Project, "Black Lives Matter: Eliminating Racial
     Inequity in the Criminal Justice System," 2015, http://sentencingproject
     .org/wp-content/uploads/2015/11/Black-Lives-Matter.pdf; United
     States Sentencing Commission, "Booker Report 2012: Part E.
     Demographic Differences in Sentencing," http://www.ussc.gov/sites
     /default/files/pdf/news/congressional-testimony-and-reports/booker
     -reports/2012-booker/Part_E.pdf.

19 U.S. Government Accountability Office, "K-12 EDUCATION: Better Use of Information Could Help Agencies Identify Disparities and Address Racial Discrimination," April 2016, http://www.gao.gov/assets/680/676745.pdf; Jonathan Kozol: *The Shame of the Nation: The Restoration of Apartheid Schooling America* (New York: Three Rivers Press, 2005).

20 Algernon Austin, "The Unfinished March: An Overview," Economic Policy Institute, June 18, 2013, http://s2.epi.org/files/2013/EPI-The-Unfinished-March-An-Overview.pdf; Ta-Nehisi Coates, "The Case for Reparations," *The Atlantic*, June 2014, http://www.theatlantic.com/magazine/archive/2014/06/the-case-for-reparations/361631/; Ian Haney López, *Dog Whistle Politics: How Coded Racial Appeals Have Reinvented Racism and Wrecked the Middle Class* (New York: Oxford University Press, 2014); Roy Eidelson, Mikhail Lyubansky, and Kathleen Malley-Morrison, "Building a Racially Just Society: Psychological Insights," *Psychology Today*, November 18, 2014, https://www.psychologytoday.com/blog/dangerous-ideas/201411/building-racially-just-society-psychological-insights.

21 Igor Volsky, "Paul Ryan Blames Poverty on Lazy 'Inner City' Men," *Think Progress*, March 12, 2014, http://thinkprogress.org/economy/2014/03/12/3394871/ryan-poverty-inner-city/.

22 Barbara Lee, "Congresswoman Lee Responds to Ryan's Racially Charged Comments," March 12, 2014, http://lee.house.gov/news/press-releases/congresswoman-lee-responds-to-ryan-s-racially-charged-comments.

23 O'Reilly Factor, "Paul Ryan's Controversial Comments," Fox News, March 25, 2014, http://www.foxnews.com/transcript/2014/03/26/paul-ryans-controversial-comments/.

24 Media Matters, "O'Reilly Defends Smear of Rep. Lee: 'Not Only Is She a Pinhead, a Race Hustler, She's a Liar,'" March 29, 2014, http://mediamatters.org/video/2014/03/29/oreilly-defends-smear-of-rep-lee-not-only-is-sh/198671.

25 Jessica Chasmar, "Dinesh D'Souza: White House Has 'Perfected Art of Manufacturing Racial Resentment,'" *Washington Times*, December 2, 2014, http://www.washingtontimes.com/news/2014/dec/2/dinesh-dsouza-white-house-has-perfected-art-of-man/.

26 Hans von Spakovsky, "What Obama and Holder Should Have Said about Ferguson Grand Jury Verdict," *Daily Signal*, December 6, 2014, http://dailysignal.com/2014/12/06/what-obama-and-holder-should-have-said-about-ferguson-grand-jury-verdict/.

27 Jake Rosenfeld, Patrick Denice, and Jennifer Laird, "Union Decline Lowers Wages of Nonunion Workers," Economic Policy Institute, August 30, 2016, http://www.epi.org/files/pdf/112811.pdf.

28 Ken Jacobs, "Americans Are Spending $153 Billion a Year to Subsidize McDonald's and Wal-Mart's Low Wage Workers," *Washington Post*, April 15, 2015, https://www.washingtonpost.com/posteverything/wp/2015/04/15/we-are-spending-153-billion-a-year-to-subsidize-mcdonalds-and-walmarts-low-wage-workers/.

29 Jim Efstathiou Jr., "Wal-Mart Accused of Illegally Firing Striking Employees," *Bloomberg Business*, January 15, 2014, http://www.bloomberg.com/news/articles/2014-01-15/wal-mart-accused-of-illegally-firing-striking-employees.

30 Worker Center Watch, "'15 Now' Protests Reveal True Intentions of Labor Activists," March 14, 2014, http://www.workercenterwatch.com/15-now-protests-reveal-true-intentions-labor-activists/.

31 William Kristol, "We Will Not Live at the Mercy of Terrorists," *Weekly Standard*, August 26, 2002, http://www.weeklystandard.com/we-will-not-live-at-the-mercy-of-terrorists/article/2860.

32 Jim Garamone, "Congress, President Agree on Iraq Resolution," DoD News, American Forces Press Service, October 2, 2002, http://archive.defense.gov/news/newsarticle.aspx?id=42660.

33 Washington Post, "Text of President Bush's 2003 State of the Union Address," January 28, 2003, http://www.washingtonpost.com/wp-srv/onpolitics/transcripts/bushtext_012803.html.

34 New York Times, "Transcript: President Bush on Iraq," October 25, 2006, http://www.nytimes.com/2006/10/25/washington/25transcript-bush.html.

35 Associated Press, "Study: Bush Led U.S. to War on 'False Pretenses,'" NBC News, January 23, 2008, http://www.nbcnews.com/id/22794451/ns/world_news-mideast_n_africa/t/study-bush-led-us-war-false-pretenses/.

36 Fox News, "Transcript: Cheney on Guantanamo Detainees," January 27, 2002, http://www.foxnews.com/story/2002/01/27/transcript-cheney-on-guantanamo-detainees.html.

37 Katharine Q. Seelye, "A Nation Challenged: Captives; Detainees Are Not P.O.W.'s, Cheney and Rumsfeld Declare," *New York Times*, January 28, 2002, http://www.nytimes.com/2002/01/28/world/a-nation-challenged-captives-detainees-are-not-pow-s-cheney-and-rumsfeld-declare.html.

38 Josh White, "U.S. Generals in Iraq Were Told of Abuse Early, Inquiry Finds," *Washington Post*, December 1, 2004, http://www.washingtonpost.com/wp-dyn/articles/A23372-2004Nov30.html.

39 Council on Foreign Relations, "New Realities in the Media Age," February 17, 2006, http://www.cfr.org/iraq/new-realities-media-age/p34024.

40 Senate Select Committee on Intelligence, *Committee Study of the Central Intelligence Agency's Detention and Interrogation Program* (publicly released December 3, 2014), http://www.feinstein.senate.gov/public/index.cfm/files/serve?File_id=7c85429a-ec38-4bb5-968f-289799bf6d0e&SK=D500C4EBC500E1D256BA519211895909.

41 Carol Rosenberg, "New Guantánamo Intelligence Upends Old 'Worst of the Worst' Assumptions," *Miami Herald*, September 30, 2016, http://www.miamiherald.com/news/nation-world/world/americas/guantanamo/article105037571.html.

42 Sworn Declaration of Col. Lawrence B. Wilkerson (Ret) in U.S. District Court for the District of Columbia, March 24, 2010, http://www.truth-out.org/files/wilkerson-sworn-declaration.pdf.

43 Gordon W. Allport, *The Nature of Prejudice* (Reading, MA: Addison-Wesley, 1954); Marilynn B. Brewer, "The Psychology of Prejudice: Ingroup Love or Outgroup Hate?" *Journal of Social Issues* 55 (1999): 429-444.

44 Rob Kurzban, "Minimal Group Experiments," *Encyclopedia of Cognitive Science* (New York: John Wiley, 2006); Michael Diehl, "The Minimal Group Paradigm: Theoretical Explanations and Empirical Findings," *European Review of Social Psychology* 1 (1990): 263-292.

45 Ian Haney López, *Dog Whistle Politics: How Coded Racial Appeals Have Reinvented Racism and Wrecked the Middle Class* (New York: Oxford University Press, 2014).

46 Naomi Klein, *No Is Not Enough: Resisting Trump's Shock Politics and Winning the World We Need* (Chicago, IL: Haymarket Books, 2017).

47 Alex Henderson, "9 Surprising Industries Getting Filthy Rich from Mass Incarceration," *Salon*, February 22, 2015, http://www.salon.com/2015/02/22/9_surprising_industries_getting_filthy_rich_from_mass_incarceration_partner/.

48 Shara Tonn, "Stanford Research Suggests Support for Incarceration Mirrors Whites' Perception of Black Prison Populations," Stanford Report, August 6, 2014, http://news.stanford.edu/news/2014/august/prison-black-laws-080614.html.

49 ACLU, "Banking on Bondage: Private Prisons and Mass Incarceration," November 2, 2011, https://www.aclu.org/banking-bondage-private-prisons-and-mass-incarceration.

50 Washington Post, "Full Text: Donald Trump Announces a Presidential Bid," June 16, 2015, http://www.washingtonpost.com/news/post-politics/wp/2015/06/16/full-text-donald-trump-announces-a-presidential-bid/.

51 Esther Yu-His Lee, "Trump Says Racially Profiling Muslims Should Be the Country's Response to San Bernardino," *Think Progress*, December 6, 2015, http://thinkprogress.org/politics/2015/12/06/3728793/donald-trump-i-think-there-can-be-profiling-muslims/.

52 Tierney Sneed, "Trump Calls for Total Ban on Muslims Entering the U.S.," *Talking Points Memo*, December 7, 2015, http://talkingpointsmemo.com/livewire/donald-trump-shutdown-muslim-immigration.

53   Lee Bergquist and Jason Stein, "Walker Looks at Showdown with State Employee Unions," *Milwaukee Journal-Sentinel*, December 7, 2010, http://www.jsonline.com/news/statepolitics/111463779.html.

54   Jason Stein and Patrick Marley, "In Film, Walker Talks of 'Divide and Conquer' Union Strategy," *Milwaukee Journal-Sentinel*, May 10, 2012, http://www.jsonline.com/news/statepolitics/in-film-walker-talks-of -divide-and-conquer-strategy-with-unions-8o57h6f-151049555.html.

55   Sylvia A. Allegretto and Lawrence Mishel, "The Teacher Pay Gap Is Wider Than Ever," Economic Policy Institute, August 9, 2016, http://www.epi.org/files/pdf/110964.pdf.

56   Jon Bershad, "Glenn Beck: Protestors 'Will Come for You, Drag You into the Streets, and Kill You,'" Mediaite, October 10, 2011, http://www.mediaite.com/online/glenn-glenn-beck-occupy-wall -street-will-come-for-you-drag-you-into-the-streets-and-kill-you/.

57   Media Matters, "Limbaugh: I Was More Self-Sufficient at Age 10 Than 'This Parade of Human Debris Calling Itself Occupy Wall Street,'" October 5, 2011, http://mediamatters.org/video/2011/10 /05/limbaugh-i-was-more-self-sufficient-at-age-10-t/183547.

58   William Bigelow, "'Occupy Unmasked' Review: Shredding the Lies of the Movement," *Breitbart*, September 20, 2012, http://www.breitbart .com/big-hollywood/2012/09/20/occupy-unmasked-rips-the-lies-of -the-movement-to-shreds/.

59   Cavan Sieczkowski, "Occupy Wall Street Protest: The Rich 1% Mock Protestors [VIDEO]," *International Business Times*, September 27, 2011, http://www.ibtimes.com/occupy-wall-street-protest-rich-1-mock -protestors-video-319174.

60   Richard Perloff, *The Dynamics of Persuasion: Communication and Attitudes in the 21st Century* (New York: Routledge, 2010).

61   Amina A. Memon, Aldert Vrij, and Ray Bull, *Psychology and Law: Truthfulness, Accuracy and Credibility* (New York: John Wiley & Sons, 2003).

62   Zaid Jilani, "Mayor Bloomberg Claims 'Occupy Wall Street' Protesters Are Targeting Bankers Who 'Are Struggling to Make Ends Meet,'" *Think Progress*, September 30, 2011, http://thinkprogress.org/economy/2011 /09/30/333038/mayor-bloomberg-wall-street-make-ends-meet/.

63   Tanya Somanader, "Trump on Occupy Wall Street Movement: 'Nobody Knows Why They're Protesting,'" *Think Progress*, October 5, 2011, https://thinkprogress.org/trump-on-occupy-wall-street-movement -nobody-knows-why-theyre-protesting-1b600f3b6322.

64   Rory Cooper, "Has Occupy Wall Street Accomplished Anything?" *Politico*, November 18, 2011, http://www.politico.com/arena/archive /has-occupy-wall-street-accomplished-anything.html.

65 Roger Pilon, "Has Occupy Wall Street Accomplished Anything?" *Politico*, November 18, 2011, http://www.politico.com/arena/archive/has-occupy-wall-street-accomplished-anything.html.

66 Senate Committee on the Judiciary, "Testimony of Attorney General John Ashcroft," December 6, 2001, http://www.justice.gov/archive/ag/testimony/2001/1206transcriptsenatejudiciarycommittee.htm.

67 Dan Balz, "Democrats Call for Rove to Apologize," *Washington Post*, June 24, 2005, http://www.washingtonpost.com/wp-dyn/content/article/2005/06/23/AR2005062301727.html.

68 David E. Sanger and Jim Rutenberg, "White House Hones a Strategy for Post-Zarqawi Era," *New York Times*, June 13, 2006, http://www.nytimes.com/2006/06/13/washington/13prexy.html.

69 Angus West, "17 Disturbing Things Snowden Has Taught Us (So Far)," *Public Radio International*, June 1, 2015, https://www.pri.org/stories/2013-07-09/17-disturbing-things-snowden-has-taught-us-so-far.

70 Wall Street Journal, "Transcript: Obama's Remarks on NSA Controversy," June 7, 2013, http://blogs.wsj.com/washwire/2013/06/07/transcript-what-obama-said-on-nsa-controversy/.

71 White House, Office of the Press Secretary, "Remarks by the President in a Press Conference," August 9, 2013, https://www.whitehouse.gov/the-press-office/2013/08/09/remarks-president-press-conference.

72 Glenn Greenwald, "Rand Paul Is Right: NSA Routinely Monitors Americans' Communications without Warrants," *The Intercept*, March 13, 2017, https://theintercept.com/2017/03/13/rand-paul-is-right-nsa-routinely-monitors-americans-communications-without-warrants/.

73 Craig Timberg and Barton Gellman, "NSA Paying U.S. Companies for Access to Communications Networks," *Washington Post*, August 29, 2013, https://www.washingtonpost.com/world/national-security/nsa-paying-us-companies-for-access-to-communications-networks/2013/08/29/5641a4b6-10c2-11e3-bdf6-e4fc677d94a1_story.html; Dana Priest and William Arkin, *Top Secret America: The Rise of the New American Security State* (Boston: Little, Brown & Company, 2011); Kenneth Lipp, "AT&T Is Spying on Americans for Profit, New Documents Reveal," *Daily Beast*, October 25, 2016, http://www.thedailybeast.com/articles/2016/10/25/at-t-is-spying-on-americans-for-profit.html.

74 Richard Esguerra, "Google CEO Eric Schmidt Dismisses the Importance of Privacy," Electric Frontier Foundation, December 10, 2009, https://www.eff.org/deeplinks/2009/12/google-ceo-eric-schmidt-dismisses-privacy.

75 In the Public Interest, "The Banks That Finance Private Prison Companies," November 2016, https://www.inthepublicinterest.org/wp-content/uploads/ITPI_BanksPrivatePrisonCompanies_Nov2016.pdf.

76   Center for Constitutional Rights, "Immigration Detention Bed Quotas: Private Prison Corporations, Government Collude to Keep Contracts Secret; Undue Corporate Influence Seen in FOIA Redactions, Attorneys Say," December 23, 2015, http://ccrjustice.org/home/press-center /press-releases/immigration-detention-bed-quotas-private-prison -corporations; Sarah Stillman, "Get Out of Jail, Inc.," *New Yorker*, June 23, 2014, http://www.newyorker.com/magazine/2014/06/23 /get-out-of-jail-inc.

77   Center for Constitutional Rights, "Second Circuit Court of Appeals Rules Corporations Cannot Stop Release of Government Documents," February 8, 2017, https://ccrjustice.org/home/press-center/press -releases/private-prison-corporations-thrown-out-court.

78   ACLU, "Banking on Bondage: Private Prisons and Mass Incarceration," November 2, 2011, https://www.aclu.org/banking-bondage-private -prisons-and-mass-incarceration.

79   National Public Radio, "Who Benefits When a Private Prison Comes to Town?" WBUR, November 5, 2011, http://www.wbur.org/npr /142058047/who-benefits-when-a-private-prison-comes-to-town.

80   Ted Hesson, "Wells Fargo Pressured over Investments in Private Prisons," *Univision*, November 12, 2012, http://npa-us.org/news /wells-fargo-pressured-over-investments-private-prisons/111212.

81   Office of the Inspector General, U.S. Department of Justice, "Review of the Federal Bureau of Prisons' Monitoring of Contract Prisons," August 2016, https://oig.justice.gov/reports/2016/e1606.pdf.

82   MSNBC, "FULL TRANSCRIPT: MSNBC Town Hall with Donald Trump Moderated by Chris Matthews," March 30, 2016, http://info .msnbc.com/_news/2016/03/30/35330907-full-transcript-msnbc -town-hall-with-donald-trump-moderated-by-chris-matthews.

83   Jen Wieczner, "Donald Trump's Election Win Is Making This Stock Soar," *Fortune*, November 9, 2016, http://fortune.com/2016/11/09 /donald-trump-stock-market-corrections-corp/.

84   Paul K. Piff, Daniel M. Stancato, Stéphane Côté, Rodolfo Mendoza- Denton, and Dacher Keltner, "Higher Social Class Predicts Increased Unethical Behavior," *PNAS* 109 (2012): 4086-4091. http://www.pnas .org/content/109/11/4086.full.pdf.

85   Kim Parker, "Yes, the Rich Are Different," Pew Research Center, August 27, 2012, http://www.pewsocialtrends.org/2012/08/27 /yes-the-rich-are-different/.

86   Walmart, "Mike Duke, President and CEO of Wal-Mart Stores, Inc.: Walmart Shareholders' Meeting 2012," June 1, 2012, http://news .walmart.com/executive-viewpoints/walmarts-enduring-values.

87   George Lakoff, *Moral Politics: How Liberals and Conservatives Think* (Chicago, IL: University of Chicago Press, 2002).

88 Michael Corkery, "Read Lloyd Blankfein's Testimony for Tuesday's 'Fab' Hearing," *Wall Street Journal*, April 26, 2010, http://blogs.wsj.com /deals/2010/04/26/read-lloyd-blankfeins-testimony-for-tuesdays -fab-hearing/.

89 Michael J. Moore and Pamela Roux, "Lloyd Blankfein Is Now a Billionaire," *Bloomberg*, July 17, 2015, http://www.bloomberg.com/news /articles/2015-07-17/blankfein-becomes-billionaire-riding-goldman-s -shares-to-riches.

90 Permanent Senate Subcommittee on Investigations, "Testimony from Lloyd C. Blankfein, Chairman and CEO, The Goldman Sachs Group, Inc.," April 27, 2010, https://www.hsgac.senate.gov/download /stmt-blankfein-lloyd-april-27-2010-goldman-sachs-hrg.

91 Greg Gordon, "How Goldman Secretly Bet on the U.S. Housing Crash," *McClatchy Newspapers*, November 1, 2009, http://www.mcclatchydc .com/news/politics-government/article24561376.html; Gretchen Morgenson and Louise Story, "Banks Bundled Bad Debt, Bet against It and Won," *New York Times*, December 23, 2009, http://www.nytimes .com/2009/12/24/business/24trading.html; Gary Rivlin and Michael Hudson, "Government by Goldman," *The Intercept*, September 17, 2017, https://theintercept.com/2017/09/17/goldman-sachs-gary-cohn -donald-trump-administration/.

92 Greg Gordon, "How Goldman Secretly Bet on the U.S. Housing Crash," *McClatchy Newspapers*, November 1, 2009, http://www.mcclatchydc .com/news/politics-government/article24561376.html.

93 Renae Merle, "Goldman Sachs Pays $5 Billion to Settle Allegations It Sold Shoddy Mortgages," *Washington Post*, April 11, 2016, https://www .washingtonpost.com/news/business/wp/2016/04/11/goldman-sachs -pays-5-billion-to-settle-allegations-it-sold-shoddy-mortgages-prior-to -financial-crisis/.

94 Matt Taibbi, "The People vs. Goldman Sachs" *Rolling Stone*, May 11, 2011, http://www.rollingstone.com/politics/news/the-people-vs -goldman-sachs-20110511; Robert Scheer, *The Great American Stickup: How Reagan Republicans and Clinton Democrats Enriched Wall Street While Mugging Main Street* (New York: Nation Books, 2010).

95 Tim Higgins and Nick Summers, "GM Recalls: How General Motors Silenced a Whistle-Blower," *Bloomberg Businessweek*, June 19, 2014, http://www.businessweek.com/articles/2014-06-18/gm-recalls-whistle -blower-was-ignored-mary-barra-faces-congress; Drew Harwell, "Why General Motors' $900 Million Fine for a Deadly Defect Is Just a Slap on the Wrist," *Washington Post*, September 17, 2015, https://www .washingtonpost.com/news/business/wp/2015/09/17/why-general -motors-900-million-fine-for-a-deadly-defect-is-just-a-slap-on-the -wrist/.

96 Ryan Jaslow, "Big Tobacco Kept Cancer Risk in Cigarettes Secret: Study," CBS News, September 30, 2011, http://www.cbsnews.com /news/big-tobacco-kept-cancer-risk-in-cigarettes-secret-study/.

97 United States Senate Health, Education, Labor and Pensions Committee, "For Profit Higher Education: The Failure to Safeguard the Federal Investment and Ensure Student Success," July 30, 2012, https://assets.documentcloud.org/documents/407797/help-senate-report.pdf.

98 John Cassidy, "Trump University: It's Worse Than You Think," *New Yorker*, June 2, 2016, http://www.newyorker.com/news/john-cassidy/trump-university-its-worse-than-you-think.

99 International Consortium of Investigative Journalists, "The Panama Papers: Politicians, Criminals and the Rogue Industry That Hides Their Cash," April 2016, https://panamapapers.icij.org; Eric Lipton and Julie Creswell, "Panama Papers Show How Rich United States Clients Hid Millions Abroad," *New York Times*, June 6, 2016, http://www.nytimes.com/2016/06/06/us/panama-papers.html.

CHAPTER 5
Superiority Mind Games: Enticing Us with Praise and Pretensions

1   F. Scott Fitzgerald, *The Great Gatsby* (New York: Charles Scribner's Sons, 1925).

2   Ben M. Tappin and Ryan T. McKay, "The Illusion of Moral Superiority," *Social Psychological and Personality Science* 8 (2017): 623-631.

3   Lee Ross, "The Intuitive Psychologist and His Shortcomings: Distortions in the Attribution Process," in *Advances in Experimental Social Psychology*, ed. Leonard Berkowitz (New York: Academic Press, 1977): 173-220.

4   Edward E. Jones and Victor A. Harris. "The Attribution of Attitudes," *Journal of Experimental Social Psychology* 3 (1967): 1-24; Lee Ross, Teresa M. Amabile, and Julia L. Steinmetz, "Social Roles, Social Control, and Biases in Social-Perception Processes," *Journal of Personality and Social Psychology* 35 (1977): 485-494.

5   Pew Charitable Trusts, "Pursuing the American Dream: Economic Mobility across Generations," July 2012, http://www.pewtrusts.org/~/media/legacy/uploadedfiles/wwwpewtrustsorg/reports/economic_mobility/PursuingAmericanDreampdf.pdf; Lauren Leatherby, "US Social Mobility Gap Continues to Widen," *Financial Times*, December 16, 2016, https://www.ft.com/content/7de9165e-c3d2-11e6-9bca-2b93a6856354.

6   Joseph E. Stiglitz, "Equal Opportunity, Our National Myth," *New York Times*, February 16, 2013, http://opinionator.blogs.nytimes.com/2013/02/16/equal-opportunity-our-national-myth/.

7   Linda Levine, *The U.S. Income Distribution and Mobility: Trends and International Comparisons*, Congressional Research Service, November 29, 2012, http://www.fas.org/sgp/crs/misc/R42400.pdf.

8   Benjamin Domenech, "The Right Needs a New Message on Income Inequality," *Wall Street Journal*, April 28, 2014, http://blogs.wsj.com/washwire/2014/04/28/what-the-right-should-learn-about-inequality/.

9   Jacob S. Hacker, *The Great Risk Shift: The Assault on American Jobs, Families, Health Care, and Retirement and How You Can Fight Back* (New York: Oxford University Press, 2006).

10   Karen Dolan and Jodi L. Carr, "The Poor Get Prison: The Alarming Spread of the Criminalization of Poverty," Institute for Policy Studies, March 2015, http://www.ips-dc.org/the-poor-get-prison-the-alarming-spread-of-the-criminalization-of-poverty/.

11   National Law Center on Homelessness & Poverty, "No Safe Place: The Criminalization of Homelessness in U.S. Cities," July 2014, http://www.nlchp.org/documents/No_Safe_Place.

12   Emily Badger, "The Double-Standard of Making the Poor Prove They're
      Worthy of Government Benefits," *Washington Post*, April 7, 2015, http://
      www.washingtonpost.com/blogs/wonkblog/wp/2015/04/07/the-double
      -standard-of-making-poor-people-prove-theyre-worthy-of-government
      -benefits/.

13   White House Office of the Press Secretary, "Remarks by the President at
      a Hillary for America Rally—Jacksonville, Florida," November 3, 2016,
      https://www.whitehouse.gov/the-press-office/2016/11/03/remarks
      -president-hillary-america-rally-jacksonville-florida.

14   Justin Miller, "Emboldened by Trump, Minimum-Wage-Hike
      Opponents Fight Back," *American Prospect*, March 14, 2017, http://
      prospect.org/article/emboldened-trump-minimum-wage-hike
      -opponents-fight-back.

15   Elise Gould, "Why America's Workers Need Faster Wage Growth—and
      What We Can Do about It," Economic Policy Institute, August 27, 2014,
      http://s4.epi.org/files/2014/why-americas-workers-need-faster-wage
      -growth-final.pdf.

16   Emmanuel Saez and Gabriel Zucman, "Wealth Inequality in the
      United States since 1913: Evidence from Capitalized Income Tax
      Data," National Bureau of Economic Research, October 2014,
      http://gabriel-zucman.eu/files/SaezZucman2014.pdf.

17   Salvatore Babones, "The Minimum Wage Is Stuck at $7.25;
      It Should Be $21.16—or Higher," Inequality.org, July 24, 2012,
      http://inequality.org/minimum-wage/.

18   Media Matters, "Fox's Stuart Varney on the Poor: 'Many of Them Have
      Things—What They Lack Is the Richness of Spirit,'" August 25, 2011,
      http://mediamatters.org/video/2011/08/25/foxs-stuart-varney-on-the
      -poor-many-of-them-hav/138530.

19   Media Matters, "Boortz: Adults Earning Minimum Wage Are
      'Incompetent,' 'Ignorant,' 'Stupid,' 'Worthless,' and 'Pathetic,'"
      August 3, 2006, http://mediamatters.org/research/2006/08/03
      /boortz-adults-earning-minimum-wage-are-incompet/136310.

20   NewsHounds, "Fox Fearmongers That Detroit Bankruptcy Is a
      'Wake Up or Else' Call," July 20, 2013, http://www.newshounds.us
      /fox_fearmongers_that_detroit_bankruptcy_is_a_wake_up_or
      _else_call_07202013#YH9CJFwlpohIQ858.99.

21   Conor Friedersdorf, "The Radical Anti-Conservatism of Stephen
      Bannon," *The Atlantic*, August 25, 2016, https://www.theatlantic.com
      /politics/archive/2016/08/the-radical-anti-conservatism-of-stephen
      -bannon/496796/.

22   Grace Wyler, "Newt Gingrich Slams Occupy Wall Street: 'Take a Bath'
      and 'Get a Job,'" *Business Insider*, November 21, 2011, http://www
      .businessinsider.com/newt-gingrich-occupy-wall-street-video-2011-11.

23 Jordan Weissmann, "Newt Gingrich Thinks School Children Should Work as Janitors," *The Atlantic*, November 21, 2011, http://www.theatlantic.com/business/archive/2011/11/newt -gingrich-thinks-school-children-should-work-as-janitors/248837/.

24 Jonathon D. Brown, "Understanding the Better Than Average Effect: Motives (Still) Matter," *Personality and Social Psychology Bulletin* 38 (2012): 209-219.

25 Felicia Pratto, James Sidanius, Lisa M. Stallworth, and Bertram F. Malle, "Social Dominance Orientation: A Personality Variable Predicting Social and Political Attitudes," *Journal of Personality and Social Psychology* 67 (1994): 741-763; James Sidanius, Sarah Cotterill, Jennifer Sheehy-Skeffington, Nour Kteily, and Héctor Carvacho, "Social Dominance Theory: Explorations in the Psychology of Oppression," in *Cambridge Handbook of the Psychology of Prejudice*, eds. Chris Sibley and Fiona K. Barlow (Cambridge, UK: Cambridge University Press, 2016), 149-187.

26 Corey Robin, *The Reactionary Mind: Conservatism from Edmund Burke to Sarah Palin* (New York: Oxford University Press, 2011).

27 Christopher Ingraham, "The 'Alt-right' Is Just Another Word for White Supremacy, Study Finds," *Washington Post*, August 16, 2017, https://www.washingtonpost.com/news/wonk/wp/2017/08/16/the -alt-right-is-just-another-word-for-white-supremacy-study-finds/.

28 Ayn Rand, *For the New Intellectual* (New York: Signet Books, 1992).

29 Michael J. De La Merced, "Schwarzman's Unfortunate War Analogy," *New York Times*, August 16, 2010, http://dealbook.nytimes.com/2010 /08/16/schwarzmans-unfortunate-war-analogy/.

30 Robert Frank, "'I Wanted the Biggest,'" *Wall Street Journal*, November 5, 2007, http://blogs.wsj.com/wealth/2007/11/05/i-wanted-the-biggest/.

31 Wall Street Journal, "Progressive Kristallnacht Coming?" Letters, January 24, 2014, http://www.wsj.com/news/articles /SB10001424052702304549504579316913982034286.

32 Wall Street Journal, "Perkinsnacht: Liberal Vituperation Makes Our Letter Writer's Point," Review & Outlook, January 29, 2014, http://www .wsj.com/articles/SB10001424052702304691904579348791505926788.

33 Bloomberg Business, "Zell: The 1% Work Harder and Should Be Emulated," February 5, 2014, http://www.bloomberg.com/news /videos/b/75f58b37-90f1-42f0-86c1-014aeb39a3e9.

34 ValueWalk, "Wilbur Ross Agrees with Tom Perkins, Sam Zell," February 11, 2014, http://www.valuewalk.com/2014/02/wilbur-ross -agrees-tom-perkins-sam-zell/.

35 Joshua Green, "Tom Perkins on Bloomberg TV: 'I Don't Regret the Message,'" *Bloomberg Businessweek*, January 28, 2014, http://www.bloomberg.com/bw/articles/2014-01-27/tom-perkins -on-bloomberg-tv-i-dont-regret-the-message.

36 Matt Phillips, "Goldman Sachs' Blankfein on Banking: 'Doing God's Work,'" *Wall Street Journal*, November 9, 2009, http://blogs.wsj.com /marketbeat/2009/11/09/goldman-sachs-blankfein-on-banking -doing-gods-work/.

37 Caroline Binham, "Goldman Sachs's Griffiths Says Inequality Helps All," *Bloomberg*, October 21, 2009.

38 Jessica Durando, "BP's Tony Hayward: 'I'd Like My Life Back,'" *USA Today*, June 1, 2010, http://content.usatoday.com/communities /greenhouse/post/2010/06/bp-tony-hayward-apology/1#.UzVhsVx6v6Q.

39 Ann Gerhart, "BP Chairman Talks about the 'Small People,' Further Angering Gulf," *Washington Post*, June 17, 2010, http://www.washingtonpost.com/wp-dyn/content/article /2010/06/16/AR2010061605528.html.

40 The Sentencing Project, "Report of The Sentencing Project to the United Nations Human Rights Committee Regarding Racial Disparities in the United States Criminal Justice System," August 2013, http://sentencingproject.org/doc/publications/rd_ICCPR%20Race %20and%20Justice%20Shadow%20Report.pdf; Chris Hedges, "The Mirage of Justice," *Truthdig*, January 17, 2016, http://www.truthdig .com/report/item/the_mirage_of_justice_20160117; Bernadette Rabuy and Daniel Kopf, "Detaining the Poor: How Money Bail Perpetuates an Endless Cycle of Poverty and Jail Time," Prison Policy Initiative, May 10, 2016, http://www.prisonpolicy.org/reports/incomejails.html.

41 Glenn Greenwald, *With Liberty and Justice for Some* (New York: Metropolitan Books, 2011).

42 Matt Taibbi, *The Divide: American Injustice in the Age of the Wealth Gap* (New York: Spiegel & Grau, 2014).

43 Janet Novack, "Federal Judges Are Cutting Rich Tax Cheats Big Sentencing Breaks," *Forbes*, May 14, 2014, http://www.forbes.com /sites/janetnovack/2014/05/14/federal-judges-are-cutting-rich-tax -cheats-big-sentencing-breaks/.

44 NPR Staff, "Fact Check: First Presidential Debate," NPR, September 27, 2016, http://www.npr.org/2016/09/27/495576599/fact-check-first -presidential-debate.

45 Laura D'Andrea Tyson and Owen Zidar, "Tax Cuts for Job Creators," *New York Times*, October 19, 2012, http://economix.blogs.nytimes .com/2012/10/19/tax-cuts-for-job-creators/; William Lajeunesse, "Billionaire Bashing Ignores Economic Reality, Say Class Warfare Critics," FoxNews.com, February 19, 2016, http://www.foxnews.com /us/2016/02/19/billionaire-bashing-ignores-economic-reality-say -class-warfare-critics.html.

46 Robert Reich, "The Four Biggest Right-Wing Lies about Inequality," May 5, 2014, http://robertreich.org/post/84828387105.

47 Nick Hanauer, "A Wealthy Capitalist on Why Money Doesn't Trickle Down," *Yes! Magazine*, September 9, 2014, http://www.yesmagazine.org /issues/the-end-of-poverty/wealthy-capitalist-nick-hanauer-on-why -money-doesn-t-trickle-down.

48 Emily Gipple and Ben Gose, "America's Generosity Divide," *Chronicle of Philanthropy*, August 19, 2012, https://philanthropy.com/article /America-s-Generosity-Divide/156175; Frank Greve, "America's Poor Are Its Most Generous Donors," *Seattle Times*, May 23, 2009, http:// www.seattletimes.com/nation-world/americas-poor-are-its-most -generous-donors/; Patricia Snell Herzog and Heather E. Price, *American Generosity: Who Gives and Why* (New York: Oxford University Press, 2016); Martin Korndörfer, Boris Egloff, and Stefan C. Schmukle, "A Large Scale Test of the Effect of Social Class on Prosocial Behavior," *PLoS ONE* 10(7) (2015): e0133193; Chuck Collins, Helen Flannery, and Josh Hoxie, "Gilded Giving: Top-Heavy Philanthropy in an Age of Extreme Inequality," Institute for Policy Studies, November 2016; http://www.ips-dc.org/wp-content/uploads/2016/11/Gilded -Giving-Final-pdf.pdf.

49 Alex Daniels, "As Wealthy Give Smaller Share of Income to Charity, Middle Class Digs Deeper," *Chronicle of Philanthropy*, October 5, 2014, https://philanthropy.com/article/As-Wealthy-Give-Smaller-Share/ 152481.

50 Emily Gipple and Ben Gose, "Rich Enclaves Are Not as Generous as the Wealthy Living Elsewhere," *Chronicle of Philanthropy*, August 19, 2012, https://philanthropy.com/article/Rich-Enclaves-Are-Not-as/156255.

51 Michael W. Kraus, Paul K. Piff, Rodolfo Mendoza-Denton, Michelle L. Rheinschmidt, and Dacher Keltner, "Social Class, Solipsism, and Contextualism: How the Rich Are Different from the Poor," *Psychological Review* 119 (2012): 546-572.

52 Jennifer E. Stellar, Vida M. Manzo, Michael W. Kraus, and Dacher Keltner, "Class and Compassion: Socioeconomic Factors Predict Responses to Suffering," *Emotion* 12 (2012): 449-459.

53 Jonas G. Miller, Sarah Kahle, and Paul D. Hastings, "Roots and Benefits of Costly Giving: Children Who Are More Altruistic Have Greater Autonomic Flexibility and Less Family Wealth," *Psychological Science* 26 (2015): 1038-1045.

54 Michael W. Kraus, Stéphane Côté, and Dacher Keltner, "Social Class, Contextualism, and Empathic Accuracy," *Psychological Science* 21 (2010): 1716-1723.

55 Nick Hanauer, "A Wealthy Capitalist on Why Money Doesn't Trickle Down," *Yes! Magazine*, September 9, 2014, http://www.yesmagazine. org/issues/the-end-of-poverty/wealthy-capitalist-nick-hanauer-on-why- money-doesn-t-trickle-down.

56   Clark McCauley, "The Psychology of Group Identification and the
      Power of Ethnic Nationalism," in *Ethnopolitical Warfare: Causes,
      Consequences, and Possible Solutions,* eds. Daniel Chirot and Martin
      E. P. Seligman (Washington: American Psychological Association
      Press, 2001), 343-362.

57   Sonia Roccas, Lilach Sagiv, Shalom Schwartz, Nir Halevy, and Roy
      Eidelson, "Toward a Unifying Model of Identification with Groups:
      Integrating Theoretical Perspectives," *Personality and Social
      Psychology Review* 12 (2008): 280-306.

58   Robert B. Cialdini, Richard J. Borden, Avril Thorne, Marcus R. Walker,
      Stephen Freeman, and Lloyd R. Sloan, "Basking in Reflected Glory:
      Three (Football) Field Studies," *Journal of Personality and Social
      Psychology* 34 (1976): 366-375.

59   White House, "National Security Strategy," February 2015,
      https://www.whitehouse.gov/sites/default/files/docs/2015
      _national_security_strategy.pdf.

60   Katie Reilly, "Read Hillary Clinton's Speech on Donald Trump and
      National Security," Time.com, June 2, 2016, http://time.com/4355797
      /hillary-clinton-donald-trump-foreign-policy-speech-transcript/.

61   Nick Gillespie, "Read/Watch the Scariest Speech from Both the
      RNC and DNC: John Allen's Unrestrained War-Mongering,"
      Reason.com, July 31, 2016, http://reason.com/blog/2016/07/31
      /readwatch-the-scariest-speech-from-both.

62   Mike Lofgren, *The Deep State: The Fall of the Constitution and
      the Rise of a Shadow Government* (New York: Viking, 2016).

63   White House, "National Security Strategy," February 2015,
      https://www.whitehouse.gov/sites/default/files/docs/2015_national_
      security_strategy.pdf.

64   Pieter D. Wezeman and Siemon T. Wezeman, "Trends in International
      Arms Transfers, 2014," Stockholm International Peace Research
      Institute Fact Sheet, March 2015, http://books.sipri.org/files/FS
      /SIPRIFS1503.pdf; Catherine A. Theohary, "Conventional Arms
      Transfers to Developing Nations, 2008-2015," Congressional
      Research Service, December 19, 2016, https://fas.org/sgp/crs
      /weapons/R44716.pdf.

65   U.S. Department of State, "Briefing on Department of State Efforts
      to Expand Defense Trade," June 14, 2012, http://m.state.gov/
      md192408.htm.

66   Zach Toombs and Jeffrey Smith, "Why Is the U.S. Selling Billions
      in Weapons to Autocrats?" *Foreign Policy*, June 21, 2012,
      http://foreignpolicy.com/2012/06/21/why-is-the-u-s-selling
      -billions-in-weapons-to-autocrats/.

67 Mark Mazzetti and Helene Cooper, "Sale of U.S. Arms Fuels the Wars of Arab States," *New York Times*, April 18, 2015, http://www.nytimes.com /2015/04/19/world/middleeast/sale-of-us-arms-fuels-the-wars-of-arab -states.html.

68 Deloitte, "2016 Global Aerospace and Defense Sector Outlook: Poised for a Rebound," January 2016, http://www2.deloitte.com/content/dam /Deloitte/global/Documents/Manufacturing/gx-manufacturing-2016 -global-ad-sector-outlook.pdf.

69 Jonathan Weisman, "U.S. Shifts Stance on Drug Pricing in Pacific Trade Pact Talks, Document Reveals," *New York Times*, June 10, 2015, http:// www.nytimes.com/2015/06/11/business/international/us-shifts-stance -on-drug-pricing-in-pacific-trade-pact-talks-document-reveals.html.

70 Médecins Sans Frontières, "1998: Big Pharma Versus Nelson Mandela," MSF Access Campaign, January 2009, http://www.msfaccess.org /content/1998-big-pharma-versus-nelson-mandela.

71 Rachel L. Swarns, "Drug Makers Drop South Africa Suit over AIDS Medicine," *New York Times*, April 20, 2001, http://www.nytimes.com /2001/04/20/world/drug-makers-drop-south-africa-suit-over-aids -medicine.html.

72 Sarah Ferris, "House Dems: White House Pushing Big Pharma Agenda in Trade Deal," *The Hill*, July 17, 2015, http://thehill.com/policy /healthcare/248322-house-dems-white-house-is-pushing-big-pharma -agenda-in-trade-deal; Paul Farmer, *Pathologies of Power: Health, Human Rights, and the New War on the Poor* (Berkeley, CA: University of California Press, 2005).

73 George Lakoff, *Whose Freedom? The Battle over America's Most Important Idea* (New York: Farrar, Strauss and Giroux, 2006).

74 Bob Cohn, "21 Charts That Explain American Values Today," *The Atlantic*, June 27, 2012, http://www.theatlantic.com/national/archive /2012/06/21-charts-that-explain-american-values-today/258990/.

75 Lydia Saad, "Americans Consider Individual Freedoms Nation's Top Virtue," Gallup, January 7, 2013, http://www.gallup.com/poll/159716 /americans-consider-individual-freedoms-nation-top-virtue.aspx.

76 Ian Millhiser, "Conservatives Have Twisted the Word 'Freedom' into Something Martin Luther King Would Never Recognize," *Think Progress*, August 28, 2013, http://thinkprogress.org/justice/2013/08 /28/2529621/mlk-freedom-equality-conservatives/.

77 Bernie Horn, "There's No Such Thing as 'Free' Markets," Campaign For America's Future, March 1, 2015, http://ourfuture.org/20150301/theres -no-such-thing-as-free-markets.

78 Robert Reich, *Saving Capitalism: For the Many, Not the Few* (New York: Vintage Books, 2015).

79 National Right to Work, "Right to Work: Frequently Asked Questions," http://www.nrtw.org/b/rtw_faq.htm.

80 Governor's Office Press Release, "Governor Scott Walker Signs Freedom to Work Legislation," March 9, 2015, http://walker.wi.gov/newsroom /press-release/governor-scott-walker-signs-freedom-work-legislation.

81 James Sherk and Andrew Kloster, "Local Governments Can Increase Job Growth and Choices by Passing Right-to-Work Laws," Heritage Foundation, August 26, 2014, http://thf_media.s3.amazonaws. com/2014/pdf/BG2947.pdf.

82 Elise Gould and Will Kimball, "'Right-To-Work' States Still Have Lower Wages," Economic Policy Institute, April 22, 2015, http://s1.epi .org/files/pdf/82934.pdf.

83 Ashley Byrd, "Trump Backs Off on Break with Party, 'Can Live with Unions at Certain Locations' (Interview)," South Carolina Radio Network, February 17, 2016, http://www.southcarolinaradionetwork .com/2016/02/17/trump-backs-off-on-break-with-party-can-live-with -unions-at-certain-locations-interview/.

84 Lee Fang, "In Statehouses Won by Republicans, the First Move Is to Consolidate Power by Weakening Unions," *The Intercept*, January 7, 2017, https://theintercept.com/2017/01/07/gop-2017-business/; Josh Eidelson, "Unions Are Losing Their Decades-Long 'Right-to-Work' Fight," *Bloomberg*, February 16, 2017, https://www.bloomberg.com /news/articles/2017-02-16/unions-are-losing-their-decades-long-right -to-work-fight.

85 Bob Altemeyer, "The Authoritarians," 2006, http://theauthoritarians .org/Downloads/TheAuthoritarians.pdf.

86 Robert T. Schatz, Ervin Staub, and Howard Lavine, "On the Varieties of National Attachment: Blind Versus Constructive Patriotism," *Political Psychology* 20 (1999): 151-174.

87 John Tierney, "The 2004 Campaign; Political Points," *New York Times*, January 11, 2004, http://www.nytimes.com/2004/01/11/us/the-2004 -campaign-political-points.html.

88 Thomas Frank, "Why They Won," *New York Times*, November 5, 2004, http://www.nytimes.com/2004/11/05/opinion/why-they-won.html; Thomas Frank, *What's the Matter with Kansas?: How Conservatives Won the Heart of America* (New York: Henry Holt, 2004).

89 Paul Waldman, *Being Right Is Not Enough: What Progressives Must Learn from Conservative Success* (New York: John Wiley & Sons, 2006).

90 Black Lives Matter, "Guiding Principles," http://blacklivesmatter.com /guiding-principles/.

91 Juliana Menasce Horowitz and Gretchen Livingston, "How Americans View the Black Lives Matter Movement," Pew Research Center, July 8, 2016, http://www.pewresearch.org/fact-tank/2016/07/08/how -americans-view-the-black-lives-matter-movement/.

92 Arturo Garcia, "Bill O'Reilly Freaks Out: #BlackLivesMatter 'Wants to Tear Down the Country,'" Raw Story, July 28, 2015, http://www.rawstory.com/2015/07/bill-oreilly-freaks-out-blacklivesmatter-wants-to-tear-down-the-country/.

93 Josh Feldman, "O'Reilly Scolds Black Lives Matter for 'Gestapo Tactics,' 'Condemning White Society,'" Mediaite, July 29, 2015, http://www.mediaite.com/tv/oreilly-scolds-black-lives-matter-for-gestapo-tactics-condemning-white-society/.

94 Tyler Cherry, "How Fox News' Primetime Lineup Demonized Black Lives Matter in 2015," Media Matters for America, December 29, 2015, http://mediamatters.org/mobile/blog/2015/12/29/how-fox-news-primetime-lineup-demonized-black-l/207637.

95 Bill O'Reilly, "How Black Lives Matter Is Killing Americans," Fox News, May 26, 2016, http://www.foxnews.com/transcript/2016/05/26/bill-oreilly-how-black-lives-matter-is-killing-americans/.

96 Bill O'Reilly, "Murdering Cops in Dallas," Fox News, July 11, 2016, http://www.foxnews.com/transcript/2016/07/11/bill-oreilly-murdering-cops-in-dallas/.

97 Fox News, "Donald Trump Lays Out Foreign and Domestic Strategies," September 9, 2015, http://www.foxnews.com/transcript/2015/09/09/donald-trump-lays-out-foreign-and-domestic-strategies/.

98 Media Matters, "Hannity Likens the Black Lives Matter Movement to the Ku Klux Klan," Fox News, October 21, 2015, http://mediamatters.org/video/2015/10/21/hannity-likens-the-black-lives-matter-movement/206339.

99 Media Matters, "Fox Regular David Clarke: Black Lives Matter Is 'Garbage,' a 'Subversive Movement' Advocating 'the Overthrow' of Our Government," October 26, 2015, http://mediamatters.org/video/2015/10/26/fox-regular-david-clarke-black-lives-matter-is/206416.

100 Media Matters, "Fox Guest: Black Lives Matter Is a 'Terrorist Group,'" October 23, 2015, http://mediamatters.org/video/2015/10/23/fox-guest-black-lives-matter-is-a-terrorist-gro/206385.

101 Brendan Gauthier, "Rudy Giuliani on 'Fox & Friends': Black Lives Matter 'Puts a Target on the Back of Police,'" Salon, July 11, 2016, http://www.salon.com/2016/07/11/rudy_giuliani_on_fox_friends_black_lives_matter_puts_a_target_on_the_back_of_police/.

102 The Movement for Black Lives, "Platform," https://policy.m4bl.org/platform/; Black Lives Matter, "Campaign Zero: Solutions," http://www.joincampaignzero.org/solutions/#solutionsoverview.

103 Pew Research Center, "Muslim Americans: No Signs of Growth in Alienation or Support for Extremism," August 2011, http://www.people-press.org/files/2011/08/muslim-american-report.pdf.

104 Pew Research Center, "Muslim Americans: No Signs of Growth in Alienation or Support for Extremism," August 30, 2011, http://www.people-press.org/2011/08/30/muslim-americans -no-signs-of-growth-in-alienation-or-support-for-extremism/.

105 Rob Morlino, "Hannity Suggested Use of Quran in Representative's Swearing-in Same as Using 'Nazi Bible' *Mein Kampf,*" *Media Matters,* December 1, 2006, http://mediamatters.org/research/2006/12/01 /hannity-suggested-use-of-quran-in-representativ/137441.

106 Brennan Suen, "Fox News Defends Ben Carson's Objection to a Muslim U.S. President," Media Matters, September 1, 2015, http://mediamatters .org/research/2015/09/21/fox-news-defends-ben-carsons-objection-to -a-mus/205688.

107 Media Matters, "Beck Guest Holton: Sharia 'Is the Biggest Threat to Our Constitutional Rights over the Next 25 Years," April 1, 2011, http://mediamatters.org/video/2011/04/01/beck-guest-holton-sharia -is-the-biggest-threat/178232.

108 Justin Berrier, "Kilmeade 'Misspoke' about 'All Terrorists' Being 'Muslims'—Twice," Media Matters, October 18, 2010, http:// mediamatters.org/research/2010/10/18/kilmeade-misspoke -about-all-terrorists-being-mu/172077.

109 Public Religion Research Institute, "Majority Say Congressional Hearings on Alleged Extremism in American Muslim Community 'Good Idea,'" February 16, 2011, http://publicreligion.org/research /2011/02/majority-say-congressional-hearings-on-alleged-extremism -in-american-muslim-community-'good-idea'/.

CHAPTER 6
Helplessness Mind Games: Manipulating Our Perceptions of What's Possible

1   James Baldwin, *Going to Meet the Man* (New York: Dial Press, 1965).

2   Albert Bandura, *Self-Efficacy: The Exercise of Control* (New York: W. H. Freeman, 1997); Bruce E. Levine, *Get Up, Stand Up: Uniting Populists, Energizing the Defeated, and Battling the Corporate Elite* (White River Junction, VT: Chelsea Green Publishing, 2011).

3   Albert O. Hirschman, *The Rhetoric of Reaction: Perversity, Futility, Jeopardy* (Cambridge, MA: Harvard University Press, 1991).

4   Judy Garber and Martin E.P. Seligman, eds., *Human Helplessness: Theory and Applications* (New York: Academic Press, 1980); Bernard Weiner, *An Attributional Theory of Motivation and Emotion* (New York: Springer-Verlag, 1986).

5   Harold Meyerson, "How to Raise American Wages," *American Prospect*, March 18, 2014, http://prospect.org/article/how-raise-americans -wages; Dean Baker, *Rigged: How Globalization and the Rules of the Modern Economy Were Structured to Make the Rich Richer*, Center for Economic and Policy Research, 2016; Dean Baker, "Is Globalization to Blame?" *Boston Review*, January 9, 2017, http://bostonreview.net /forum/dean-baker-globalization-blame.

6   Joseph E. Stiglitz, "Of the 1%, by the 1%, for the 1%," *Vanity Fair*, March 31, 2011, http://www.vanityfair.com/news/2011/05/top-one -percent-201105.

7   United Nations Development Programme, Human Development Report 1999 (New York: Oxford University Press, 1999).

8   Thomas L. Friedman, "Foreign Affairs; Senseless in Seattle," *New York Times*, December 1, 1999, http://www.nytimes.com/1999/12/01 /opinion/foreign-affairs-senseless-in-seattle.html.

9   Cam Simpson, "Victoria's Secret Revealed in Child Picking Burkina Faso Cotton," *Bloomberg Business*, December 15, 2011, http://www .bloomberg.com/news/articles/2011-12-15/victoria-s-secret-revealed -in-child-picking-burkina-faso-cotton.

10 Noam Chomsky, *Profit over People: Neoliberalism and Global Order* (New York: Seven Stories Press, 1999); Arundhati Roy, *War Talk* (Boston: South End Press, 2003).

11 Josh Bivens, "Everybody Wins, Except for Most of Us: What Economics Teaches about Globalization," Economic Policy Institute, November 2008, http://www.epi.org/publication/everybody_wins_except_for _most_of_us/; Sherrod Brown, *Myths of Free Trade: Why American Trade Policy Has Failed* (New York: The New Press, 2006).

12   Wendell Potter, *Deadly Spin: An Insurance Company Insider Speaks Out on How Corporate PR Is Killing Health Care and Deceiving Americans* (New York: Bloomsbury Press, 2010).

13   Austin Frakt, "Hospitals Are Wrong about Shifting Costs to Private Insurers," *New York Times*, March 18, 2014, http://www.nytimes.com /2015/03/24/upshot/why-hospitals-are-wrong-about-shifting-costs-to -private-insurers.html.

14   Ge Bai and Gerald F. Anderson, "Extreme Markup: The Fifty US Hospitals with the Highest Charge-to-Cost Ratios," *Health Affairs* 34 (2015): 922- 928, http://content.healthaffairs.org/content/34/6/922.abstract.

15   Wendell Potter, "For-Profit Hospitals Mark Up Prices by More Than 1,000 Percent Because There's Nothing to Stop Them," June 15, 2015, http://wendellpotter.com/2015/06/for-profit-hospitals-mark-up-prices -by-more-yhan-1000-percent-because-theres-nothing-to-stop-them/.

16   Ben Hirschler, "Exclusive - Transatlantic Divide: How U.S. Pays Three Times More for Drugs," *Reuters*, October 12, 2015, http://uk .reuters.com/article/2015/10/12/us-pharmaceuticals-usa-comparison -idUKKCN0S61KU20151012.

17   Robert Reich, "Why We Allow Big Pharma to Rip Us Off," October 5, 2014, http://robertreich.org/post/99279814665; Jonathan Cohn, "Here's How Congress Is Helping Big Pharma Keep Drug Prices High," *Huffington Post*, April 29, 2016, http://www.huffingtonpost.com/entry /medicare-prescription-drug_us_57238466e4b0b49df6ab1e61.

18   Andrew Pollack, "Mylan Raised EpiPen's Price before the Expected Arrival of a Generic," *New York Times*, August 24, 2016, http://www. nytimes.com/2016/08/25/business/mylan-raised-epipens-price-before -the-expected-arrival-of-a-generic.html; Ariana Eunjung Cha, "U.S. Lawmakers Demand Investigation of $100 Price Hike of Lifesaving EpiPens," *Washington Post*, August 23, 2016, https://www.washingtonpost .com/news/to-your-health/wp/2016/08/23/u-s-lawmakers-demand -investigation-of-100-price-hike-of-life-saving-epipens/.

19   Toni Clarke and Ransdell Pierson, "Mylan Offers Discounts on EpiPen Amid Wave of Criticism," *Reuters*, August 25, 2016, http://www.reuters.com/article/us-mylan-nl-pricing-idUSKCN11017J.

20   Dan Mangan and Anita Balakrishnan, "Mylan CEO Bresch: 'No One's More Frustrated than Me' about EpiPen Price Furor," CNBC, August 25, 2016, http://www.cnbc.com/2016/08/25/mylan-expands-epipen-cost -cutting-programs-after-charges-of-price-gouging.html.

21   House of Representatives' Committee on Oversight and Government Reform Memo, http://democrats.oversight.house.gov/sites/democrats .oversight.house.gov/files/documents/Memo%20on%20Turing%20 Documents.pdf.

22 The Economist, "Painful Pills," September 26, 2015, http://www.
    economist.com/news/business-and-finance/21665436-dramatic-rises
    -price-some-medicines-prompt-calls-action-hillary-clinton-promises.

23 Peter Singer, *The Expanding Circle: Ethics, Evolution, and Moral
    Progress* (Princeton, NJ: Princeton University Press, 2011).

24 Richard H. Thaler and Cass R. Sunstein, *Nudge: Improving Decisions
    about Health, Wealth, and Happiness* (New Haven, CT: Yale University
    Press, 2009).

25 Mark Egan, "Nudge Database v1.2," https://www.stir.ac.uk/media
    /schools/management/documents/economics/Nudge%20Database
    %201.2.pdf.

26 Deborah A. Prentice and Dale T. Miller, "Pluralistic Ignorance and
    Alcohol Use on Campus: Some Consequences of Misperceiving the
    Social Norm," *Journal of Personality and Social Psychology* 64 (1993):
    243-256.

27 Timur Kuran, *Private Truths, Public Lies: The Social Consequences
    of Preference Falsification* (Cambridge, MA: Harvard University
    Press, 1997); Elisabeth Noelle-Newman, *The Spiral of Silence: Public
    Opinion—Our Second Skin* (Chicago, IL: University of Chicago Press,
    1984).

28 Lee Fang, "Gun Industry Executives Say Mass Shootings Are Good
    for Business," *The Intercept*, December 3, 2015, https://theintercept
    .com/2015/12/03/mass-shooting-wall-st/.

29 Adrienne Lafrance, "America's Top Killing Machine," *The Atlantic*,
    January 12, 2015, http://www.theatlantic.com/technology/archive
    /2015/01/americas-top-killing-machine/384440/.

30 Wayne LaPierre, "Stand and Fight," *Daily Caller*, February 13, 2013,
    http://dailycaller.com/2013/02/13/stand-and-fight/.

31 Peter Overby, "NRA: 'Only Thing That Stops a Bad Guy with a Gun Is
    a Good Guy with a Gun,'" NPR, December 21, 2012, http://www.npr.org
    /2012/12/21/167824766/nra-only-thing-that-stops-a-bad-guy-with-a
    -gun-is-a-good-guy-with-a-gun.

32 C-SPAN, "2014 Conservative Political Action Conference, Wayne
    LaPierre, National Rifle Association," March 6, 2014, https://www.c
    -span.org/video/?318134-8/wayne-lapierre-addresses-cpac.

33 Josh Sugarmann, "The NRA: Gun Industry Trade Association
    Masquerading as a Shooting Sports Foundation," *Huffington Post*,
    June 25, 2014, http://www.huffingtonpost.com/josh-sugarmann
    /the-nra-gun-industry-trad_b_5212780.html.

34 John Lott, "Gun Restrictions Leave People Vulnerable and Helpless,"
    U.S. News & World Report, December 19, 2012, http://www.usnews
    .com/debate-club/did-the-sandy-hook-shooting-prove-the-need-for
    -more-gun-control/gun-restrictions-leave-people-vulnerable-and
    -helpless.

35 Gregor Aisch and Josh Keller, "Gun Sales Soar after Obama Calls for New Restrictions," *New York Times*, March 18, 2016, http://www .nytimes.com/interactive/2015/12/10/us/gun-sales-terrorism-obama -restrictions.html.

36 Evan DeFilippis and Devin Hughes, "Shooting Down the Gun Lobby's Favorite 'Academic': A Lott of Lies," Armed With Reason, December 1, 2014, http://www.armedwithreason.com/shooting-down-the-gun -lobbys-favorite-academic-a-lott-of-lies/.

37 Abhay Aneja, John J. Donohue III, and Alexandria Zhang, "The Impact of Right to Carry Laws and the NRC Report: The Latest Lessons for the Empirical Evaluation of Law and Policy," Stanford Law and Economics Olin Working Paper No. 461, September 4, 2014, http://papers.ssrn .com/sol3/papers.cfm?abstract_id=2443681; Harvard Injury Control Research Center, "Homicide," Harvard T.H. Chan School of Public Health, http://www.hsph.harvard.edu/hicrc/firearms-research /guns-and-death/.

38 Mike Spies, "The NRA's Straight-A Students," *The Trace*, November 4, 2016, https://www.thetrace.org/2016/11/nra-gun-record-rating-system -straight-a-students/.

39 Andrew Kohut, "Despite Lower Crime Rates, Support for Gun Rights Increases," Pew Research Center, April 17, 2015, http://www .pewresearch.org/fact-tank/2015/04/17/despite-lower-crime-rates -support-for-gun-rights-increases/.

40 CNN Press Room, "Donald Trump Calls into SOTU, Says What Hillary Clinton Has Done 'Is Criminal,'" July 26, 2015, http://cnnpressroom .blogs.cnn.com/2015/07/26/donald-trump-calls-into-sotu-says-what -hillary-clinton-has-done-is-criminal/.

41 Lee Fang, "How Private Prisons Game the Immigration System," *The Nation*, February 27, 2013, http://www.thenation.com/article /how-private-prisons-game-immigration-system/.

42 Immigration Policy Center, *Giving Facts a Fighting Chance: Answers to the Toughest Immigration Questions*, October 2010, http://www .immigrationpolicy.org/sites/default/files/docs/Giving_Facts_a _Fighting_Chance_101210.pdf.

43 U.S. Congressman John Culberson, "Culberson Tells Obama Immigration Official, When Law Says 'Shall' It's Not Optional," Press Release, April 15, 2015, http://culberson.house.gov/news /documentsingle.aspx?DocumentID=398234.

44 Dawy Rkasnuam and Conchita Garcia, "Banking on Detention: 2016 Update," Detention Watch Network & Center for Constitutional Rights, 2016, http://www.detentionwatchnetwork.org/sites/default/files /reports/Banking%20on%20Detention%202016%20Update_DWN, %20CCR.pdf.

45 Melissa del Bosque, "ICE Director to U.S. Rep. Culberson: We Can't Just Put People in Detention for 'the Heck of It,'" *Texas Observer*, April 20, 2015, http://www.texasobserver.org/ice-director-culberson -immigrant-detention/.

46 Donald Trump, *Great Again: How to Fix Our Crippled America* (New York: Threshold Editions, 2016).

47 Sari Horwitz and Maria Sacchetti, "Attorney General Jeff Sessions Repeats Trump Threat That 'Sanctuary Cities' Could Lose Justice Department Grants," *Washington Post*, March 27, 2017, https://www .washingtonpost.com/world/national-security/attorney-general-jeff -sessions-repeats-trump-threat-that-sanctuary-cities-could-lose -justice-department-grants/2017/03/27/1fa38e2a-1315-11e7-9e4f -09aa75d3ec57_story.html.

48 Tom K. Wong, "The Effects of Sanctuary Policies on Crime and the Economy," Center for American Progress, January 26, 2017, https:// www.americanprogress.org/issues/immigration/reports/2017/01/26 /297366/the-effects-of-sanctuary-policies-on-crime-and-the-economy/.

49 Donald Trump, *Great Again: How to Fix Our Crippled America* (New York: Threshold Editions, 2016).

50 Governor's Office, "Governor McCrory Signs the Protect North Carolina Workers Act," October 28, 2015, http://governor.nc.gov/press-release /governor-mccrory-signs-protect-north-carolina-workers-act.

51 Mark Krikorian, "A Third Way," Center for Immigration Studies, May 2006, http://cis.org/node/419.

52 Robert Reich, "The Morality of a $15 Minimum," October 19, 2015, http://robertreich.org/post/131476708345.

53 Donald Cohen, "Minimum Wage Doomsayers Are Still Wrong after 74 Years," *Huffington Post*, June 25, 2012, http://www.huffingtonpost.com /donald-cohen/minimum-wage_b_1621767.html.

54 Michael Saltsman, "The 'Fight for $15' Is a Job Killer," Employment Policies Institute, April 2013, https://www.epionline.org/oped/the -fight-for-15-is-a-job-killer/.

55 Employment Policies Institute, "The Faces of $15: Consequences of Minimum Wage Hikes," https://www.facesof15.com.

56 Robert Reich, "The Morality of a $15 Minimum," October 19, 2015, http://robertreich.org/post/131476708345.

57 Naomi Klein, *The Shock Doctrine: The Rise of Disaster Capitalism* (New York: Metropolitan Books, 2008); Naomi Klein, "Get Ready for the First Shocks of Trump's Disaster Capitalism," *The Intercept*, January 24, 2017, https://theintercept.com/2017/01/24/get -ready-for-the-first-shocks-of-trumps-disaster-capitalism/.

58 Carol Tavris and Elliot Aronson, *Mistakes Were Made (but Not by Me): Why We Justify Foolish Beliefs, Bad Decisions, and Hurtful Acts* (Boston, MA: Houghton Mifflin Harcourt, 2015).

59   Leon Festinger, Henry Riecken, and Stanley Schachter, *When Prophecy Fails: A Social and Psychological Study of a Modern Group That Predicted the Destruction of the World* (New York: Harper-Torchbooks, 1956).

60   Mark D. Alicke, "Culpable Control and the Psychology of Blame," *Psychological Bulletin* 126 (2000): 556-574.

61   Donald J. Trump (@realDonaldTrump), "We have done a great job with the almost impossible situation in Puerto Rico. Outside of the Fake News or politically motivated ingrates,...," Twitter, October 1, 2017, 8:22 a.m., https://twitter.com/realdonaldtrump/status/914465475777695744

62   Eliza Relman, "Trump on Puerto Rican crisis: 'This Is an island surrounded by water, big water, ocean water,'" Business Insider, September 29, 2017, http://www.businessinsider.com/trump-puerto -rico-hurricane-maria-island-water-2017-9.

63   Donald J. Trump (@realDonaldTrump), "...Such poor leadership ability by the Mayor of San Juan, and others in Puerto Rico, who are not able to get their workers to help. They....," Twitter, September 30, 2017, 7:26 a.m., https://twitter.com/realdonaldtrump/status/914089003745468417

64   Abby Phillip, Ed O'Keefe, Nick Miroff, and Damian Paletta, "Lost Weekend: How Trump's Time at His Golf Club Hurt the Response to Maria," *Washington Post*, September 29, 2017, https://www .washingtonpost.com/politics/lost-weekend-how-trumps-time-at-his -golf-club-hurt-the-response-to-maria/2017/09/29/ce92ed0a-a522 -11e7-8c37-e1d99ad6aa22_story.html; Eliza Relman, "Trump on Puerto Rican Crisis: 'This Is an Island Surrounded by Water, Big Water, Ocean Water,'" *Business Insider*, September 29, 2017, http:// www.businessinsider.com/trump-puerto-rico-hurricane-maria -island-water-2017-9; Gabriel Stargardter and Dave Graham, "Trump Lays Blame on Puerto Ricans for Slow Hurricane Response," *Reuters*, September 30, 2017, http://www.reuters.com/article/us-usa-puertorico -trump/trump-lays-blame-on-puerto-ricans-for-slow-hurricane -response-idUSKCN1C50GQ.

65   Joby Warrick, "White House Got Early Warning on Katrina," *Washington Post*, January 24, 2006, http://www.washingtonpost.com /wpdyn/content/article/2006/01/23/AR2006012301711.html.

66   CNN, "Chertoff: Katrina Scenario Did Not Exist," September 5, 2005, http://www.cnn.com/2005/US/09/03/katrina.chertoff/.

67   Cain Burdeau and Holbrook Mohr, "BP Downplayed Possibility of Major Oil Spill," Boston.com, May 1, 2010, http://www.boston.com /news/science/articles/2010/05/01/bp_downplayed_possibility_of _major_oil_spill/.

68   Associated Press, "BP Executive Defends Oil Firm's Record," *Dallas Morning News*, May 3, 2010, http://www.dallasnews.com/news/state /headlines/20100503-BP-executive-defends-oil-firm-s-6104.ece.

69 Clifford Krauss, "Oil Spill's Blow to BP's Image May Eclipse Costs," *New York Times*, April 29, 2010, http://www.nytimes.com/2010/04 /30/business/30bp.html.

70 Abrahm Lustgarten and Ryan Knutson, "Years of Internal BP Probes Warned That Neglect Could Lead to Accidents," ProPublica, June 7, 2010, http://www.propublica.org/article/years-of-internal-bp-probes -warned-that-neglect-could-lead-to-accidents.

71 Brad Johnson, "BP Calls Blowout Disaster 'Inconceivable,' 'Unprecedented,' and 'Unforeseeable,'" Climate Progress, May 3, 2010, http://thinkprogress .org/climate/2010/05/03/174659/bp-plays-stupid/.

72 Jim Hightower, "What Really Poisoned the Water in Flint, Michigan," *AlterNet*, February 3, 2016, http://www.alternet.org/news-amp-politics /jim-hightower-what-really-poisoned-water-flint-michigan.

73 Lindsey Smith, "Leaked Internal Memo Shows Federal Regulator's Concerns about Lead in Flint's Water," Michigan Radio, *All Things Considered*, July 13, 2015, http://michiganradio.org/post/leaked -internal-memo-shows-federal-regulator-s-concerns-about-lead -flint-s-water.

74 Tim Dickinson, "WTF Is Happening in the Flint Water Crisis, Explained," *Rolling Stone*, January 22, 2016, http://www.rollingstone.com/politics/ news/wtf-is-happening-in-the-flint-water-crisis-explained-20160122.

75 Alexandra Ossola, "Lead in Water: What Are the Health Effects and Dangers?" *Popular Science*, January 18, 2016, http://www.popsci.com /lead-water-what-are-health-effects-dangers.

76 John Eligon, "A Question of Environmental Racism in Flint," *New York Times*, January 21, 2016, http://www.nytimes.com/2016/01/22/us/a -question-of-environmental-racism-in-flint.html; Office of Governor Rick Snyder, "Final Report of the Flint Water Advisory Task Force," March 2016, https://www.michigan.gov/documents/snyder/FWATF_FINAL_REPORT _21March2016_517805_7.pdf; Chris Hedges, "Flint's Crisis Is about More Than Water," *Truthdig*, February 7, 2016, http://www.truthdig.com/report /item/flints_crisis_is_about_more_than_water_20160207.

77 Glenn Greenwald, "The 'Nobody Could Have Known' Excuse and Iraq," *Salon*, August 31, 2010, http://www.salon.com/2010/08/31/burns_3/.

78 Dan Collins, "'99 Report Warned of Suicide Hijacking," CBS News, May 17, 2002, http://www.cbsnews.com/news/99-report-warned-of -suicide-hijacking/.

79 Kurt Eichenwald, "The Deafness before the Storm," *New York Times*, September 10, 2012, http://www.nytimes.com/2012/09/11/opinion /the-bush-white-house-was-deaf-to-9-11-warnings.html.

80 Eric Alterman and George Zornick, "Think Again: Iraqi Weapons of Mass Destruction: Did 'Everyone' Agree?" Center for American Progress, June 12, 2008, https://www.americanprogress.org/issues/general/news/2008 /06/12/4534/think-again-iraqi-weapons-of-mass-destruction/.

81   Eric Alterman and George Zornick, "Think Again: Iraqi Weapons of Mass Destruction: Did 'Everyone' Agree?" Center for American Progress, June 12, 2008, https://www.americanprogress.org/issues/general/news /2008/06/12/4534/think-again-iraqi-weapons-of-mass-destruction/.

82   PBS NewsHour, "Troops Question Secretary of Defense Donald Rumsfeld about Armor," December 9, 2004, http://www.pbs.org /newshour/bb/military-july-dec04-armor_12-9/.

83   White House, "Vice President's Remarks at the Gerald R. Ford Journalism Prize Luncheon Followed by Q&A," June 19, 2006, http://georgewbush-whitehouse.archives.gov/news/releases/2006 /06/20060619-10.html.

84   Zeke Miller, "Mike Bloomberg: Blame Congress, Not Banks for the Mortgage Crisis," *Business Insider*, November 1, 2011, http://www .businessinsider.com/mike-bloomberg-blame-congress-not-banks -for-the-mortgage-crisis-2011-11.

85   Barry Ritholtz, "What Caused the Financial Crisis? The Big Lie Goes Viral," *Washington Post*, November 5, 2011, https://www.washingtonpost .com/business/what-caused-the-financial-crisis-the-big-lie-goes-viral /2011/10/31/gIQAXlSOqM_story.html; Carl Levin, "Wall Street and the Financial Crisis: The Role of Investment Banks," *The Hill*, April 27, 2010, http://thehill.com/blogs/congress-blog/campaign/94549-wall-street -and-the-financial-crisis-the-role-of-investment-banks-sen-carl-levin.

86   Jason Linkins, "High Church Hustle," *The Baffler*, No. 21, 2012, http://thebaffler.com/salvos/high-church-hustle.

87   Dean Starkma, "No, Americans Are Not All to Blame for the Financial Crisis," *New Republic*, March 9, 2014, http://www.newrepublic.com /article/116919/big-lie-haunts-post-crash-economy.

88   Charles Gasparino, "Robert Rubin's Agony," *Daily Beast*, August 19, 2009, https://www.thedailybeast.com/robert-rubins-agony; Jeff Faux, *The Servant Economy: Where America's Elite Is Sending the Middle Class* (New York: John Wiley & Sons, 2012); Robert Scheer, *The Great American Stickup: How Reagan Republicans and Clinton Democrats Enriched Wall Street While Mugging Main Street* (New York: Nation Books, 2010).

89   Zachary Mider, "Nominating Mnuchin for Treasury Will Dredge Up Mortgage Meltdown Controversies," *Bloomberg Politics*, November 22, 2016, https://www.bloomberg.com/politics/articles/2016-11-22/trump -treasury-contender-mnuchin-found-profits-in-mortgage-mess; Lorraine Woellert, "Trump Treasury Pick Made Millions after His Bank Foreclosed on Homeowners," *Politico*, December 1, 2016, http://www.politico.com /story/2016/12/trump-treasury-foreclosed-homes-mnuchin-232038; Paul Kiel and Jesse Eisinger, "Trump's Treasury Pick Excelled at Kicking People Out of Their Homes," ProPublica, December 27, 2016, https:// www.propublica.org/article/trump-treasury-pick-excelled-at-kicking -elderly-out-of-their-homes; David Dayen, "Treasury Nominee Steve

Mnuchin's Bank Accused of 'Widespread Misconduct' in Leaked Memo," *The Intercept*, January 3, 2017, https://theintercept.com/2017/01/03/treasury-nominee-steve-mnuchins-bank-accused-of-widespread-misconduct-in-leaked-memo/.

90 Karl E. Weick, "Small Wins: Redefining the Scale of Social Problems," *American Psychologist* 39 (1984): 40-49; Bernice Lott and Kate Webster, "Carry the Banner Where It Can Be Seen: Small Wins for Social Justice," *Social Justice Research* 19 (2006): 123-133; Leonard A. Jason, *Principles of Social Change* (New York: Oxford University Press, 2013).

91 Teresa Amabile and Steven J. Kramer, "The Power of Small Wins," *Harvard Business Review*, May 2011, https://hbr.org/2011/05/the-power-of-small-wins.

92 Carl T. Rowan, "The Rehabilitation of George Wallace," Washington Post, September 5, 1991, https://www.washingtonpost.com/wp-srv/politics/daily/sept98/wallace090591.htm.

93 Ta-Nehisi Coates, *Between the World and Me* (New York: Speigel & Grau, 2015); Sarah Stillman, "Get Out of Jail, Inc.: Does the Alternatives-to-Incarceration Industry Profit from Injustice?" *New Yorker*, June 23, 2014, http://www.newyorker.com/magazine/2014/06/23/get-out-of-jail-inc.

94 Michelle Alexander, *The New Jim Crow: Mass Incarceration in the Age of Colorblindness* (New York: The New Press, 2010).

95 Katie Rose Quandt, "1 in 13 African-American Adults Prohibited from Voting in the United States," Moyers & Company, March 24, 2015, http://billmoyers.com/2015/03/24/felon-disenfranchisement/.

96 Maggie McCarty, Gene Falk, Randy Alison Aussenberg, and David H. Carpenter, "Drug Testing and Crime-Related Restrictions in TANF, SNAP, and Housing Assistance," Congressional Research Service, October 18, 2015, https://www.fas.org/sgp/crs/misc/R42394.pdf.

97 Leadership Conference on Civil and Human Rights, "Justice on Trial: Racial Disparities in the American Criminal Justice System," 2000, http://www.protectcivilrights.org/pdf/reports/justice.pdf.

98 Terrell J. Starr, "Top Black Voter Disenfranchisement Tactics," NewsOne, 2012, http://newsone.com/1703995/black-voter-disenfranchisement-tactics-voter-id-redistricting/.

99 National Conference of State Legislatures, "At-Will Presumptions and Exceptions to the Rule," http://www.ncsl.org/research/labor-and-employment/at-will-employment-overview.aspx.

100 Paul Davidson, "Some Businesses Use Part-Time to Meet Health Law," *USA Today*, December 30, 2014, http://www.usatoday.com/story/money/business/2014/12/30/health-law-impact/21067751/.

101 American Association of University Professors, "Background Facts on Contingent Faculty," http://www.aaup.org/issues/contingency/background-facts.

102 Dominic Gates, "Boeing Deal Won't End Company's Tough Bargaining," *Seattle Times*, January 4, 2014, http://www.seattletimes.com/business/boeing-deal-wonrsquot-end-companyrsquos-tough-bargaining/.

103 Alex Lach, "5 Facts about Overseas Outsourcing: Trend Continues to Grow as American Workers Suffer," Center for American Progress, July 9, 2012, https://www.americanprogress.org/issues/labor/news/2012/07/09/11898/5-facts-about-overseas-outsourcing/.

104 Jim Hightower, "4 Ways Amazon's Ruthless Practices Are Crushing Local Economies," *AlterNet*, September 25, 2014, http://www.alternet.org/corporate-accountability-and-workplace/4-ways-amazons-ruthless-practices-are-crushing-local.

105 Stacy Mitchell, "New Analysis: Amazon Warehouses Impose Hidden Costs on Communities," Institute for Local Self-Reliance, October 22, 2015, https://ilsr.org/new-analysis-amazon-warehouses-impose-hidden-costs-on-communities/; Olivia LaVecchia and Stacy Mitchell, "Amazon's Stranglehold: How the Company's Tightening Grip Is Stifling Competition, Eroding Jobs, and Threatening Communities," Institute for Local Self-Reliance, November 2016, https://ilsr.org/wp-content/uploads/2016/11/ILSR_AmazonReport_final.pdf.

106 David Streitfield "A New Book Portrays Amazon as Bully," *New York Times*, October 22, 2013, http://bits.blogs.nytimes.com/2013/10/22/a-new-book-portrays-amazon-as-bully/.

107 Nicholas Confessore and Megan Thee-Brenan, "Poll Shows Americans Favor an Overhaul of Campaign Financing," *New York Times*, June 2, 2015, http://www.nytimes.com/2015/06/03/us/politics/poll-shows-americans-favor-overhaul-of-campaign-financing.html.

108 For important overviews of the problem, see John Nichols and Robert W. McChesney, *Dollarocracy: How the Money and Media Election Complex Is Destroying America* (New York: Nation Books, 2013); Lawrence Lessig, *Republic, Lost: How Money Corrupts Congress— and a Plan to Stop It* (New York: Twelve, 2011).

109 Gabrielle Levy, "How Citizens United Has Changed Politics in 5 Years," *U.S. News & World Report*, January 21, 2015, http://www.usnews.com/news/articles/2015/01/21/5-years-later-citizens-united-has-remade-us-politics; Wesleyan Media Project & Center for Responsive Politics, *Special Report on Outside Group Activity, 2000-2016: Super PACs Dominate 2016; "Dark Money" a Consistent but Growing Presence since 2000*, August 2016, http://mediaproject.wesleyan.edu/wp-content/uploads/2016/08/DisclosureReport_FINAL.pdf.

110 Ian Vandewalker, "Shadow Campaigns: The Shift in Presidential Campaign Funding to Outside Groups," Brennan Center For Justice, 2015, https://www.brennancenter.org/sites/default/files/analysis /Shadow_Campaigns.pdf.

111 Chisun Lee, Brent Ferguson, and David Earley, "After Citizens United: The Story in the States," Brennan Center for Justice, New York University School of Law, 2014, https://www.brennancenter.org/sites /default/files/publications/After%20Citizens%20United_Web_Final.pdf.

112 Richard L. Hasen, "Super-Soft Money: How Justice Kennedy Paved the Way for 'SuperPACS' and the Return of Soft Money," *Slate*, October 25, 2011, http://www.slate.com/articles/news_and_politics/jurisprudence /2011/10/citizens_united_how_justice_kennedy_has_paved_the_way _for_the_re.html.

113 Adam Lioz and Karen Shanton, "The Money Chase: Moving from Big Money Dominance in the 2014 Midterms to a Small Donor Democracy," (Demos, January 14, 2015), http://www.demos.org/publication/money -chase-moving-big-money-dominance-2014-midterms-small-donor -democracy.

CHAPTER 7
Countering the Mind Games, Building a Better Society

1   Frances Fox Piven, *Challenging Authority: How Ordinary People Change America* (Lanham, MD: Rowman & Littlefield Publishers, 2006).

2   See, for example, the following polls: http://www.nytimes.com /interactive/2015/06/03/business/income-inequality-workers-rights -international-trade-poll.html; http://www.motherjones.com/politics /2015/05/senator-bernie-sanders-policy-platform-presidential -campaign; https://s3.amazonaws.com/s3.documentcloud.org /documents/1512693/global-warming-poll.pdf; http://www.scribd.com /doc/267409090/CBS-News-New-York-Times-money-and-politics-poll; http://www.gallup.com/poll/182426/americans-say-low-income -earners-pay-taxes.aspx; http://www.nytimes.com/interactive/2014/12 /19/us/19procedures-full-poll.html; http://www.gallup.com/poll /182441/americans-say-higher-education-not-affordable.aspx; http:// www.gallup.com/poll/175646/favor-federal-funds-expand-pre- education.aspx; http://publicreligion.org/site/wp-content/uploads/2015 /11/PRRI-AVS-2015.pdf; http://www.gallup.com/poll/217331/labor -union-approval-best-2003.aspx.

3   Noam Chomsky, *Necessary Illusions: Thought Control in Democratic Societies* (New York: South End Press, 1989).

4   William J. McGuire, "The Effectiveness of Supportive and Refutational Defenses in Immunizing and Restoring Beliefs against Persuasion," *Sociometry* 24 (1961): 184–197; William J. McGuire and Demetrios Papageorgis, "The Relative Efficacy of Various Types of Prior Belief Defense in Producing Immunity against Persuasion," *Journal of Abnormal and Social Psychology* 62 (1961): 327–337; John A. Banas and Stephen A. Rains, "A Meta-Analysis of Research on Inoculation Theory," *Communication Monographs* 77 (2010): 281–311; John Cook and Stephan Lewandowsky, *The Debunking Handbook* (St. Lucia, Australia: University of Queensland, 2011), https://skepticalscience. com/docs/Debunking_Handbook.pdf; John Cook, Stephan Lewandowsky, and Ullrich K. H. Ecker. Neutralizing misinformation through inoculation: Exposing misleading argumentation techniques reduces their influence. PLoS ONE, 12 (2017), https://doi.org/10.1371 /journal.pone.0175799; Bobi Ivanov, Stephen A. Rains, Sarah A. Geegan, Sarah C. Vos, Nigel D. Haarstad, and Kimberly A. Parker, "Beyond Simple Inoculation: Examining the Persuasive Value of Inoculation for Audiences with Initially Neutral or Opposing Attitudes," *Western Journal of Communication* 81 (2017): 105-126; Thomas Wood and Ethan Porter, "The Elusive Backfire Effect: Mass Attitudes' Steadfast Factual Adherence," *Political Behavior* (forthcoming), https://papers.ssrn.com/sol3/papers.cfm?abstract_id=2819073.

5   Anthony Pratkanis and Elliot Aronson: *Age of Propaganda: The Everyday Use and Abuse of Persuasion* (New York: Henry Holt & Company, 2001).

6   Bobi Ivanov, Stephen A. Rains, Sarah A. Geegan, Sarah C. Vos, Nigel D. Haarstad, and Kimberly A. Parker, "Beyond Simple Inoculation: Examining the Persuasive Value of Inoculation for Audiences with Initially Neutral or Opposing Attitudes," *Western Journal of Communication* 81 (2017): 105-126.

7   Josh Eidelson, "How a $15 Minimum Wage Went from Fringe to Mainstream," *Bloomberg Businessweek*, March 29, 2016, http://www .bloomberg.com/politics/articles/2016-03-29/how-a-15-minimum -wage-went-from-fringe-to-mainstream; Steven Greenhouse, "How the $15 Minimum Wage Went from Laughable to Viable," *New York Times*, April 3, 2016, http://www.nytimes.com/2016/04/03/opinion/sunday /how-the-15-minimum-wage-went-from-laughable-to-viable.html.

8   Roy Eidelson, "The Sustaining Fires of Standing Rock: A Movement Grows," *Counterpunch*, March 16, 2017, http://www.counterpunch.org /2017/03/16/the-sustaining-fires-of-standing-rock-a-movement-grows/.

9   Clare Foran, "Poll: U.S. Support Slipping for Fracking, Keystone," *The Atlantic*, November 12, 2014, http://www.theatlantic.com/politics /archive/2014/11/poll-us-support-slipping-for-fracking-keystone /443721/; Cliff Weathers, "What Really Killed Fracking in NY?" *AlterNet*, December 22, 2014, http://www.alternet.org/fracking/who -killed-fracking-ny; John Schwartz, "Environmental Activists Take to Local Protests for Global Results," *New York Times*, March 19, 2016, http://www.nytimes.com/2016/03/20/science/earth/environmental -activists-take-to-local-protests-for-global-results.html.

10   Diane Brooks, "These Seattle Teachers Boycotted Standardized Testing— and Sparked a Nationwide Movement," *Yes! Magazine*, March 14, 2014, http://www.yesmagazine.org/issues/education-uprising/pencils-down; Gerstein-Bocian-Agne Strategies, "New Poll Results on Charter Schools," January 29, 2016, http://www.inthepublicinterest.org/wp-content /uploads/ITPI-CPD-NationalCharterPoll-1-29-2016.pdf.

11   Nick Timiraos and William Mauldin, "Odds Worsen for TPP Trade Deal," *Wall Street Journal*, July 29, 2016, http://www.wsj.com/articles /tpp-trade-deals-odds-fade-1469822992; Janine Jackson, "'These Agreements Depend on Secrecy in Order to Pass,'" Fairness & Accuracy in Reporting, July 30, 2016, http://fair.org/home/these-agreements -depend-on-secrecy-in-order-to-pass/; Jared Bernstein and Lori Wallach, "The New Rules of the Road: A Progressive Approach to Globalization," *American Prospect*, September 22, 2016, http:// prospect.org/article/new-rules-road-progressive-approach -globalization; Dave Johnson, "Trump Declares TPP Still Dead. So Now What?" OurFuture.org, January 25, 2017, https://ourfuture .org/20170125/trump-declares-tpp-still-dead-so-now-what.

12 Yamiche Alcindor, "Black Lives Matter Coalition Makes Demands as Campaign Heats Up," *New York Times*, August 1, 2016, http://www .nytimes.com/2016/08/02/us/politics/black-lives-matter-campaign .html; Paul Street "People over For-Profit Prisons: A Social Movement in Gary, Indiana," *Counterpunch*, April 8, 2016, http://www.counterpunch .org/2016/04/08/people-over-for-profit-prisons-a-social-movement-in -gary-indiana/; James Kilgore, "Opposing Mass Incarceration Is 'Trendy,' but Can We Stop the Train of Piecemeal Reform?" *Truthout*, June 3, 2016, http://www.truth-out.org/opinion/item/36277-opposing-mass -incarceration-is-trendy-but-can-we-stop-the-train-of-piecemeal-reform.

13 Max Ehrenfreund, "Bernie Sanders Is Profoundly Changing How Millennials Think about Politics, Poll Shows," *Washington Post*, April 25, 2016, https://www.washingtonpost.com/news/wonk/wp/2016/04 /25/bernie-sanders-is-profoundly-changing-how-millennials-think -about-politics-poll-shows/.

14 Sarah Frostenson, "The Women's Marches May Have Been the Largest Demonstration in US History," *Vox*, January 31, 2017, http://www.vox .com/2017/1/22/14350808/womens-marches-largest-demonstration -us-history-map.

15 Andy Newman, "Highlights: Reaction to Trump's Travel Ban," *New York Times*, January 29, 2017, https://www.nytimes.com/2017 /01/29/nyregion/trump-travel-ban-protests-briefing.html.

16 Josh Eidelson, "How a $15 Minimum Wage Went from Fringe to Mainstream," *Bloomberg Businessweek*, March 29, 2016, http://www .bloomberg.com/politics/articles/2016-03-29/how-a-15-minimum -wage-went-from-fringe-to-mainstream; Steven Greenhouse, "How the $15 Minimum Wage Went from Laughable to Viable," *New York Times*, April 3, 2016, http://www.nytimes.com/2016/04/03/opinion/sunday /how-the-15-minimum-wage-went-from-laughable-to-viable.html; Peter Dreier, "How the Fight for 15 Won," *American Prospect*, April 4, 2016, http://prospect.org/article/how-fight-15-won.

17 Cliff Weathers, "What Really Killed Fracking in NY?" *AlterNet*, December 22, 2014, http://www.alternet.org/fracking/who-killed -fracking-ny; John Schwartz, "Environmental Activists Take to Local Protests for Global Results," *New York Times*, March 19, 2016, http:// www.nytimes.com/2016/03/20/science/earth/environmental-activists -take-to-local-protests-for-global-results.html; Roy Eidelson, "The Sustaining Fires of Standing Rock: A Movement Grows," *Counterpunch*, March 16, 2017, http://www.counterpunch.org/2017/03/16/the -sustaining-fires-of-standing-rock-a-movement-grows/; Clare Foran, "Poll: U.S. Support Slipping for Fracking, Keystone," *The Atlantic*, November 12, 2014, http://www.theatlantic.com/politics/archive/2014 /11/poll-us-support-slipping-for-fracking-keystone/443721/; Philip Bump, "Don't Look Now, but Reality Is Winning the Climate Debate," *Washington Post*, March 15, 2017, https://www.washingtonpost.com /news/politics/wp/2017/03/15/dont-look-now-but-reality-is-winning -the-climate-debate/.

18   Peter Aldhous, "How Six Rebel Psychologists Fought a Decade-Long War on Torture—and Won," *Buzzfeed*, August 7, 2015, https://www.buzzfeed.com/peteraldhous/the-dissidents; Roy Eidelson, "Psychologists Are Facing Consequences for Helping with Torture. It's Not Enough." *Washington Post*, October 13, 2017, https://www.washingtonpost.com/outlook/psychologists-are-facing -consequences-for-helping-with-torture-its-not-enough/2017/10/13 /2756b734-ad14-11e7-9e58-e6288544af98_story.html.

19   Sarah Dougherty and Scott Allen, "Nuremberg Betrayed: Human Experimentation and the CIA Torture Program," Physicians for Human Rights, June 2017, http://physiciansforhumanrights.org /assets/multimedia/phr_humanexperimentation_report.pdf.

20   Roy Eidelson and Jean Maria Arrigo, "How the American Psychological Association Lost Its Way," *Los Angeles Times*, July 30, 2015, http://www.latimes.com/opinion/op-ed/la-oe-arrigo-psychologists -apa-report-20150729-story.html.

21   Kenneth S. Pope, "Are the American Psychological Association's Detainee Interrogation Policies Ethical and Effective? Key Claims, Documents, and Results," Zeitschrift für Psychologie/Journal of Psychology 219 (2011): 150-158.

22   Democracy Now!, "Psychological Warfare? A Debate on the Role of Mental Health Professionals in Military Interrogations at Guantanamo, Abu Ghraib and Beyond," August 11, 2005, https://www.democracynow .org/2005/8/11/psychological_warfare_a_debate_on_the.

23   Gerald P. Koocher, "Speaking against Torture," Monitor on Psychology, February 2006, http://www.apa.org/monitor/feb06/pc.aspx.

24   Larry C. James, Fixing Hell: An Army Psychologist Confronts Abu Ghraib (New York: Grand Central Publishing, 2008).

25   Mark Engler and Paul Engler, *This Is an Uprising: How Nonviolent Revolt Is Shaping the Twenty-first Century* (New York: Nation Books, 2016); Erica Chenoweth and Maria J. Stephan, *Why Civil Resistance Works: The Strategic Logic of Nonviolent Conflict* (New York: Columbia University Press, 2011).

26   Jim Hightower, "The Simple Secret to Making a Difference—No Matter What Your Cause Is," *AlterNet*, April 15, 2016, http://www.alternet.org /activism/simple-secret-making-difference-no-matter-what-your-cause.

27   Jonathan Matthew Smucker, *Hegemony How-To: A Roadmap for Radicals* (Oakland, CA: AK Press, 2017).

28   Rod Serling, dir., The Twilight Zone, Season 1, episode 22, "The Monsters Are Due on Maple Street," aired March 4, 1960, on CBS, https://vimeo.com/168014736.

29 Chris Hedges, *Wages of Rebellion: The Moral Imperative of Revolt* (New York: Nation Books, 2015); Sarah Leonard and Bhaskar Sunkara, *The Future We Want: Radical Ideas for the New Century* (New York: Metropolitan Books, 2016); Roy J. Eidelson, "Inequality, Shared Outrage, and Social Change," *Peace Review* 23 (2011): 4-11.

30 Emma F. Thomas, Craig McGarty, and Kenneth I. Mavor, "Transforming 'Apathy into Movement': The Role of Prosocial Emotions in Motivating Action for Social Change," *Personality and Social Psychology Review* 13 (2009): 310-333.

31 Chuck Collins, *Born on Third Base: A One Percenter Makes the Case for Tackling Inequality, Bringing Wealth Home, and Committing to the Common Good* (White River Junction, VT: Chelsea Green, 2016).

32 Barry Yeoman, "Can Moral Mondays Produce Victorious Tuesdays?" *American Prospect*, January 19, 2015, http://prospect.org/article/can -moral-mondays-produce-victorious-tuesdays; William J. Barber II, *The Third Reconstruction: Moral Mondays, Fusion Politics, and the Rise of a New Justice Movement* (Boston, MA: Beacon Press, 2016).

33 Katrina vanden Heuvel, "The Antidote to Cynical Politics," *Washington Post*, December 1, 2015, https://www.washingtonpost.com/opinions /the-antidote-to-cynical-politics/2015/12/01/064f69c6-97a1-11e5-94f0 -9eeaff906ef3_story.html.

34 Daniel Marans, "Elizabeth Warren Gives Progressives in Congress a Rousing Call to Arms against Trump," *Huffington Post*, February 4, 2017, http://www.huffingtonpost.com/entry/elizabeth-warren-congressional -progressives_us_5895e6b5e4b0406131373015.

INDEX

Garza, Alicia, 145 (*see also* Black
Lives Matter)
gas industry (*see* fossil fuel industry)
General Dynamics, 28, 37
General Electric, 80
General Motors, 45, 50, 115, 172
GEO Group, 108, 109, 164-165
gerrymandering, 179 (*see also*
elections, voter fraud, voter
suppression)
Gingrich, Newt, 66-67, 125
Giuliani, Rudy, 76, 146
global warming (*see* climate change)
globalization, 154-156
glyphosate, 44
Goldman Sachs, 49, 81, 113-114, 129,
175-176 (*see also* finance industry)
Google, 108
Göring, Hermann, 25
Great Recession, 3, 50, 67, 105,
114, 128, 132, 170, 174-176 (*see also*
finance industry, Occupy Wall
Street)
Green, Melanie, 18
Greenwald, Glenn, 130
Guantánamo Bay detention center,
83, 84, 96-97, 195
gun control, 16, 32, 162-164 (*see also*
National Rifle Association)
Halliburton, 28
Hanauer, Nick, 132, 134
Haney López, Ian, 99
Hannity, Sean, 146, 147
Hardee's, 73 (*see also* fast food
industry)
Hayes, Chris, 6, 59
Hayward, Tony, 130, 171 (*see also*
fossil fuel industry)
healthcare, 4, 34-36, 79, 139, 156-
159, 186-187 (*see also* Affordable
Care Act, Medicaid, Medicare)
Heartland Institute, 41-42, 122
Heller, Joseph, 18
Heritage Foundation, 62, 72, 81-82,
94, 105, 140-141
Hetey, Rebecca, 99
Hirschman, Albert, 152
Hitler, Adolf, 128, 147

HIV, 138, 158
Hoffman Report, 196-197
Hood, James, 177
Hoover, J. Edgar, 88
House Armed Services Committee,
37, 83, 84
House Committee on
Appropriations, 165
Hurricane Katrina, 66-67, 126,
170-171
Hurricane Maria, 170
Hussein, Saddam, 26, 28, 95-96, 173
(*see also* Iraq War)
Hyatt 100, 124-125
U.S. Immigration and Customs
Enforcement (ICE), 165 (*see also*
immigration)
immigration, 16, 47, 91, 100, 109,
142, 162, 164-166, 187
incarceration
abuse of prisoners in Abu Ghraib,
82-84, 195-197
activism against, 186, 190
drug-related sentences, 28-29,
178
economic disparities, 3, 123,
130-131
private prisons, 28, 29, 99, 100,
108-110, 164-166
racial disparities, 93, 99-100,
130-131, 178
treatment of prisoners in
Guantánamo Bay detention
center, 96-97, 195-197
income gap, *see* inequality
inequality, 3-4, 7, 13, 19, 38, 52, 61,
80-82, 94, 120, 121-125, 149, 176
defense of, 6, 31, 56, 65, 71, 84,
85, 88, 97, 102-103, 110, 124, 127,
129, 132, 141, 143, 152, 159, 167,
182, 185, 198
impact from globalization, 155
and Obama, Barack, 123
protests of, 5, 51, 134, 200
and Walker, Scott, 101
See also Occupy Wall Street
Inhofe, James, 41, 83-84
Institute for Policy Studies, 201

ABOUT THE AUTHOR

ROY EIDELSON, PHD is the former executive director of the University of Pennsylvania's Solomon Asch Center for Study of Ethnopolitical Conflict and a past president of Psychologists for Social Responsibility. His work focuses on applying psychological knowledge to issues of social justice and political change. His writing has appeared in a variety of scholarly peer-reviewed journals and other outlets including the *Washington Post* and *Los Angeles Times*. Follow him online at royeidelson.com and @royeidelson.

Made in the USA
Middletown, DE
14 August 2020